THE FIGHTING COMMODORES

by the same author

The Fighting Captain (Leo Cooper, 1993)

THE FIGHTING COMMODORES

The Convoy Commanders in the Second World War

by

ALAN BURN

'Britain...will depend as far ahead as we can see, not on the
Royal Navy but on the merchant ships that actually carry
(the) basic requirements both in peace and in war.'

A.T. Mahan

NAVAL INSTITUTE PRESS
ANNAPOLIS, MARYLAND

First published in Great Britain in 1999 by Leo Cooper,
an imprint of Pen & Sword Books, Ltd.,
47 Church Street, Barnsley, South Yorkshire S70 2AS.

Published and distributed in the United States of America
and Canada by the Naval Institute Press, 291 Wood Road,
Annapolis, MD 21402-5035

Library of Congress Catalog Card No. 98-68697
ISBN 1-55750-283-8

This edition is authorized for sale only in the United States,
its territories and possessions, and Canada

Printed in England by Redwood Books Ltd., Trowbridge, Wilts

DEDICATION

This book is dedicated to the officers and men from the British, Allied and neutral merchant services, who sailed in the merchant ships that kept Britain alive and freed Europe during the Second World War. In particular, it is dedicated to the Convoy Commodores who came back from retirement to lead the many thousands of convoys, and to the Consigs, their signals staff.

CONTENTS

PUBLISHER'S NOTE

Sadly, shortly after he had delivered the first draft of this book the author suffered an incapacitating stroke and was unable to do any more work on the text. It was thought, however, that the book was sufficiently near to completion to justify publication, particularly in view of the enthusiastic reception of, and continuing demand for, his previous work, *The Fighting Captain* the story of Captain Frederic Walker. The publishers crave the readers' indulgence for such rough edges as remain.

The help and advice of Len Bridge have been invaluable.

GLOSSARY

A/S	Anti-submarine
BdU	*Befehlshaben der U-boote* (U-boat Command)
COMINCH	C-in-C United States Fleet
Connav	Convoy Navigator
DBS	Distressed British Seaman
DCNS	Deputy Chief of the Naval Staff
DEMS	Defensively Equipped Merchant Ship
D/F	Direction Finding
DNI	Director of Naval Intelligence
EG	Escort Group
FAT	*Federapparattorpedo*
HF/DF	High Frequency Direction Finding
HO	Hostilities Only
LST	Landing Ship Tank
NCSO	Naval Control Service Operation
OIC	Operational Intelligence Centre
OOW	Officer of the Watch
RCN	Royal Canadian Navy
RMO	Recruitment and Manning Organization
RNB	Royal Naval Barracks
RNLI	Royal Naval Lifeboat Institution
RNR	Royal Naval Reserve
RNVR	Royal Naval Volunteer Reserve
Sigint	Special Intelligence derived from Ultra decrypts
SOE	Senior Officer of Escort
VLR	Very Long Range (aircraft)
WOMP	Western Ocean Meeting Point

Chapter 1

STARVATION OR SURRENDER

'If an enemy wishes to conquer us, not a man needs to be landed, not a bomb dropped on our territory. Cut our sea communications and we are left with a choice of starvation or surrender.'
Vice-Admiral Sir Gilbert Stephenson, when he opened HMS *Eaglet*, the shore base of the Royal Naval Reserve in Liverpool in 1971.

In 1940, before Hitler made the disastrous mistake of invading Russia, the outcome of the Second World War depended on the ability of the British to survive and to provide a platform from which, eventually, the might of the German armies could be challenged and the Allies could return to the offensive and drive them out of the conquered countries of Europe.

Britain's ability to hold out alone and to resist invasion depended on seaborne supplies of food and fuel, and on raw materials both for armaments and to keep her vital industries going. None of these activities could have been maintained without enormous regular seaborne cargo movements.[1]* Frugal Defence budgets had left the Royal Navy woefully short of warships and the Admiralty may be criticized for over-emphasis on building large ships, but the Trade Division of the Admiralty had worked methodically to set up a complicated worldwide system to control the merchant ships that would carry these supplies. The personnel had been nominated and trained in their

------

* See Notes, p. 241.

1

duties, and arrangements made to put them in their stations as soon as war broke out. This was the Naval Control Service Operation (NCSO).

After the German armies swept through Europe ocean-going ships could not be risked in the English Channel or on the east coast. Imports had to be brought in to the west coast ports and much of the cargo transferred to coastal ships for onward distribution. The First World War had shown that the problem of distribution started at the port of origin and did not finish until the goods reached their destination in this country. It had taken three years, from 1914 to 1917, for Lord Milner to overcome the resistance of British shipowners to any intervention in, or control of, their activities, the latter stubbornly maintaining that they had a right to direct their ships where they liked. However, the Ministry of Shipping had been wound up in April, 1921. All controls had been dropped and armaments removed from merchant ships to make space for more cargo.

In 1939, without overall control of the distribution system by ocean, coast, road and rail, the lesson had to be learnt all over again. Because of the restrictions on the east and south coast ports, the road and rail services were not able to cope with the extra load and the goods that could no longer be delivered to them were transhipped at west coast ports to coastal convoys, many of which had to face the long journey round the northern tip of Scotland and down the east coast.

The first regular convoys ran between the Thames estuary and the Firth of Forth on 6 September, 1939, and outward-bound ocean convoys (including the first Gibraltar convoy) started from Liverpool and London the next day.

With the introduction of convoys, the efficiency of the ships fell dramatically. There were delays while the ships in each convoy were sorted out according to characteristics, capacity, speed and destination. There were delays as the ships took up their sea-going stations. Each convoy could only travel at the speed of the slowest ship; breakdowns were frequent and delayed all ships, and there were bottlenecks in the ports caused by air raids. When a large convoy arrived at the port of destination there was a scramble for the available berths and offloading facilities. At the same time the volume of cargo to be carried by sea increased enormously. Planners had estimated that, if all ports between the Tyne and Southampton were unusable, the additional rail transport needed would mean an increase of one sixth of the rail systems' carrying capacity, equivalent to nearly one million ton-miles per annum.

To keep London alone supplied with food would take up an additional 375 trains per week.[2] The railways were already at full capacity and couldn't hope to deal with this additional load, so by October, 1939, 25% of the east and south coast trade had been diverted to coastal convoys. Because of the delays in the shipping sector of the distribution system, imports fell to 50% of peacetime levels. The shipowners used these circumstances as a reason for continuing to fight stubbornly against Government controls.

The whole weight of this extraordinary additional load fell on the merchant ships, their masters and their crews. Many ships past their normal lifespans, which had been lying idle up creeks and rivers, came back into service. It had been thought that market pressures would cause the neutral shipowners to provide ships for British services, but German policy was to sink neutrals in convoys, so freight rates rose rapidly and neutrals saw no point in chartering their ships to the British when they could be earning better money elsewhere at less risk. The merchant fleets of the Allies were already in existence in 1939, with their peacetime masters and crews, but Britain, from the very first day of hostilities, had to find enough seamen and officers with the necessary experience and skill not only to man her ships but also to command the convoys.

Apart from the war risks, masters did not relish the idea of sailing in close company in foul weather and being ordered about. No merchant seaman of any race had chosen a career at sea to fight a war and none of them saw in it any prospect of glory or advancement. All that convoys meant to them was a very considerable increase in the workload of their small crews, continuous additional strain on their watchkeeping officers trying to keep out of the way of other helmsmen ahead, astern or abeam, and the prospect of acting as defenceless bait for E-boats, U-boats, surface raiders or bombers. The navigational dangers of fogs, shoals, ice and rocks were multiplied by intense

3

enemy minelaying activity around the coast and safe channels were restricted by our own minefields.[3]

It was vital in convoy that all ships proceeded at the same speed, but most ships have an optimum speed and even this varies with different wind and sea conditions. Moreover, a ship behaves in a very different fashion when 'in ballast', or lightly laden, to when fully loaded with a deck cargo. Like most averages, the course and speed never suited any ship exactly. For some it was too fast, for some too slow, and for some it was impossible because many ships have a critical speed which varies according to their load. At this speed vibration can be not only uncomfortable but can also develop into a serious problem. In the extreme conditions often experienced in the North Atlantic and the Norwegian Sea during the winter, it needed experience and judgment to find the balance between going too fast, which resulted in green seas sweeping over the bows, smashing the deck cargo and damaging the ship itself, and going too slow so that the ship would not answer her rudder.[4]

In operating convoys, therefore, not only had the traditional freedom of the shipowners to be overcome, but also the natural resentment of their masters at the additional problems which they faced in running and handling their ships at sea, and of the foreign masters whose allegiance to the Allies and their cause could not be taken for granted. After all, at that time it was widely believed abroad that it wouldn't be long before Britain also went under.

When Churchill returned to the Admiralty on 3 September, 1939, full pressure was brought to bear on the neutral ships. None were permitted to take on fuel or indeed to use any facilities from British sources without a warrant from the reborn Ministry of Shipping and these warrants were only issued in return for an undertaking to place the ship under the control of the Ministry and to abstain from trading with the Germans.

On 26 August, 1939, the Admiralty had taken over control of all British shipping. There were two main types of trade convoy, the coastal convoys and the ocean convoys. The tasks and problems of the two differed greatly. Coastal convoys generally consisted of small ships designed for their special trades with a capacity of 2,000 tons and less, engaged in the inshore routes on journeys of a few days. They covered shorter distances and experienced different conditions and dangers. The masters, mates and crew knew their own routes between the ports of the British Isles, the surrounding seas, and every rock and shoal. Their task was extremely hazardous and exacting, but their horizons did not need to extend to the oceans and ports of the world. As the coxswains and crew of an RNLI lifeboat, often drawn from the ranks of local fishermen, must know every shoal, rock and tidal eddy in their radius of operation, but not far beyond, so the masters of the ships in the coastal convoys needed in-depth knowledge of their own waters, but not of the oceans beyond.

In contrast the ocean convoys operated offshore, setting out from the west coast down to Gibraltar, Freetown or beyond, across the Atlantic to Halifax, and onwards to the east coast ports of the Americas and Canada. They ranged from North Russia to the Cape of Good Hope, up the Persian Gulf and, on the other side of the world, to Australia and New Zealand. The journeys of the ships in these convoys could take weeks rather than days and depended on the speed of the slowest ship and the weather conditions. Butting into the foul weather which was a characteristic of the northern oceans in the war years, these convoys sometimes made good only 50 miles in 24 hours, half the average speed of Nelson's square-riggers when chasing the French fleet from the West Indies. The U-boats never turned back a convoy, but the weather broke up a few, turned back many vessels and sunk a few more.

The ships that made up the ocean convoys were larger, sometimes much larger, and built for ocean conditions. They demanded greater depth of water in which to operate; the number of ports in Britain where they could be loaded, offloaded and if necessary docked and repaired, were limited. Their cargoes were usually of greater value, their masters and officers needed foreign-going offshore experience, as well as cargo, seamanship and navigational skills that were not demanded by the coastal lines. Every effort was made to keep the ocean-going ships off the coastal routes to avoid the additional dangers that they would experience if this last leg was added to their journey. Some of the ocean-going ships were brand new out of the shipyards, but others were ancient coal-burners, lacking some of the most basic equipment necessary for a ship in convoy. The shortage was such that almost anything that could float was pressed into service.

The situation was no better in the German and British Navies; they too were unready for war. Neither had sufficient modern warships adequately armed. The Germans hadn't got enough U-boats and the Royal Navy hadn't got enough escort vessels. The Royal Navy hadn't got enough properly equipped mine sweepers and the Germans hadn't got enough mines of the right sort. Nevertheless, vicious attacks on the small ships in the coastal convoys started at once and the German offensive against the ocean convoys kicked off with some remarkable successes by Dönitz and his U-boats against both the merchant ships and the Royal Navy's capital ships. The U-boats were at sea on station when war was declared and on the first day sunk the passenger liner *Athenia*, with the loss of 112 lives. The aircraft carrier *Courageous* was next to go and the Navy's base at Scapa Flow was penetrated by *U-47* which sank the battleship *Royal Oak*. 262,697 tons (79 ships) went down in the first four months.

The Admiralty had been hamstrung between the wars by budget cuts and the Ten Year Rule of August, 1919, which stipulated that 'For the purposes of framing revised estimates, the British Empire will not be engaged in any great war during the next ten years,' a doctrine that continued to govern Naval expenditure for the next fifteen years.

Not one exercise or rehearsal of a trade convoy, with merchant ships of different nationalities and warships operating together without lights under simulated attack, was carried out in the interwar years. Nevertheless, the Trade Division of the Admiralty had done the best it could with the resources at its disposal, charged, as it was, with the planning and administration of the convoy system which would come into operation immediately war was declared. It was to become one of the largest organizations within the naval staff, under an Assistant Chief of Naval Staff, reporting ultimately to the First Sea Lord. The Trade Division was responsible for the conduct of convoys at sea, the routes of all shipping, the organization of the escorts and the instruction of all masters.

Among those trained, with their bags packed, were the first of

6

the Ocean Convoy Commodores. Thirty of them had been attending a series of training conferences at the Greenwich Naval College, at which the basic principles and essential practical moves for the control of convoys had been worked out.

They were based on Liverpool, the most important and busiest port for the trade convoys. During the war years Liverpool's docks handled an average of 13,000 ships per annum and a total shipping tonnage of 120 million tons, plus 23 million tons of coastal trade, distributing 57 million tons of imports.[5] Nearly all these ships and their cargoes moved in convoys.

The table below gives the number of convoys that sailed in the North Atlantic during the period of hostilities and the number of convoys that suffered losses:

Ocean Convoys Sailed and Losses

	Total Convoys	Convoys With losses	
North Atlantic	1480	186	12.5%
Gibraltar	653	68	10.5%
Arctic	78	21	27 %
	2311	275	12.5%

The total number of convoys of all sorts is much larger than this. The Secretary of the Admiralty called for figures of convoys sailed after five years of hostilities from the main convoy ports of the United Kingdom which included Methil, Southend (London), Solent Area, Plymouth, Milford Haven, Greenock, Aultbea, Liverpool, Belfast and Oban. The return showed that 4,025 ocean convoys and 10,025 coastal convoys sailed out of these ports.[6] The number of convoys that sailed into the same ports is not listed, but whenever a convoy was at sea, whether it was inward or outward bound, it had at least one escorting warship and the convoy itself was run by a Commodore or the master of a merchant ship acting as Commodore.

Chapter Two

THE MAKING OF A COMMODORE

The Ocean Commodores[1] were attached to HMS *Eaglet* in Liverpool. The Senior Officer of the Escort Group (SOE) was in command of the convoy. The Commodore was in command of the ships in the convoy. 181 Ocean Commodores are listed on 4 June, 1943, of whom 102 came from the Royal Navy, eight from the Dominions Navies, four from Allied Navies and fifty-seven from the Royal Naval Reserve. Among them were eleven retired Admirals, thirty-three Vice-Admirals, fifty-three Rear Admirals, thirteen Captains RN, two Norwegians, two Dutch, four Canadians, three Indians, and one New Zealander, one Commander, one Lieutenant Commander and fifty-seven very senior and experienced Captains from the Royal Naval Reserve.

In August, 1939, masters of merchant ships were going peaceably about their work on the oceans of the world, as they had done without interference for the past twenty years. If they had golden rules, they were to keep as far away from any other ship as they could and to shine a bright light at night. Once at sea they were their own bosses: no one in a ship under their command could refuse their orders: by law their orders must be carried out and the sole right of subordinate officers, crew or passengers was to do what they were told and complain afterwards.

On the outbreak of war on 3 September the Royal Navy took command. The masters were herded together in blacked-out ships, not allowed to show navigation lights and ordered about by naval officers, some of whom were half their age.

It takes quite a while to build a ship: it takes some years to

8

train a corps of officers to run a fleet of ships; it takes half a lifetime to develop the skills of a Commodore to run a convoy in whatever weather from the Atlantic to the equator, under fire and in darkness and to command instant obedience from fully qualified seagoing captains, used to running their own ships at their own speed, in their own way.

The breeding of these men started in the 1880s and 1890s. Their training began when they were fourteen years old and thereafter they lived a life of the sea until advancing years forced them to retire to make way for the next generation, or the war caught them.

With a few exceptions, there were two sources from which they came – the Royal Navy and the merchant service. They differed greatly in their methods of command, but they had two common characteristics – the all-embracing and undefinable skill called seamanship, and respect for and love of the sea.

To understand how Britain was able to deploy so many top-level officers at such short notice, we have to go back to their earliest days, and to do so we will follow the career of one of the best-known of the Commodores, who rose to be a Vice-Admiral.

He was not a very bright boy at school. Just a very ordinary schoolboy whose father died while he was young. He was brought up by his mother who lived in a large Victorian house in London. She was very beautiful, spoke French and played the piano. He was described as quiet and timid. In the last years of the nineteenth century, when he was a boy, the Royal Navy was at the height of its powers. Its supremacy was such that it had not been defeated, or even involved in any major war or campaign, during the life of any serving officer. In the quiet of his room, before he was bundled off to school at the age of eight, he read the great adventure stories about naval life.

But there was a feeling of unrest in the air. The Royal Navy's traditional enemy, the French Fleet, had crept back to a position where it could challenge the total supremacy of the British Empire's seapower. There were many disputes and some sabre-rattling over colonial questions and matters as remote as the boundaries of Siam. Since there was no actual fighting, the morale of the fleets was maintained by constant competitions, some to do with the upkeep and external appearance of the ships, some with sport and competitions between ships, but few that reflected the changing nature of the task of the Senior Service in the world at the start of the twentieth century. The competitions 'kept the lads on their toes' and demonstrated the comparative efficiency between the divisions in a ship and between the ships in a fleet, but they did nothing to increase their effectiveness as fighting units. The navies of the world were going through a time of major change, from sail to steam and then from coal to oil. The science of communication was not yet born and Flag Officers in charge of squadrons still relied on visual signals by flags, lights and semaphore. Since these were often obscured by spray, low visibility and fog, and since they were in any case immediately rendered ineffective by the smoke and flame of battle as soon as action was joined, fleet actions were governed by rigid procedures laid down in the Fighting Instructions which allowed the minimum discretion and initiative to the Commanding Officers of the men of war.

It needed a nomination to put a cadet through *Britannia* at Dartmouth, and many candidates failed the examination, which was necessarily competitive as the Navy was seen as a suitable career for the sons of the prosperous upper middle-class business and professional classes of that time. On this occasion seventy were admitted and our timid fourteen-year-old failed at his first attempt, but managed to squeeze through because a number of successful candidates didn't take up their vacancies.

The training and accommodation for the young cadets was provided on board two old wooden hulks, HM Ships *Britannia* and *Hindustan*, moored in Dartmouth harbour, and connected by a gangway that led from the bow of *Britannia* to the stern of *Hindustan*. The conditions were primitive, worse even than the facilities for which parents paid considerable sums to gain their sons the right to suffer in the Public Schools of that generation.

The cadet was soon introduced to the driving forces of the Navy – competition, seniority, and 'Zeal', a word that appears with monotonous regularity in the Service Records of all chosen officers of that generation. The word 'temperate' also makes a frequent appearance. All officers, apparently, were temperate until found out, but, flipping through the contemporary records, one finds that one of these temperate officers assaulted the vicar after morning service and another fell drunkenly into the grave of one of his colleagues' relations at a funeral. Both became Flag Officers who served at sea as Convoy Commodores.

The cadet's day started with a cold bath. So that he should never forget that he was supposed to be at sea, he slept in a hammock slung tight up to the deckhead where ventilation was minimal, so close to his fellow sufferers on either side that he couldn't climb in or out without disturbing them. He learnt how important this hammock would be in action, stowed as a protection against the flying wooden splinters when the round shot shattered the ship's side. He was taught how to sail a boat and to row a heavy cutter. He was given no practical experience in pilotage, or the handling of boats or ships under power in varied sea, wind and tide conditions. He didn't like bullying, but bullying was the order of the day: the cadets were thrashed on the slightest pretext, not only by cadet captains, but also by older cadets in their third and fourth terms.[2]

Boxing, a very practical way of taking exercise when confined on board a small ship, was compulsory. This was one of the few parts of his early instruction that would be of any practical use to him in his naval career, teaching him the need to control his temper and enabling him to protect himself against the bullying.

If the arbitrary discipline imposed on him by his peers in the gunroom was not enough to subdue him, there was a set scale of harsh official punishments, culminating in corporal punishment in the presence of the Surgeon and the Officer of the Day. This experience would, it was reckoned, harden him to ignore the harsh punishments handed out to the ratings on the lower deck.

He was given no opportunity to study the problems of man management, of command, of organization, of delegation, of strategy or of tactics. He was given little or no responsibility. He was deliberately discouraged from independent thought and action.[3] Instead he was taught to splice ropes, tie knots, climb up the rigging, scrub decks, obey orders and never ask questions. For the rest, most of the time was spent in academic learning in the classroom, and learning blind, instant obedience and respect for rank and status for its own sake.

Britannia's standards in the subjects taught were high, and the results achieved made a difference to each cadet's seniority as a midshipman, which would be significant throughout the rest of his naval career. Two officers of the same rank meeting at sea would reach for the Navy List, which set out these vital facts and determined who took command.

He first went to sea in a 10,000-ton cruiser, after he had been promoted to midshipman (snotty), almost the lowest form of animal life in the Royal Navy. (A lower breed of the same animal was thriving in the Second World War, the Acting Temporary Midshipman, Royal Naval Volunteer Reserve.) At this time, in 1895, most of the modern ships built under the Navy Defence Act of 1887 had been commissioned and the Navy had almost completed its evolution from sail to steam, but, true to tradition, he was required to spend his last year as a snotty in HMS *Active* and HMS *Raleigh* under sail, as midshipman of the maintop, supervising the setting and furling of the sails on the mainmast and adding further to his store of anachronistic knowledge.

He was to have a period of fourteen years, until 1912, before he rose to the rank of Commander, in which capacity he was actually in command of the battleship HMS *Duncan* in the temporary absence of her captain. In 1916 he was promoted to Acting Captain, and in the last year of the First World War reached the rank of Captain, RN. In 1925 he took command of the battleship HMS *Revenge*.

He had 'arrived' – after a long journey. To have command of a battleship was a leap forward, not only because of the professional and social status that went with the appointment but because command of a major ship at sea was an essential part of the pathway to the highest ranks in the Service.

Naval officers were automatically socially acceptable throughout the Empire and led a very busy social life flying the flag around the world. They had a wonderful life, though they worked extremely hard. But this was a bad time for all officers, particularly senior officers looking for command. In 1925 108 Post Captains, all of whom had served in that rank in the Grand Fleet, were present at a dinner for Admirals Jellicoe and Beatty.

There were too few ships in commission, drastic cuts in the budgets and massive scrapping of old warships without replacement. The Ten Year Rule was in operation and nobody wanted or was prepared to face up to the possibility of another World War. If an officer, like our Commodore, was good enough to get command at sea, he knew that this would probably be his last, and when that appointment ended he would have to take what was available ashore or join the Promotion on Retired List.

Our Commodore's last job before he was put out to grass was Commodore in Command of the Royal Naval Barracks (RNB) at Portsmouth, a crowded gathering of frustrated seamen with not enough to do, full of equally frustrated officers, and run by the crushers and the jaunties for their own benefit and that of the barrack stanchions. These were non-commissioned ratings serving out their time ashore from which comes the naval ditty:

> I was wandering through the Dockyard bright and early
> When I met a sailor old and grey.
> On his back he bore his bag and hammock
> And this is what I heard him say,
> 'Oh I wonder, yes I wonder
> If the Jaunty made a blunder,
> When he sent this draft chit down to me.
> I've been a barracks stanchion
> In the house of Jago's Mansion.[4]
> And I do not want to go to sea.'

RNB was a dreadful place. No rating was allowed to be seen above the ground except at the double. In the Second World War ratings passing through RNB between ships helped to clear bombed houses, under the control of established barracks 'stanchions', the naval equivalent of the wartime civilian 'spiv'.

At the age of fifty he joined the ranks of the so-called Yellow Squadron, made up from captains who, although they would not be employed again and would never fly their flag at sea, were automatically promoted to Rear Admiral and put on the retired list, a system that was devised to make way for younger officers, who would otherwise have been blocked for ever more.

He was still in his prime. Like Nelson himself and the Naval captains of the generations after the Revolutionary and Napoleonic Wars, his life had now to be built round retired pay and his local community. The Commodore filled in his time pottering about in small boats, running boxing clubs, Toc H, the Church Council, the Navy League, Boys' Clubs and the Portsmouth Boy Scouts, a busy life, punctuated by occasional visits to the Admiralty, cap in hand, to see if there was any chance of getting back to sea.[5]

Most of the retired Royal Naval captains and admirals had similar backgrounds. They had experienced as young men the exciting opening years of the twentieth century when Admiral Fisher was First Sea Lord and all the navies of the world were undergoing enormous changes. The younger ones had benefited in their training from the replacement of the two rotting old hulks by the fine Royal Naval College at Dartmouth and a second naval training establishment at Osborne.

In the autumn of 1939 they were suddenly in demand again, although they were now past middle age and out of touch; some had even lost their sea legs and would suffer once again from seasickness. Nevertheless they answered the call, dusted off their old uniforms, packed their bags and went back to sea to do a very different job from that which they had known.

There were a few, a very few, who had continued on the active list, surviving the Geddes Axe and serving right through the years from 1919 until the outbreak of the Second World War in increasingly important appointments. Frederic Dreyer was one of eleven young cadets who would eventually reach the rank of Admiral and serve as an ocean Commodore. He was born on 8 January, 1878, privately educated and sent to HMS *Britannia* at the age of thirteen and a half. He was marked out for high things from the start, passing out two years later having achieved first classes in all subjects, thus gaining twelve months' seniority over the less talented (and less zealous!). He too was subjected to a curriculum which included training in the sailing ship HMS *Cruiser*, where it was not unusual for seamen to fall from the rigging, sometimes to their death, all presumably in the interests of character-building and the development of 'officer-like qualities'. His time was spent in big ships in the days when specialization in gunnery was the way to promotion. In the last year of the century he went to Greenwich, then to the gunnery school on board HMS *Excellent*[6] and on to the gunnery school at Sheerness for a series of long courses. At this time rangefinders made their appearance in ships, but without any method of transmitting the ranges to the guns which were getting bigger and bigger and more and more numerous, notwithstanding the fact that some battleships were still fitted with rams!

In 1907, at the age of twenty-nine, Dreyer was appointed by Admiral Jackie Fisher to be Experimental Gunnery Officer on HMS *Dreadnought*, and so he came under the eye of this formidable officer, then First Sea Lord.

Thereafter his career was all upwards until the outbreak of the First World War. His first command was HMS *Amphion*, a new light cruiser, and he moved on from there to be Flag Captain to Rear Admiral Arbuthnot in the 22,500-ton Dreadnought, HMS *Orion*. At the age of thirty-six he was in command of this ship at the Fleet Review by King George V in July of 1914, having reached a position of great importance at exactly the right time. There were fifty-seven battleships and battle cruisers present at the review.

He was both a very competitive and a very competent officer, demanding and getting high levels of performance from all his officers and ship's company. He would expect and get instant obedience, respect, immaculate turn-out and perfect execution of each and every manoeuvre that he called for. If he moved, he would have his surrounding cluster of staff at his beck and call. His Secretary, a Paymaster Commander, would go with him, also his Flag Lieutenant and his Steward. His accommodation would be spotless, spacious and comfortable, his clothes and uniforms pressed and laid out with the medals in place. In reality he was lord of all he surveyed – unless he was seasick, like Nelson.

If he needed battle experience to round off his qualifications, they were to be picked up in the next four years. He commanded Admiral Jellicoe's flagship, HMS *Iron Duke* in the Battle of Jutland. If he lacked experience of strategic control at the highest level, he gained that when Jellicoe was appointed First Sea Lord and Dreyer went with him. Here at the Admiralty, he was involved in the great controversy about setting up the convoy system and in December, 1916, was a member of Jellicoe's newly created Anti-Submarine Division of the Naval Staff. Then he was appointed Director of Naval Ordnance.

15

This was our Commodore in 1919. He had 20 years to survive in peacetime conditions in a Navy on which every possible pressure was being brought to bear to avoid new building and to cut down costs. In spite of this he continued to operate at full steam almost without a break. By 1920 he was Director of the Gunnery and Torpedo Division of the Naval Staff, where his deputy was Captain, later Admiral Sir, H.J. Studholme Brownrigg, who also was to serve as a convoy commodore. In 1922 he relieved Captain Dudley Pound to take command of the battlecruiser *Repulse* and in 1923, now forty-five, he was promoted to Rear Admiral.

His career between the wars is hard to believe, showing as it does the wonderful life that a competent, hard-working, senior naval officer could lead in the interwar years. He became Assistant Chief of Naval Staff, commanded the Battle Cruiser Squadron, was promoted to Vice-Admiral on 1 March, 1929, and came back to the Admiralty in 1930 as Deputy Chief of Naval Staff.

He was advised that he would be C-in-C, Atlantic Station, the necessary last step on the ladder to qualify him for consideration for appointment to Admiral of the Fleet. He went aboard HMS *Nelson* to see his new quarters and chose a Chief of Staff, (Brownrigg again) and a Flag Captain.

One black cloud marred the perfection of his horizon. In 1931 the country was suffering under the Great Depression. On 21 July cuts in pay to all three Armed Services, schoolteachers, police forces and unemployed were proposed by the Government and vigorously opposed by the Admiralty. These cuts would break pledges made to naval personnel. The details were released first to the newspapers, revealing that the cuts would hit the Navy hardest of all. There were problems with some of the ships at Invergordon. The First Sea Lord told Dreyer that he must remain with the other Sea Lords until the matter was cleared up, so he could not take up his appointment. Dreyer was thus deprived of any chance of final promotion to First Sea Lord, but nevertheless none of the five Sea Lords suffered greatly from this sorry episode in the history of the Royal Navy. Indeed they did very well.

In Dreyer's own words:

Sir Bolton Eyres-Monsell, who then became First Lord until 5 June, 1936, was an ex-naval officer, and saw to it that the five Sea Lords at the time of the Invergordon Mutiny were not made scapegoats for the misdeeds of the First National Government:

– The First Lord (Field) was promoted to Admiral of the Fleet and awarded the Military Grand Cross of the Bath.

– The Second Sea Lord (Fuller), who was already a KCB and had been C-in-C America and West Indies, was offered the post of C-in-C Plymouth but preferred not to accept it.

– The Third Sea Lord (Roger Backhouse) had already been appointed Second-in-Command Mediterranean Fleet. He became a KCB. Later he was C-in-C Home Fleet, and was then appointed First Sea Lord, promoted to Admiral of the Fleet, and awarded the GCB.

– The Fourth Sea Lord (Preston) was appointed Commandant of the Imperial Defence College and awarded the Military KCB.

The Deputy Chief of Naval Staff (myself) was awarded the military KCB in June, 1932, promoted to full Admiral in December, 1932, and in January, 1933, left the Board of Admiralty and sailed to become C-in-C China Station for three years instead of the usual two. In June, 1937, I was awarded the Grand Cross of the British Empire.[7]

This was a good example of the old naval custom that, if an officer wants to rise in the Service, he must make some mistake, face a court martial, incur Their Lordships' Displeasure and be dismissed from his ship. The way is then clear for him to get a better job, rise up the ranks and take command of a bigger and better ship.

The enormous energy that the commodore put into his work, and his play, in the last three years of his time on the active list is scarcely credible. His position was specifically defined as 'the principal authority responsible for maintaining the Protection of British Life and Property on the China Station', and he himself says in his autobiography that 'My visits to British ports were planned . . . with the object of showing the Flag for the benefit of British subjects, and also to enable me to judge the value of each port in the event of war'.

He tried, and nearly succeeded, in doing a survey of, and

writing a report on, every port on his station, not forgetting a 1,000-mile journey up the Yangtze to Nanking, Hankow and Ichang, four visits to Japan, visits to Formosa, Manila, Singapore, Penang, Bangkok, Shanghai, Borneo, Macao, Hong Kong, Swatow, Foochow, Weihaiwei, and Sumatra. Although he had access to the hundreds of British masters who had used these ports and waters for decades in the course of their trading, to put together such a work was a mammoth undertaking.

Wherever he went he was royally entertained by Governors, Emperors, Rajas, Generals, Admirals or just distinguished old friends. He took with him, whenever possible, his dispatch vessel, the sloop HMS *Falmouth*, with his wife and staff on board.

In May, 1939, after forty-eight years in the Royal Navy, Admiral Sir Frederic Dreyer, GBE, KCB, was placed on the retired list at the age of sixty-one. Few officers could look back on such a distinguished career. He had commanded a battleship, fought in the Battle of Jutland, reached the rank of Admiral, held the appointments of the Commander-in-Chief of the China Station and of the Assistant Chief of Naval Staff, and served close to the most influential Admirals of the time. Because of his questing mind and inherent discontent with the state of the service that he loved, and because he had done more than most to bring the ships and their management up to date, he was not always popular, but he was still full of life and ideas, too active to retire to the Hampshire countryside.

With war imminent, he volunteered to serve with the ocean convoys and was one of the first band of officers who went off to Greenwich to get ready for the next task. In common with all convoy commodores, he dropped his rank to Commodore 2nd Class, Royal Naval Reserve, on 15 September, 1939. He sailed from Southend as commodore of OA 19, his first convoy of merchant ships, on Friday, 13 October, 1939, and on his first ocean convoy from Liverpool to Nova Scotia on 25 October.

The training and apprenticeship of professional Merchant Service officers was, in some respects, similar to that of their Royal Naval counterparts. At an early age they were packed off to one of the training ships, or to Pangbourne, a public school where the education was geared to the production of cadets who would eventually qualify to be officers in the British merchant service. Pangbourne differed from other public schools in that, instead of reciting sonnets by heart before breakfast, the young men might be found reciting a section of the International Regulations for the Prevention of Collision at Sea. Instead of suits the cadets wore uniforms, polished their boots and were regularly drilled under the supervision of a lance corporal in the Royal Marines. Their education was a down-to-earth study of the business of running a merchant ship on the oceans of the world.

Although the merchant service tried to emulate the Royal Navy and outwardly had a similar hierarchy, in nearly every other way it differed greatly. The attempt to rechristen the merchant service the Merchant Navy was never successful because the merchant service has never been a single entity. It consisted then, and consists now, of a number of commercial shipping firms whose ships and practices differ as much as the practices of commercial firms ashore. The passenger liners ran services to regular schedules on regular routes. They were the smartest ships and depended for their livelihood on the maximum degree of service and comfort. The larger, faster and more comfortable the ship, the better the cuisine, the cleaner the cabins, the better trained the stewards and the more it resembled a five-star hotel, the higher it ranked and the greater the prestige of the captain and his officers. The big passenger ships tended to emulate the Royal Navy in standards of appearance and of discipline. They wore uniforms with the appropriate stripes on the sleeves and scrambled egg on their caps, and distinguished clearly between the deck, engineering and catering branches.

The passenger liners made their money by carrying passengers and the Royal Mail. They dealt with passengers in the same way as the railways, with first, second and third class accommodation, unashamedly differentiating between those who were prepared and able to pay for the best, and for a seat at the captain's table, and those who were not. The wealthiest had cabins on the upper decks on the port side on the journey out to the Far East, and on the starboard side on the way back, to avoid the full heat of the sun on the journey. Hence the expression 'POSH' (Port Out, Starboard Home), which was printed on the tickets of the Peninsular and Orient Line passenger ships: posh was a symbol of something bought with money by the wealthy, and is still defined in the dictionary as 'socially exclusive or fashionable'.

Next in the scale came the cargo liners, which operated regular schedules on established routes and made their money out of carrying commercial cargoes, and sometimes a few passengers if the cargo was not too incompatible – few passengers would choose to travel on a ship carrying bird droppings from the west coast of South America. Then there were the tankers, the larger the better for commercial reasons, comfortable for their crews, but intensely boring, since they never got much chance to go ashore in a pleasant port; they were also potential funeral pyres in wartime. Last on the list of the ocean-going ships came the tramp ships which connected all the ports of the world, picking up whatever cargoes they could. In a different category again came the little coastal craft and the coal-scuttle brigade of the east coast of Britain, running on a shoestring for hard-nosed owners.

All the shipping lines were in the business to make money and there were firms and individuals who operated old ships to the minimum standards they could get away with in order to enable them to compete in a highly competitive market. In wartime, as we have seen, ships were brought back from the estuaries and creeks where they had been laid up because they were badly needed and because the rocketing freight rates made shipping a very attractive business for the owners. The more successful the shipping line, the more they could afford to be benevolent and paternal. Some were; some were not.

The second-class social standing of merchant service officers carried on into the other ranks, the seamen, stokers, oilers, cooks and stewards, among whom there was a strong hierarchy and boundaries almost as strong as the caste system that ruled in the Indian crews. Ashore, the merchant seaman had no uniform: he was not recognized and even at home in wartime could be asked why he wasn't in the services fighting for his Country.

The song

> All the nice girls love a sailor,
> All the nice girls love a tar . . .
> For there's something about a sailor,
> Because you know what sailors are

was written for Jack, the seaman in the Royal Navy, not for the seaman in the merchant service.

In contrast, W.S. Gilbert wrote the song:

> The *Ballyshannon* foundered off the coast of Cariboo
> And down in fathoms many went the Captain and the crew;
> Down went the owners – greedy men, whom hope
> of gain allured:
> Oh, dry the starting tear, for they were heavily insured.

It wasn't just a question of uniforms: many officers and crew were paid the bare minimum wage by parsimonious ship-owners, put to sea in dangerously overladen ships and were fed appallingly.

The one thing that all the officers and crews in merchant ships had in common was the love of life at sea, the age-old pride of seafaring men who carry out their work against an element that can be very unforgiving and cruel, but also very beautiful. It was in those days one of the only ways for adventurous young men to see the world and be paid for it. In return they chose to face the daily marine hazards of collision, shipwreck and fire, it is often forgotten that, unlike their opposite numbers in the Royal Navy, they had not chosen to go to sea to fight a war and face, in addition, the perils of attacks in ill-found and defenceless ships.

The commodores of the convoys, if they came from a Royal Naval background, were part of a world-wide club, with its own conventions and a tendency to understate problems. A long career of not offending the powers above had left its mark on them, but they had little or no experience of handling slow single-screw ships in ballast in Atlantic weather. Those who came from a merchant service background did not belong to this club and were apt to be much more forthright in their comments and reports. They were better fitted to the task they were to perform in having spent more time at sea and understanding from experience life in the merchant ships they commanded and the difficulties of handling the motley collection of ships and multi-national crews that made up a convoy. If a naval officer wanted to know any details of the flotilla that he commanded – say the turning circle of a warship – he could look it up in a reference book, but there were no such statistics available for all the different types of merchant ships in various load conditions. In bad weather the speed of the convoy was often dictated by the handling characteristics of one or more ships and was a matter of judgment for the commodore. In many cases, shipowners had claimed a higher speed than their ships could achieve in order to reduce the risk of being relegated to slow convoys, which were more vulnerable. Sometimes ships couldn't keep up because their chandlers had supplied them with bad coal. Sometimes they were short of stokers. Sometimes, unlike the Duke of Plaza Toro, ships pressed on ahead to escape pursuing U-boats, or just to get ashore before the pubs closed.

The variations between the Royal Navy and the merchant service naturally arose from the differences in the tasks which they performed. For centuries the Royal Navy's senior officers had been Britain's ambassadors to all the ports of the world, and this led to a profound difference in social status. Merchant seamen, even masters of ships, were not automatically entertained in foreign ports. Some, at the end of their seagoing careers, will tell you that they had never once been invited into a private home abroad. Irrespective of professional competence, the Merchant Service always ranked second to the Royal Navy, in the same way that qualified reserve officers always ranked below Royal Navy officers of equivalent rank and seniority on board HM ships, though the distinction became more blurred as the war progressed.

Chapter Three

THE CONVOY SIGNALMEN

Now we come to the convoy commodores' eyes and ears, the convoy signalmen, an extraordinary body of unsung heroes, carrying out an absolutely vital job, about which very little has ever been said or written.

> This Petty Officer has been my continuous and only source of help in my work for many a tedious and weary voyage and I feel that my debt to him can never really be repaid. He volunteered to serve, leaving a well-paid and steady job, the minute hostilities broke out. His patriotism does one good to contemplate. I admire him immensely.

These are the words of Vice-Admiral Goldsmith about Yeoman of Signals Pell. They could be applied to many of the Convoy Yeomen and their teams of signalmen.

None of the commodores were young men. All of them flew their broad pennants[1] from, and were accommodated in, merchant ships which did not normally carry trained signalmen. To do his job the commodore had to have a trained team of signalmen, and, most important of all, an experienced Yeoman of Signals, versed in the ways of the Navy, to lead them. Without them he had no eyes and no ears and could not communicate either with the Senior Officer of the escorts or with any of the ships in the convoy for which he was responsible. These were the convoy signalmen, the young men who manned the signal halyards and the Aldis lamps on the bridges of the commodores' ships, led by a Yeoman of Signals who often went from ship to ship with their commodores.

23

In 1939 James Graves, who finished the war with a commission, was in the London Division of the Royal Naval Volunteer Reserve, trained as a signalman like his grandfather before him. On 30 August he was mobilized with eighty other RNVR ratings and sent to Chatham Barracks. After training, he went with six others to join the staff of a convoy commodore at Southend, which was the assembly point for all the convoys outward bound from the Thames estuary.

Jim tells us what happened. At the convoy conference, attended by the commodore and senior officer of the escorts and run by the NCSO, the masters, radio operators and signalmen were given their instructions on convoy conduct and signalling, but, 'It appeared that few of the Masters cared much about signal procedure, having quite enough to do in navigating their ships.'

Shortly before convoy OA 19 sailed Commodore Dreyer arrived. Since we read about him, he had voluntarily dropped his rank to Commodore and the numbers of his staff to three, Chief Yeoman of Signals John Lancaster, RN Retired, Petty Officer Telegraphist Warner RN

and myself, Ordinary Signalman RNVR. . . . To my eyes the Commodore seemed to be rather old, in his sixties I believe. He was a very energetic man, still fiery enough to awe a young signalman and for three days he kept us busy, correcting our signal books and making his plans for the conduct of the convoy.

The Commodore and his team found that their ship, *Clan Macbrayne*, was the smallest ship of the Clan line, manned by British officers and lascar crewmen muffled up to the eyebrows on a chilly day, but

going about their duties with bare feet! . . . The Commodore asked the master to reduce speed to allow the joining ships to catch up. The Master called one of the apprentices, 'My salaams to the chief engineer and ask him to reduce five revolutions. The apprentice scampered down the ladders and along the decks . . . apart from the engine room telegraphs there appeared to be no other way of communication from the bridge.

24

The next convoy was an ocean convoy. To the young Ordinary Signalman, attending the convoy conference before sailing on his first and one of the earliest Atlantic convoys bound across the Atlantic to Halifax (OB 25),

> the age of some of the masters was surprising – in their sixties and seventies dressed in dark suits (Navy blue nuts) with bowler hats, looking like City businessmen.

On arrival in Halifax in the early days the convoy signalmen stayed in the luxury of the Halifax Hotel where the level of central heating was almost unbearable to the bunting tossers in their blue serge and jerseys, but very acceptable to the ladies in the hotel who would discard their long johns the moment they were indoors and sit around in summer frocks with rolled stockings showing a disconcerting length of thigh. But this didn't last for long: on the next trip it was the freezing cold Naval Barracks, huddled in greatcoats 'borrowed' from reluctant Canadian storemen.

Jim Graves was in a strong position to know what was going on: one of his duties was to write up the Commodore's diary. He remembers on the return journey passing a ship on an opposite course flying the Swedish flag. A couple of hours later the Commodore had a signal from the escorting warship that they had intercepted a signal giving an accurate report of the convoy's position, course and speed, which could have emanated from this ship. This gave rise to the first of many score of signals that he would hoist before dusk over the years, warning the ships that emergency alterations of course would be made after dark, with other timed alterations during the night to move the ships off their predicted line of advance.

It wasn't long before he and his Commodore were exposed to another deadly enemy of the Atlantic convoys, the vicious, merciless and all-powerful Atlantic weather at its fiercest. A cargo of oil drums broke adrift, pursued by the mate and the deck hands – a deadly game of Russian roulette as the ship pitched and rolled its guts out. A huge sea whipped over the after deckhouse and stove in the door, leaving the accommodation open to the weather. The carpenter set about repairing it. The next wave got him and swept him over the side. Panic broke out, led by the second mate and some of the crew who tried to persuade the Master to let them launch a boat to recover the carpenter, a crazy plan in those seas. Instead the Master decided to alter course.

> This alteration of course was a dangerous manoeuvre in the giant seas, and the ship rolled terribly. For one moment I thought the steel anti-aircraft shelter on the bridge was breaking loose but it was only the wheelhouse door swinging wildly on its hinges. The carpenter was not seen again and the ship resumed its course with a very saddened crew. We came up the Channel in a dense fog, each ship following a buoy streamed astern and in the fog met an outward-bound convoy. There was a collision between two of the ships.[2]

Treachery, hurricane, shifting cargo, man overboard, death, fog and collision in one return trip – the early signals staff and their commodores were given a baptism of fire.

In contrast, the next trip was to Gibraltar, where the Commodore stayed in luxury with the Commander-in-Chief, the weather was warm and sunny and the water so blue and clear that, when alongside, they could see the piles of old tins and empty bottles lying on the seabed beneath the ship.[3] Only bureaucracy and security spoilt it all: the Spanish dancing girls were whisked back across the border before midnight when the border closed, and German agents reported the movement of every ship through the Straits.

After the Gibraltar convoy Jim Graves' days as a convoy signalman came to an end. He was now, in terms of the war years, an experienced signalman, and they were as rare as gold. He was whisked off to a Fleet minesweeper and replaced by a much-maligned part-time sailor, an HO (Hostilities Only) rating, one of the thousands who, with a little bit of help from his friends, was to win the war when the going got tough.

Jim Graves says of his Commodore:

> I'm sure Admiral Dreyer would have agreed that he was a diffi-cult man to deal with but I suppose every senior officer is. I

remember when we were joined by additional staff, a midshipman RNVR and a signalman RNVR. One day in the middle of the Atlantic, the Admiral said, 'What's the time, Midshipman?' 'Half eleven, Sir,' he replied. The Admiral exploded and sent him off the bridge for the remainder of the watch. Had it been a sailing ship, I'm sure he would have been sent to the masthead.

The Admiral was a gentleman, a man I could respect and I never fell foul of him and, as I kept his diary for him, I was fully in the picture. One day on the bridge he said to me, 'Graves, he who lives with a tiger learns to stroke fur the right way.' This I took to be a very neat compliment. It was only afterwards that I learnt that he had recommended me for a commission.

Commodore Dreyer was luckier than many convoy commodores, who suffered not only from sailing in woefully ill-equipped ships but also from a shortage of trained signalmen. As more and more ships put to sea in convoy and the number of convoys increased correspondingly, each had a commodore and each commodore had a real need for a minimum of five staff: a Yeoman, a Petty Officer Telegraphist, a Leading Signalman and two Signalmen. Even before the convoy system was in full operation, there was a serious shortage. The Fleets got first priority, the Senior Officers of Escort (SOE) second, the escort vessels third and then, in spite of protestations, came the commodores. When the supply of RNR and RNVR reservists was exhausted, young men were recruited and sent on intensive specialized signalling courses at one of Billy Butlin's holiday camps at Skegness which had been taken over and renamed HMS *Royal Arthur*.

An Admiralty Fleet Order issued in September, 1939, laid down arrangements for 500 men to be trained in ten classes of fifty. Most of these trainees came straight from civilian life, some straight from school; some had picked up a little knowledge of the sea from their membership of the Sea Scouts, some from mucking about in boats on the rivers and estuaries. Very few knew much about the Royal Navy or about ships, the sea or the oceans of the world.

After four months' training in the ways of the Navy and

emphasis on semaphore signalling, morse signalling by Aldis lamp, flag hoists, and a grounding in the International Code of Signals and coding, they were sent to sea.

As they completed their shore training, these first 500 relieved the regular signalmen for duties in the Fleets, where their experience was badly needed. Further batches followed, and training classes were also started at HMS *Leigh* in Southend. Between 1940 and 1944 thirty-four classes (twenty-eight at *Royal Arthur* and six at *Leigh*) comprising 1190 convoy signalmen, had been trained and sent to sea where they served on the staffs of the commodores. They covered all the oceans of the world, wherever convoys ran. Many of them came back for further training as leading signalmen and convoy Yeomen of Signals, eventually taking over all these duties from the active service ratings. Of the first 500, over 20% (101) and another 26 RN signal staff lost their lives.[4]

As the war progressed, these HO signalmen took over nearly all the convoy work, releasing the pensioners and reserve naval signalmen to man the warships, escort carriers, minesweepers, and the new Escort and Support Groups. In the early days it was very hard both on the commodores, used to professional dedicated naval signalmen, brought up in naval traditions, and on the signalmen themselves, pitchforked into a new world and working in very close quarters with men two or even three times their age who had reached and passed the peak of their careers.

Ernest Dunhill, who joined through the Boy Scouts Association, recalls:

> For my first convoy I was posted to the staff of a Rear Admiral (retired). He was a white-haired old gentleman in his seventies, and had captained a cruiser during the First World War [just before Ernest was born]. I was a lad of 20 who a few months previously had been a junior clerk in a Chartered Accountant's office. The Commodore's staff consisted of a Chief Yeoman, a Petty Officer Telegraphist, both pensioners who had been recalled, and three signalmen who had never been to sea before.

Ernest went on to serve in about sixty ocean convoys in the Atlantic and the Mediterranean, more even than the top-ranking

Commodore Manners, (Rear Admiral Sir Errol Manners KBE RN Retd) who completed fifty-two ocean convoys, including ONM 249 which consisted of 153 ships. Most of these convoys were dismal, grey and boring, but on this occasion it was one of the rare sunny days in the Atlantic:

> The Commodore's ship was a medium-sized merchant ship carrying about 100 passengers, many of whom were taking the opportunity to sunbathe in the warm sunshine. It was difficult to believe that there was a war on. I had the afternoon watch, and the first indication of anything unusual happening was a signal to say that a battleship was overtaking us and would pass through the convoy. HMS *Prince of Wales* steamed through the convoy flying the following signal: CHURCHILL WISHES YOU A PLEASANT VOYAGE.
>
> Having passed through the convoy, *Prince of Wales* turned and passed through again. The Prime Minister was returning home after a meeting with President Roosevelt on board an American battleship which resulted in the Atlantic Charter. Our Chief Yeoman suggested that we fly the white flag with a diagonal scarlet cross – the V flag. The warship on our starboard side took her cue and an identical row of flags fluttered out as every ship in the convoy hoisted the 'V' for Victory flag. I felt quite important sending and receiving signals between my Commodore and the Prime Minister, the First Sea Lord, the Chief of the Imperial General Staff, etc.

Pageantry like this was rare in the Atlantic and Arctic Oceans and the North Sea, but the responsibility that the convoy signalmen bore was much greater than that of ratings of equivalent rank in any other branch of the Service, and the burden was more onerous because they were not operating in an established naval environment, with plenty of advice, supervision and instruction available to them; in a merchant service environment where they were on their own and had to make their own decisions. Whereas most of the commodores expected them to maintain naval standards of discipline and conventions, the officers and crews of the ships in which they sailed were usually much less formal. The convoy signalmen were never part of that wonderful self-contained body of people, the happy ship's company of one of HM Ships, which builds up tribal loyalty and community spirit from the date that a ship commissions. After each convoy, consigs moved on to other British, Allied or neutral ships. The lucky ones occasionally picked up ships which maintained peacetime standards.

Commodores tried to keep their teams with them from convoy to convoy, but the principle was not accepted by the Trade Division of the Admiralty on the grounds that the commodores got more time ashore in which to write up their reports, be briefed or debriefed and to travel from job to job than was proper for young signalmen. Where a feeling of close confidence had built up, commodores often fought hard to hold on to the same Yeoman from ship to ship, and sometimes managed to succeed, but this made it worse for the signalmen, who might suffer a change of Petty Officer, a change of ship, and often a change of convoy route after each convoy.

As a branch of the Armed Services, the convoy signalmen probably saw more of the different aspects of the war at sea than any other branch, because of the variety of officers they served under, the variety of masters and mates in the ships, the different nationalities and the different oceans and seas in which they sailed.

Sometimes they were thrown in at the deep end. There is a story of one man who went to the Boy Scouts' Headquarters at 25 Buckingham Palace Road, SW1, where they were pleading for volunteers who had some idea of signalling. He was asked to fill in a form giving various personal details including the nature of his job in civilian life. He filled it in quite correctly as 'signalman'. He was taken into the Royal Navy as an ordinary signalman and, to his dismay, almost at once found himself at sea as part of a crusty Admiral's staff in a merchant ship. He then had to explain that his previous signalling experience had been confined to the Southern Railways signal box at Clapham Junction.

An idea of the variety of their life can be obtained from a summary of a year's work recorded in Len Matthews' log.

1942

November: Troop convoy in *Narkunda* for Torch landings.
Sunk by bombing at Bougie on 14 December.

December: Convoy JW 51B to Russia in *Empire Archer*. Attacked by *Lützow*, *Hipper* and 6 Destroyers. Commodore Melhuish breaks only pair of glasses. Captain Sherbrooke, HMS *Onslow*, awarded the VC.

1943

January: Attacked by ski troops while transferring to Murmansk in an armoured train.

February: Convoy RA52 from Russia in Daldorch.

March: Convoy to New York in *Prometheus* takes 23 days.

April: Collisions in ice on convoy to Halifax in *Empire Southey*.

June: Troop convoy to Sicily, Bombed and damaged.

July: Mediterranean convoy in *Letitia*.

August: Based Gibraltar.

September: Decoy convoy Gibraltar to UK in *Merkland*; attacked for 17 days by aircraft and U-boats.

October: Convoy to Halifax in *Saluta*.

The value of the consigs and of the Yeomen of Signals to their commodores can best be gauged from the recommendation written by Vice-Admiral Sir Malcolm Goldsmith KBE DSO when recommending Convoy Yeoman Bob Pell for a Distinguished Service Medal:

I am very anxious that the services of this admirable Petty Officer should be rewarded by a DSM. He has been my right-hand man from the very beginning, and has always shown a good and gallant example under all and the most trying circumstances.

In April, 1940, I took a convoy with guns and ammunition to Andalsnes in Norway. We were heavily bombed for the best part of two days. All the ships suffered and all had to be docked for repairs on return to England. The Master of the *Delius* (my ship) was awarded the CBE, Petty Officer Pell's example and cool-headed leadership were conspicuous.

In June, 1940, I was evacuating the troops from St Nazaire. Again we were heavily bombed. The *Lancastria* was sunk by bombs. Again Petty Officer Pell behaved admirably and set a fine example.

In January and March, 1943, I took a convoy to and from Murmansk. The convoy was bombed and attacked by submarines. The weather was appalling. Petty Officer Pell cheerfully did far more than his duty as usual.

31

Besides these occasions on which the ships were in jeopardy from bombs and from aircraft Petty Officer Pell has been my continuous and only source of help in my work for many a tedious and weary voyage and I feel that my debt to him can never really be repaid.

He volunteered to serve, leaving a well-paid and steady job, the minute hostilities broke out. His patriotism does one good to contemplate. I admire him immensely.

I earnestly hope my request that he be given the DSM will be granted. He deserves it far better than I deserved my Knighthood and infinitely better than the master of the *Delius* deserved his CBE.

Admiral Goldsmith, who made this glowing recommendation, was born on 22 August, 1880, and his way up the ladder was not without some setbacks. He was involved in a collision in 1918, he 'exercised insufficient care with the custody of the Confidential Books' and managed to incur the expression of Their Lordships' Severe Displeasure.

However, his successes and service outweighed his peccadilloes. He commanded a division of the 9th Destroyer Flotilla at the Battle of Jutland, sailed his 15-ton yacht *Rame* single-handed to Malta to take up his appointment as King's Harbour Master and had reached high rank before he was placed on the retired list in 1931. He was back as an ocean commodore on 4 September, 1939, taking his first convoy out on 7 September, 1939, and completing thirty-eight convoys, plus a number of military convoys, before the end of the war.

In 1943, Commodore Goldsmith said, 'I hate my job like poison. My life is so dull.' At that time he claimed to have convoyed 1,500 ships and only lost 'two or three'. He died on board his yacht, *Diotima*, off Greece in 1955, having been become a Knight of the Order of the Sword of Sweden and a member of the Order of Stanilas and St Vladimir of Russia.

Chapter Four

SIR KENELM CREIGHTON

'For a dyed-in-the-wool Royal Naval officer like myself, it was a difficult task to get to know these merchant seamen, what went on in their minds and how to persuade them to unbend . . . a gulf seemed to separate the officers and men of the two services.'

Six hundred and thirty-two Allied Merchant ships, over one million tons, were lost during the Second World War due to 'unknown and other causes', one out of every eight ships sunk. A few were overwhelmed by the sea, but most went aground, hit ice or collided due to human error, not enemy action. Commodore Sir Kenelm Creighton (Rear Admiral Sir K.E.L. Creighton KBE MVO RN), born in 1882, was a specialist navigator, an admirable background for the job of convoy commodore. The navigation and seamanship skills required to bring a great body of very slow ships across the Atlantic through foul weather, bad visibility, fog and ice and to make a safe landfall through minefields after weeks at sea without sight of sun or star, maintaining radio silence, would be beyond the capability of most officers today, if they were deprived of their satellite navigation aids, which are now bought by most offshore yachtsmen for a few hundred pounds and, provided the satellites are available, save all the trouble and skill involved in celestial navigation.[1] In his training as a specialist navigator he was exposed not only to an extensive technical education but also to practical handling of large ships with different characteristics in close company. Indeed he spent most of his time during the First World War at sea on the bridge of big warships in close company.

As a cadet he had the same training as other officers of that generation, followed by a prolonged period of preparation as a junior officer. The training was a fine mixture of theory and practice; among other duties he had carried out the first survey of the north coast of Borneo since Captain Cook's, working from a small ship still equipped with sails, as well as a single screw, using the Dyak headhunters when ashore to carry his gear through the jungle. The job of a navigator brought him in close contact with many of the most senior officers in the days when the Royal Navy was at its strongest. His responsibilities included not only navigation but advising Commanding Officers and Flag Officers on the handling characteristics of their ships under all weather conditions. He rose steadily through the Navy, becoming Master of the Fleet under Admiral Beatty in the battleship, HMS *Queen Elizabeth*. He fought in the Battle of Jutland and was on the bridge of that ship in the Firth of Forth when Admiral Beatty took the German High Seas Fleet's surrender in 1919 and had the satisfaction of seeing the German ships proceeding to anchor in the berths which he had prepared for them.

After this long and competitive apprenticeship he was promoted to Captain on 31 December, 1921, and rose to command the battleship *Royal Sovereign*, in the Mediterranean. During Mussolini's time he 'heard the strutting Fascists prating about Mare Nostrum', as the new stylish Italian fast and heavily-armed warships came into commission.

But after the First World War there were too many senior officers for the few ships in commission. So, like many of his contemporaries, he swallowed the hook and in 1934 retired to live in a small house bordering one of the creeks that stretch inland along the coast near Portsmouth. From the Wharf House in Emsworth he could see the ebb and flow of the tides, sail his boat, look after his garden and sit on the local magistrate's bench twice a week. On a retired officer's pay with two children to educate, he was short of money, so he took up an offer to don RAF uniform and to help in the selection of pilots, with the exalted rank of Honorary Flight Lieutenant RAFVR. His sciatica came back to bring him to a halt and leave him doubled up in a dingy hotel bedroom between his stints of interviewing, but two weeks' hard treatment at the Royal Naval Hospital at Haslar put him right and able to respond to a call from the Admiralty when summoned, with a score of retired Admirals, to Greenwich to take part in a series of five-day courses to prepare them for the job of ocean Convoy Commodore. When he looked round the circle of weather-beaten old faces it seemed more like a gardeners' outing than a Convoy Commodores' Conference.

Having completed the course, he was still recruiting for the RAF when he heard the news of the sinking of the *Athenia* on 4 September, 1939, and made his way to the Admiralty. He changed back from his RAF uniform to his naval uniform, carefully preserved in mothballs and took a drop in his naval rank from Rear Admiral, Royal Navy, to Commodore Second Class in the Royal Naval Reserve. Having been a useless expense to the Admiralty for five years, he was suddenly in immediate demand, with just a few days to get ready to go back to sea. His wife repaired the ravages of the moths on his old uniforms, and Gieves in Portsmouth replaced the gold braid on his five jackets with the broad band of a Commodore Royal Naval Reserve. Then he hurried off to the town to buy himself a seaman's kitbag.

A telegram ordered him to report to Southend, where he found frantic activity to put into effect the long-laid plans for the huge network of convoys which had been worked out so carefully and thoroughly by the Trade Division of the Admiralty in preparation for that day. Confusion reigned when he first arrived – the plans were paper plans and had not been rehearsed by a single exercise involving merchant ships between the wars – but a week later he was immersed in the first of his convoy conferences, presided over by the Naval Officer in Charge and attended by the Masters of the six small ships that would make up convoy OA 13, led by the ancient rusty tramp, *Merchant Prince*, which would have the honour of flying his Commodore's broad pennant.

Four years and seven months had gone by since he had handled a ship, but here he was.

clambering up the vertical wire ladder dangling over the side. I chuckled inwardly, contrasting my present position with the pomp and circumstance that attended my arrival aboard my last

35

command, the battleship *Royal Sovereign*, with her well-scrubbed gangway and mahogany rails, bosun's pipes shrilling and the officer of the watch and quarterdeck staff rigidly at attention. . . . The Chief Officer yanked me inboard, my other hand collecting a lump of thick black grease on the way.

Then for the first time he met his staff, not this time budding young commanders and ambitious young Flag Lieutenants determined to prove how zealous they were, but a trio consisting of a signalman and a telegraphist led by Yeoman of Signals Stanford. The only cabin available close to the bridge was a small rabbit hutch next to the master's cabin, which compared unfavourably with the spacious suite of cabins that he and his staff would have occupied in the Royal Navy. There was moisture and rust all over the deckhead and the cabin bulkheads, with a few hooks and some drawers under the bunk for his gear. On this ship, as on many others, he learned that it was the poor standard of food that was going to be the hardest thing to bear.

He led an uneventful convoy of small ships under flags of many nations with one single escort as far as nine degrees west at which point he ordered the convoy to disperse with most of the ships bound for Halifax. While in convoy he had chosen the simplest zigzag diagram from the twenty options provided and used no other during his three years as convoy commodore. He saw little point in zigzags in a slow convoy, since they gave rise to an enhanced risk of collision, particularly at night and in bad visibility, and lengthened the time at sea. (Several years later, when Admiral Horton took over as C-in-C Western Approaches, he amended the convoy instructions to reduce the zigzagging in slow convoys.)

In the Royal Navy HM ships fly a distinguishing Flag when a Flag Officer is on board (hence the expression – Flag Officer). In the good ship *Merchant Prince*, the Master, impressed by the responsibility of being Commodore's ship wore a bowler hat in honour of the Commodore's broad pennant, but replaced it by the traditional cloth cap when the Commodore dispersed the convoy and lowered his pennant.

The weather treated the westward-bound Atlantic convoys

very harshly, increasing the passage time and potential storm damage, because the ships were often in ballast and had to fight not only against a prevailing head wind but also against the Gulf Stream. At the end of the journey the ships faced ice in the winter and fog on the Labrador Banks for many months. To give them a little time to recover in Halifax the Commodores stayed in the Nova Scotia Hotel, in fine rooms with bathroom attached and a Commodores' club room, stocked with drinks supplied by the generous Haligonians. The Commodores usually had ten days in port, during which they and their staff could write up their reports, swop experiences with their colleagues and relax.

It was different for the masters and officers of the merchant ships, who were not provided with comfortable hotels to go to and in any case had little opportunity to get away and recover from the transatlantic passage. For the masters of the merchant ships, arrival was the start of another period of activity, during which they dealt with the problems of finding berths, of loading and unloading cargo and preparing the ships for the return journey. Crew problems, usually brought to a head by excess of alcohol in the dockside bars, had to be resolved, deserters replaced and repairs effected.

In Halifax, where the Bedford Basin can hold several hundred ships, our Commodore met Commander Oland who had retired after 17 years in the Royal Canadian Navy. He was brought back in 1937 to set up the Naval Control Service, a 'fine rock of a man, as sure, serene and strong as his native Nova Scotia'. We will hear more of his huge contribution to the convoy system.

While he was in Halifax a reporter from a Canadian newspaper wrote about his first sight of a gaggle of convoy commodores:

Through the years, like all sailors, high or low, they no doubt dreamed of their retirement to a little home by the sea; of a wife whom they would see every day, a small garden, children, grandchildren. This happy life they have left to go to sea again, to face sudden death.

My first recollection of them was when I saw three elderly men in naval uniform, slowly climbing the stairs to the Control Office. Weathered, grizzled, they had a look of command, of race, for all their weariness and veteran aspect. Each wore on his chest a blaze of ribbons; each on his sleeves carried the broad band of commodore.

Halfway up they paused, like ageing horses on a hill. 'The old pump,' said one, 'isn't so good as it used to be.' Three pairs of eyes, amazingly young in wrinkled faces, exchanged amused glances of agreement. The three pairs of legs, grown slow and a bit unsteady stumped up to my office. These are the elders of the sea who command our convoys.

Commodore Creighton returned home in a convoy of fifty-two ships. This was exceptionally large for the early days. At the conference before the ships sailed the assembled masters of the merchant ships were given their orders. One instruction stated baldly that if a ship was torpedoed no other ship must stop to pick up survivors.[2] In this, and every other early convoy, this grim reminder of the realities of war was a major test of the merchant seamen's morale and sometimes, gallantly but rashly, a master ignored this order with disastrous results.

On the return voyage Creighton travelled as Rear Commodore, leading one column and heading up one section of the convoy, ready to take over if the Commodore's ship was damaged or sunk. These two early convoys came as a great shock to one who had known nothing in his previous life at sea except the Royal Navy with its pomp and swagger. He reported when he got back:

For a dyed-in-the-wool Royal Naval officer like myself, it was a difficult task to get to know these merchant seamen, what went on in their minds and how to persuade them to unbend . . . a gulf seemed to separate the officers and men of the two services.[3]

Nevertheless the amount of vital practical information related to the running of convoys that the Commodore picked up in his return journey to Halifax and relayed back to the Trade Division, was quite amazing. The Commodore learnt of the huge gap in the disciplinary powers of the master of a merchant ship over the mates and the seamen. In theory he had absolute power over everybody on board, but he found in practice that

> [The masters of the merchant ships] upheld discipline by sheer character and personality, for their powers of discipline under Board of Trade Regulations are almost non-existent.

He saw a recalcitrant seaman knocked down the bridge ladder to persuade him to go on look-out duty. He became conscious of the very limited manpower resources in a merchant ship, and the cheese-paring attitude of many ship owners towards the maintenance of their ships and their responsibilities to the crew. He learnt that revolution counters were unknown in some merchant ships and that orders for small alterations in speed took the form of verbal requests from the master to the chief engineer, relayed by word of mouth by the junior apprentice.

He knew that smoke from the funnel could sometimes be seen fifty miles away by a waiting U-boat, but he learnt now that an engineer burdened with bunkers of northern coal of doubtful quality would have little chance of avoiding making smoke compared with one bunkered with good Welsh coal, and the master would get bolshy if bombarded with signals to increase speed.

He saw first-hand the best and the worst masters of merchant ships: 'when they were good they were very very good, and when they were bad they were horrible'. On a convoy from Gibraltar the master of the Commodore's ship, before sailing, had visited most of the bars in Main Street and had to be sent below by the mate, fortunately a big man, on the orders of the commodore who was a small man. When convoy SL 13 left Sierra Leone under his command in December, escorted, as was not unusual, by a solitary sloop, he found surly unwelcoming officers, led by an openly hostile young master quite indifferent to the need to navigate his ship. It fell to the Commodore to bring the convoy up the Channel in thick fog and his first certain knowledge of land was a welcome from an aircraft sent out to meet them, telling them that they were five miles south-west of the Owers Light Vessel, having passed the Isle of Wight without seeing it.

Modestly he described the job of the Commodore thus:

> The Commodore's position was like that of an old ram leading a flock of sheep. When the commander-in-chief heard of danger in store for the convoy, like the shepherd, he told his most trusted sheepdog – the escort commander. The escort commander told

the Commodore, who, gathering his flock together, turned away from the danger. The trusted sheepdog chivvied up the stragglers and stood-by to drive off the Wolf Pack.

He was too modest. In that convoy he had first to bridge the gap between the merchant service and the Royal Navy and adjust to different standards after nearly forty years in the Senior Service. He had to establish his position as an 'old ram' that the wary master mariners would follow. Twice he had been forced to take over command of the ship in which he was supposed to be a passenger because of the ship's officers' incompetence.

For three years of convoy duty his life, like that of most of the merchant seamen, was a boring and exacting routine, sometimes waiting for days for convoys to assemble in those most unfriendly and barren anchorages in the inlets of Iceland, and sometimes plodding, rolling and pitching along day after day in the perpetually grey and sunless waters of the North Atlantic. When his convoy came back to a British port he was allowed a few days at home; if he was lucky the telegram ordering him back to sea would specify 'hot' which meant a trip down to the warm waters on the way to Gibraltar, or on to Sierra Leone, with never a sight of a U-boat or of a German aircraft.

During the period shortly after France fell it was a different and sadder story. The shock of losing an ally alongside whom Britain had fought from 1914 to 1918 was compounded by the need to put the French fleet out of reach of the hands of the Germans or of the Vichy Government. He became involved in the problem of repatriating thousands of French soldiers who had escaped from the beaches of Dunkirk but wanted no part of future fighting, and who were consuming food and resources in internment camps in Britain. The action Oran[4] was completed when the Commodore was on his way with a convoy of fifteen ships carrying 15,000 French troops to be landed at Casablanca. He was flying his broad pennant in *Balfe*, whose master was Captain Woods.

Captain Woods was in his late sixties, white haired . . . typical of all that is best in our Merchant Navy masters. He was quiet, a good Christian and took life as it came.

40

As he approached Casablanca, the escorts left him. The Frenchmen on board were armed, but the officers and crews of the merchant ships were unarmed. The French were decidedly, overtly (and understandably) anti-British. His ships were surrounded a few miles off Casablanca by French naval patrols who ordered him to stop. He was boarded by a burly French officer with three armed bodyguards:

> They marched straight to the bridge where the Capitaine was most disagreeable. He asked me if we had a wireless office. I replied that we had. Whereupon he ordered one of his men to lock it up. He then strode across the bridge elbowing my dear old master, Captain Woods, out of the way as he did so. This made me see red. I rushed up to him, grabbed him by the lapels of his coat and said that I objected to his insulting attitude towards the master and took strong exception to the way he was behaving.

The Commodore obtained permission to go in and land the French troops, guided by a pilot who deliberately bumped his ship into the jetty. Once alongside, the French Admiral attempted to impound the ships. He sought advice from the C-in-C Gibraltar and received no reply. As soon as he had disembarked the French troops, he and his ships were put under arrest by the resident French Admiral and told that he would not be released until each of his ships had taken on board 1000 British refugees from Gibraltar. To release these valuable ships, the Commodore asked permission from the C-in-C Gibraltar to bring these Gibraltarians back (by letter since the Wireless room was still locked up). This was refused, but the Commodore ignored the refusal and took them back to Gibraltar and then on to England, with just two lifeboats per ship and any spare life-rafts and lifebelts that could be scrounged from Gibraltar. The conditions on board were appalling and, if the ship had been attacked, the loss of life would have been very heavy, but by good fortune the convoy arrived without serious incident.

In September, 1941, after two years of convoy duties, there came a break in his routine when he was engaged on the HG convoys between Britain and Gibraltar. Many of the ships were old and small coal-burners carrying iron ore. *Avoceta*, his ship on convoy HG 73, was a 3000-ton cargo liner, fitted out to carry passengers as well, which was most unfortunate for him as the passengers included 128 foreign refugees, sixty of whom were children or babies who had been stranded in Europe when the Germans overran France and the Low Countries. Most of the remainder were disillusioned foreign women who had married men of British citizenship. The convoy was well escorted by a destroyer, two sloops, eight corvettes and the catapult ship *Springbank*, carrying a Hawker Hurricane aircraft which could be sent off, but only once, to deal with a shadowing aircraft. The pilot then had two options – to ditch close to an escort and hope to be picked up, or to make for the nearest friendly airfield, in this case Gibraltar.

By the summer of 1941 the number of U-boats in commission had started to rise rapidly, increasing in a year from forty-nine to 124 and then rocketing to 239 in December. This was not reflected by the number of operational boats because of Dönitz's insistence on a very high standard of training before the U-boats went to war. In September there were 190 in commission, of which 115 were under training and only seventy-five in service.[3] During that summer the squadron of Focke-Wulf Condors, K.G.40, had been transferred to the Fliegerführer Atlantic and a series of actions against convoys started where strong forces of U-boats and the Condors were working together, which was quite unusual. These actions were concentrated in the seas off the coast of Spain and Portugal, out of range of Allied fighter protection for the convoys from Gibraltar or England, but within range of the four-engined long-distance German reconnaissance planes. The convoy was first spotted by an Italian submarine, another rare event, which brought in the Condors. For four days these menacing aircraft, the vultures of the convoy routes, circled the convoy, out of reach of the anti-aircraft fire, guiding the wolf pack to its prey. Unimpeded by aircraft cover, the U-boats travelled at high speed on the surface to get ahead of the merchant ships and position them-selves for an attack in darkness. If an escort chased them on the surface, the U-boats were several knots faster than the corvettes and almost as fast as the sloops. The Hawker Hurricane was launched from the catapult ship *Springbank*, and chased the shadower for a short while, but it wasn't fast enough to do any damage and had to limp back to Gibraltar as the last few gallons of fuel petered out.

In spite of the strong escort, Commodore Creighton judged that his ships were in for a very bad time. Heavy wireless traffic warned of U-boats ahead and he estimated that the last opportunity for an attack would be just after the moon set on 25 September and that the convoy could only hope to escape if there was a fog or a violent storm. He had 128 passengers and forty crew on board and brought the women and children up to the smoking room under the bridge, where Yeoman Stanford did his best to cheer them up, working with a young priest of thirty-five, who was praying with them and hearing confessions in one corner of the saloon which he had turned into a chapel.

They liked Stanford, with his friendly smile, and his great bulk reassured them. He loved children and was always joking and playing games with them. Creighton remembers him coming to the bridge and saying:

> When we started this trip, sir, a Jew was a Jew and an R.C. was an R.C. and a good few had never been inside a church in their lives, but they all came drifting into the saloon to pray and hear that priest. We've found a common religion there.

The Commodore's premonitions were accurate. On the night of 25 September the moon set just before midnight. Shortly afterwards *U-203* loosed off a spread of four torpedoes. The first hit *Varangberg* and the third and fourth hit *Cortes* with heavy loss of life. The second caught *Avoceta* in the engine room. The Commodore and Signalman Erskine were hurled across the bridge; when they came to they picked themselves up and stumbled across to set off the distress rockets. *Avoceta*'s bow reared up until they were standing on the front surface of the bridge, while below them the water cascaded down the almost vertical deck, sweeping the passengers and children from the smoking room. The night was hideous with screams and the roar of escaping steam, *Avoceta* hung there for a short time and then plunged stern first below the waves just four minutes after she had been hit, taking forty-three of the crew, four gunners and seventy-six of the 128 passengers with her, among them many of the children. One of those who perished was the priest who had worked so hard to give comfort and hope to so many in their last hours.[5]

The Commodore was dragged down with her, entangled in the rigging of the foremast, and was close to drowning when his lifebelt and an escaping bubble of air blew him to the surface, fifty yards from a crowded raft, stone deaf but still able to swim. He hung on to the raft for three hours with the temperature down to 42°F, shivering and dizzy. One by one the occupants of the raft, dazed and choking on oil fuel, slid off and disappeared.

As the cold bit into him and he gave up hope for the second time the corvette *Periwinkle* appeared out of the darkness, nosed up alongside and he was hauled up the scrambling nets onto the deck. Two of his staff of convoy signalmen were not so lucky. A young Ulsterman and a Canadian, Larson, were lost, but Signalman Erskine and Yeoman Stanford survived.

Creighton, still deaf and badly shaken, called upon his Vice Commodore to take over command for the remaining miles. The slaughter continued throughout the following two nights and days and the U-boat commanders claimed to have sunk eighteen ships. This was a gross over-estimate, but of the twenty-five ships that sailed only sixteen survived.

Creighton lost all his gear, so carefully darned by his wife in the first week of the war, and his seaman's kitbag, but when he got ashore in Liverpool, in the course of one day he was treated to a dinner by the Operational Intelligence Centre, condemned to everlasting deafness by the doctor ('There is nothing that can be done'), attended Admiral Noble's Court of Inquiry, got on the train, met his wife in London, arrived back home at Wharf House and there, home at last, fell into a deep sleep from which he woke thirty-six hours later in time to get to his local church on Sunday to give thanks to God. He found the same old people there, sitting in the same pews and praying for those who had gone to defend their country.

He didn't hang around for long. His hearing returned in a week and by November he and Stanford were back at sea together, with Stanford as cheerful as ever, 'all merry and bright' in a slow convoy of forty-one ships, heading into the usual westerly gales. The ship was carrying a big consignment of whisky. The dockers in Liverpool, when loading these cargoes, were in the habit of claiming 'temptation money'. If not paid, the fragile glass bottles were apt to get smashed during the loading process and the leaking contents were mopped up and disposed of by the thirsty dockers. The officers in the Commodore's ship seem to have picked up the same habits on the trip across the Atlantic. When they emerged from the fog off the Labrador Banks they found themselves forty miles out in their landfall and the Commodore was on the bridge with his sextant to get them back on course, employing his rusty skills as a navigator.

A military convoy of eighteen ships carrying many troops and materials of war left Gourock for the Mediterranean on 10 June, 1942, under his command, protected by a big contingent of warships with the battleship HMS *Nelson* in the middle. A thick fog descended and he and the convoy were ordered by the SOE to make an emergency turn of ninety degrees. The ships in the convoy took their orders from the commodore, but he refused to execute this unseamanlike order and advised *Nelson* and the ships in the convoy accordingly. Nothing happened and nothing more was said.

Between these incidents there were many thousands of miles of boring and monotonous steaming, always with the threat of the unseen submarine below the waves with its torpedoes. As we have seen, it was natural that most commodores, if they developed a good understanding with their yeomen, tried to keep the same one on each succeeding convoy. A keen young petty officer had to get back into the Fleet to obtain promotion and some needed the money. Nevertheless, while some changed partners frequently, other pairs managed to stay together for years. A particularly close bond had developed between Creighton and Stanford and, in spite of official policy, they managed, by devious means, to stay together like a pair of yoked work horses for three years. In the late summer of 1942 the Admiral decided he was getting past it and that it was time to give up. Creighton told Stanford, who agreed with his decision and he asked to be relieved of his appointment, a request that was granted on 28 September, 1942, three years and twelve days after his first appointment and after completing twenty-five convoys. In each of those three years he had spent an average of seven months actually at sea. Stanford and he had been together all this time.

Creighton said of his oppo, 'He had served me well and we had become good friends: he never failed me in any small way. He was a most tactful man and very popular with the officers and crews of the merchant ships. Loyal, dependable and unfailingly good humoured, I could not have wished for a more able lieutenant in those hard years.' He went back to general service for the rest of the war and became Chief Yeoman of Signals in an aircraft carrier. When his time was up he left the Navy to run a dairy farm in Devon.

Many of the Convoy Commodores and their Yeomen of Signals, through many hours of discomfort and danger spent together, developed this strong bond of interdependence and trust. Some of the Yeomen felt in their hearts, in a good-humoured and friendly way, that they were really there to make sure that the old boys didn't get into trouble. And the Commodores felt that the young lads were coming along quite nicely and might one day become seamen. The fact remains that Creighton and Stanford played chess together to pass away some of the worst times of waiting, and young Stanford usually won.

After a short period ashore Creighton was appointed Director-General of Lights and Ports Administration for Egypt, the Red Sea and Cairo, and sailed with his wife to take up his new appointment, but his ship, the 20,000 ton Dutch liner *Marnix Van Sint Aldegonde*, carrying 3,000 troops, was torpedoed and sunk. The drill of the ships crew and the discipline of the troops on board was so good that not a single life was lost, and the Admiral, for the second time, and his wife, for the first, survived to complete their journey.

Chapter Five

THE COASTAL CONVOYS

In spite of the shortage of escorting warships, of commodores to command them and of signalmen to support the commodores, the network of coastal convoys also started to run from the first day of hostilities. The merchant seamen and ship's companies who sailed in them were under attack immediately, because they were a vital link in Britain's distribution system. For them there was no 'phoney war'.

Before the outbreak of war many of the larger ocean-going ships which brought in the vital food, fuel and raw material imports from abroad docked in London, the east coast or south coast ports. As the war progressed, more and more of these ships docked in the west coast ports to reduce the risk of further losses in the North Sea or in the English Channel. But land transport facilities from the west coast ports, by road or rail, were already unable to carry the load: the Great North Road in 1939 was a two-track lane that wound its way through the old coaching towns; the rail system was already working at full capacity and had not sufficient waggons to carry this additional freight.

The shipping and ports on the east coast of Britain were already hard-pressed: the power stations of London and the south coast alone needed 40,000 tons of coal weekly from the coalfields of County Durham and Yorkshire, which was shipped through the ports of Blyth, Newcastle, Sunderland, Hartlepool and Middlesbrough, and carried with the other bulk general cargo in coasters down the east coast.

Before 1939 solving the problem of protecting this shipping had not received a very high priority, although it was not difficult

47

Orkney Islands
Scapa Flow
Outer Hebrides
The Minch
Aultbea
Inner Hebrides
Aberdeen
SCOTLAND
Oban
Methil
Firth of Forth
Greenock
Glasgow
Edinburgh
NORTH SEA
North Channel
Newcastle upon Tyne
Belfast
Middlesbrough
Flamborough Head
IRISH SEA
Hull
R. Humber
Dublin
Liverpool
The Wash
IRELAND
ENGLAND
Cromer
WALES
Gorleston
Yarmouth
Lowestoft
Aldeburgh
St George's Channel
Milford Haven
Felixstowe
Harwich
London
R. Thames
ATLANTIC OCEAN
Bristol Channel
Southampton
Plymouth
English Channel

Southend
Shoeburyness
The Nore
Ooze Deep
Sheerness
I. of Sheppey
Miles
0   5
The Thames Estuary

to foresee that shipping on the east and south coasts of Britain would be exposed to unusually high risks. They would, in fact, be in the front line of battle. Whereas the Admiralty was obsessed with the concept that the safety of the country would depend on having more big ships and bigger guns than the enemy, the coastal trade, although an essential part in the whole distribution system of Britain, depended on many dirty little ships. These small coasters were not armed at the start – and never adequately armed, even at the end – and were escorted by too few escort vessels which were not in much better shape.

The ships that carried these cargoes were of course exposed to the usual marine hazards of collision, fire, fog and tempest. Along the east coast, from the Firth of Forth to the Humber, on past the Wash, the shoals off Cromer, the shifting sands of the Thames estuary, round the North Foreland, inside the Goodwin Banks, the ships were threatened with the constant menace of cross-currents, shifting sands, the dreaded lee shore, stranding and collision. The North Sea is a cold, unfriendly sea, with short aggressive waves and an unusually high occurrence of fog and mist; a balmy, sunlit day merits a special entry in the log with the certainty that payment will be required in the form of more suffering on the morrow. From the first day of war these 'normal' perils were multiplied many times over. The requirement to sail in convoy meant close proximity to many other ships with different characteristics of speed and manoeuvrability; shore aids, lightships and navigation lights were either switched off or only available intermittently; many of the shipping channels were closed to navigation. Darkened ships sailed without lights in narrow swept channels. In the coastal trade ships were expected to sail in convoy, to keep close station, to double their number of lookouts and to respond instantly to the orders of the Commodore or the escorting warships. But this trade was highly competitive, and the ship owners were not keen to increase their crew costs to provide for the additional lookouts and watchkeepers needed to cope with wartime convoy sailing, even when experienced officers and crew could be found.

They came under enemy attack from bombing and from E-boats. To the westward of the North Foreland, after France fell and before the English Channel was closed, the big German guns behind Cap Gris Nez carried out target practice on the little coasters as they paraded slowly along the south coast on a set course at a set range, like ducks in a tub in a village fair. The range was known, the narrow swept channels were plotted and the German guns were well dug in and firing from steady platforms. Fortunately they were not able to use the dome of Boulogne Cathedral as an observation and fire control point because, so the local story goes, when the dome was built in Napoleon's time the architect was anti-British and ordered the builders to stop taking the tower any higher so that they could not see England.

In the early months there was no effective air cover for the coastal convoys. RAF Coastal Command's first priority was to watch the exits from the North Sea to the Atlantic to detect any attempt by the German surface raiders to break out. (Though, had they detected any such breakout they would not have had the numbers or the fire power to take any effective action; continuous surveillance was in any case impossible due to the weather conditions which prevail in the North Sea.) Their second priority was to carry out anti-submarine patrols. Even the four Trade Protection Squadrons of Blenheims formed on 17 October, 1939, under Fighter Command had been transferred by December to other duties and replaced by short-range single-seater fighter aircraft. These planes were quite unsuited to this duty: they had little endurance and too often took off and arrived with the convoys after the German raiders had come, made their attacks and gone home.

For most of their length the swept 'safe' channels accommodated both north- and south-bound convoys. The channels were so narrow, a mile or less from side to side, that the ships were deployed in only two columns, which could stretch from van to rear for 20 miles or more. Sometimes, due to shortage of minesweepers or damage to their sweeps, the ships had to be further elongated into one single column, a difficult and slow manoeuvre at any time, but made hazardous in bad visibility or by night in a high wind and driving rain. To re-form these slow ships into two columns took for ever.

The Commodore at the head of his long 'snake' of ships threading their way down these narrow alleys could rarely see all his charges, and often did not know what was happening to the tail-end charlies, miles astern and sometimes sailing in different weather conditions and under attack. There were not enough aircraft to provide continuous cover, they could not always find the convoys and when they arrived they were liable to be fired on by trigger-happy convoy ships as they appeared out of the clouds. When the first convoys were attacked by aircraft, neither the masters of the merchant ships, nor their officers, nor their commodores, nor the aircraft pilots had any experience of working together, nor did they have the training, equipment or skills to communicate between single-seater fighter aircraft and surface escorts. As a result it was quite common for fighters to be in the air 'covering' one section of a convoy, but quite unaware that another section a few miles astern was under attack.

The ordeal of the coasters did not end when they docked: they were sitting targets when they were in port, immobilized alongside, or at moorings, loading, unloading, under repair or waiting to join convoys, 100,000 tons of shipping could be lying off Southend pier waiting to sail, and another 100,000 tons lying off the Downs in the examination anchorage.

Nevertheless the first regular trade convoys in operation were the east coast convoys, starting on 6 September, 1939, running between Methil in the Firth of Forth and the east coast ports to the great convoy assembly and dispersal point off the Nore and Southend in the Thames estuary inside the Yantlet Gate.[1]

These east coast convoys were coded FN northward, and FS southward. They ran on a two-day cycle in each direction, starting with FN 1 and FS 1, progressing to FN 100 and FS 100 and then restarting time after time as the war rolled on. They were escorted by the destroyers, sloops and A/S trawlers of the Rosyth Escort Force, under the command of the Commanders-in-Chief of the Nore, among whom were Admirals Sir H.J.S. Brownrigg and Admiral Sir Reginald Plunkett-Ernle-Earle-Drax, who both became Commodores of ocean convoys. Many of the Commodores of the ocean convoys working from Liverpool did their 'apprenticeship' on coastal convoys.

It is difficult to arrive at an accurate total for the convoys that sailed during the Second World War. There were Trade convoys

51

and Military convoys and since a convoy was defined as any merchant ship escorted by one or more warships, it is impossible to say accurately how many sailed. After five years of war the Secretary of the Admiralty called for a report of the numbers of convoys sailed from the principal convoy ports in the United Kingdom and also of the number of ships that sailed independently. The returns showed 4,025 ocean convoys, 10,025 coastal convoys and 174,215 independents, an average of almost eight convoys every day, nearly all under the command of a commodore, and nearly one hundred ships daily unescorted, varying from the majestic Queens ploughing across the Atlantic with a Division of troops on board to the old sailing barges creeping round the coast.

Southend was the main centre of activity for coastal convoys. The activity in the great Port of London and its anchorages at that time is difficult to imagine. The thought of this great number of ships milling around in shoal waters within easy range of German bombers and navigating in narrow channels visited by mine-laying aircraft leaves one breathless. Nevertheless, 61,155 ships cleared from Southend with losses that averaged only two per thousand over the whole war. The thousandth convoy sailed in May, 1942, after which the losses fell to one per thousand.[2]

Most of the Southend-Rosyth convoys were under the command of a commodore, sometimes supported by a vice-commodore. The commodores were usually drawn from the ranks of Lieutenant-Commanders or Commanders in the Royal Naval Reserve, who were qualified and experienced masters of merchant ships, holding Board of Trade masters' or extra-masters' certificates, who had undergone annual training in the Royal Navy. It was a very demanding and onerous appointment. The commodores and their staff of signalmen were not always welcomed when they came aboard the little coasters. Many of the coasters simply did not have room, facilities or food for this influx, and the masters were not used to having anybody senior to themselves in their little kingdoms, breathing down their necks and laying down the law. Some were tactful, some were not.

From the outset of the so-called 'phoney war' when most people in Britain were wondering what it was all about, the men who manned the little ships around the coasts of Britain, particularly the east and south coasts, were risking and losing their lives. The main killer was the German mine. Not just once in a while, but daily and nightly, the Germans laid mines. They laid them with fair accuracy in the narrow channels conveniently marked with navigation buoys for the convenience of the shipping, particularly in the narrow constricted approaches to the ports of London, Felixstowe and Hull. They laid them from E-boats, and sometimes from disguised surface craft which dodged the watch provided by the overstretched Auxiliary Patrol lines. They scattered them with equal frequency, but with less accuracy from aircraft. Many of these fell on land. Occasionally they laid them from seaplanes which alighted unopposed to sow their deadly crop close inshore. They laid them from U-boats, which were being used as submersible torpedo boats operating on the surface, where they could not be detected by Asdics, and disappearing if attacked, tactics in which they had been thoroughly trained by Admiral Karl Dönitz at his training centre in Swinemünde on the Baltic Sea during the interwar years.

Mines were a particularly nasty form of attack. The threat of their presence, like that of the U-boat, hovered like an evil smell on the water, invisible but ever-present. When a mine struck, there was no way in which the ship could hit back; indeed it was sometimes impossible for the victims to know what had hit their ship.

While the Admiralty discussed big ships and big guns, the Germans laid mines. The Royal Navy's small and quite inadequate minesweeping fleet was equipped solely to deal with mines moored to the bottom, which exploded when something hit them – contact mines. In the first week of hostilities it became evident that mines were exploding close by ships but not after being struck. Something was horribly wrong.

On 16 September, 1939, *City of Paris* was so severely shaken by an external explosion that her crew abandoned ship. But she did not sink and, when reboarded, it was found that no part of her hull was holed. It was now clear to the specialists in HMS *Vernon*, the Navy's shore base which dealt with mines, and the Mine Design Department that acoustic or magnetic mines were being used. This was devastating news.

There were many variations and combinations of acoustic and

53

magnetic mines,[3] but the counter-measures, although developed and known, could not be put into production until a mine was actually recovered and dissected. Only then would it be known which of the many possible variations were being used by the Germans. To make the task of analysis more difficult and more hazardous for the mine-detection teams the Germans introduced double and triple booby traps to explode in the faces of the experts trying to dissect any mines that fell on the sandbanks or mudflats, or were revealed by the falling tide. They even dropped dummy mines that had no other purpose than to kill the mine-detector teams.

For two months the Royal Navy had no answer to the magnetic mine. No progress was made until, on 22 November, 1939, a parachute mine was seen to land on the mud at Shoeburyness. A very brave officer, Lieutenant-Commander J.G.D. Ouvry, and his team, disarmed it and turned it over to the bomb-disposal experts who established that it contained 650 pounds of Hexanite explosive and that it was activated by the magnetic field of a ship passing overhead.

But there was no effective short-term solution available. The coastline and the ports were scoured for wooden ships to act as spotters to pinpoint where the mines were laid and attempts were made to set them off by the use of very large magnets: maybe positive thinking, but not at all successful.

The longer-term solutions were to demagnetize all ships by passing a powerful electric current round each ship (wiping), which provided a temporary solution for a few months, or to reverse the magnetism (degaussing). To wipe or to degauss all ships presented a mammoth problem. 3,000 ocean-going ships and 1,500 coasters carried Britain's supplies. On any day 2,500 were at sea, not counting hundreds of fishing boats and trawlers. Either of these solutions gave rise to further problems, since most of the ships depended on magnetic compasses, which were not always reliable even before these drastic measures were taken to alter ships' magnetic fields.

Meanwhile the Germans complicated the problem by extending the areas of minelaying and by laying both moored contact mines and magnetic mines in the same areas. Contact minesweepers sweeping for moored mines could be blown up by magnetic mines, and magnetic sweepers could be blown up by moored mines. Meanwhile both warships and merchant ships could be and were blown up by either and endured great slaughter.

The Germans profited vastly from our lack of preparation. The lightships and channel buoys were still in position, making it much easier for them to lay their mines with great accuracy in the shipping channels. By the end of October nineteen ships (59,027 tons) and in November another twenty-seven (120,958 tons) and a destroyer had been sunk by mines and many more damaged. In under four months since the outbreak of the war, while the war ashore smouldered, the Germans had sunk seventy-nine ships (292,697 tons) and inflicted dreadful casualties on the Merchant Service officers and men who manned them. They had filled the shipyards with damaged ships and succeeded in closing the greatest port in the world. On 21 November all navigation lights were extinguished and night sailings stopped in the Thames estuary. The situation was so critical that two of the three navigation channels, and for a short time all three channels, into the Port of London were closed. The Big Ships of the Royal Navy were powerless to help as the Germans started to throttle the British.

These initial casualties were devastating. Had sinkings continued at this rate the supplies to the South of England power stations and industry in Greater London would have petered out.

How did we recover from this early crisis? Fortunately for Britain, in this respect the Germans were not much better prepared than the Allies at the start of the war. They had stocks of 20,000 contact mines, but only 1,500 magnetic mines and they very soon ran out. By the time they had replenished their supplies the counter-measures were beginning to have an effect, and the lightships and shore lights no longer guided the enemy to their targets.

On 28 March, 1940, the first of the LL mine-sweeping trawlers began to operate.[4] They did the job, but they were not very popular with their crews at first, because they caused almost as much damage to their crews' nerves as to the mines they exploded. The ships were specially strengthened, but this was scant consolation to the crews, who could look forward with certainty to a very severe shake-up whenever they were successful in blowing up a mine.

In May, 1940, the spotlight shifted from the east coast to the battle off the coasts of Holland, Belgium and France, as Hitler's tanks swept through Europe. The ship and aircraft resources were concentrated on the evacuation of the Army from Dunkirk. Nevertheless the battle of mines and counter-measures continued. The Germans changed the polarity of their mines, then introduced delayed-action devices. In August, 1940, they brought in the acoustic mine, which was set off by the noise of the ship's propellers. The counter to this was a Kango hammer in a huge bucket lowered over the bow. Unfortunately the range of the Kango hammer was very limited and the mines exploded quite close ahead. It required a quartermaster with nerves of steel to steer straight into the water dead ahead where a mine had just exploded and the hill of water thrown up had not yet subsided. Finally, at the very end, the Germans started to use pressure mines to which there was no known answer which could be applied in the short term.

Once a convoy was outside the maze of the channels among the shoals off Norfolk and the mouth of the Thames estuary, the ships crept from one to another of the dimly lit buoys which marked the swept channels, though the buoys were often either missing or out of position. During the long winter nights too often their lights were not working and the normal marine hazards were increased by exceptionally bad weather. The port of Hull was blocked with twelve feet of ice and, in the worst weather, even by day the fog, rain, snow and vicious short seas obscured the buoys which could only be spotted when it was too late to avoid hitting them.

A well-armed and reliable escort on the east coast was HMS *Valorous*, one of the renowned V and W destroyers that played such a significant part in the Second World War. She was long in the tooth, having been built – very well built – in 1917, but recently refitted with useful twin 4-inch dual-purpose anti-aircraft guns. She held a very proud record of convoys sailed. She was well known and always recognized by the coal-scuttle brigade[5] because of her distinguishing pendants, L 00, prominently painted on either bow. On one black winter's night

56

in the middle watch she was leading an FS convoy down across the mouth of the Wash; the current was setting across the course line, pushing her over to port, mightily aided by a great gale from the starboard beam. The combined effect at low speed was to shove her along like a blind crab. There was no sign of the next buoy when a vicious gust and rain squall came down to blind her, so that the Kango hammer on the bows disappeared and visibility was suddenly nil. On the open unprotected bridge, in the driving spray and hail, the only way to protect the eyes was to look through the wrong end of a megaphone, a time to grit the teeth and not call for mother – things would get better. As each squall swept through, the Officer of the Watch and Duty Signalman peered over the side of the bridge into the wet bitter darkness.

'Object close alongside to port sir!' bellowed the port lookout.

A few feet away, separated by the bow wave from the ship's side and tossing slowly down the length of the forecastle and the upper deck, was the unlit buoy, seemingly dragged in towards the ship's side by the sideways drift of the ship.

'Hard a'port. Full ahead both engines!'

'Wheel's hard a'port, Sir. Both engines full ahead.'

The buoy bobbed along, very close under the bridge structure; the stern swung out to starboard, just clear and the buoy disappeared into the murk astern.

'Close one, Sir,' said the Duty Signalman and sucked his teeth.

At breakfast the next morning the coxswain took his orders from Buster Brown, the First Lieutenant. As he turned to leave the wardroom, he hesitated a moment, with his hand on the door latch.

'During the middle watch we stuffed a couple of hammocks into that slit in the ship's side in the Chiefs' mess, Sir. I think it will hold; not much water coming in and it's above the water-line.'

'Thankyou, coxswain. I'll be along to have a look.'

The door closed. There was a silence.

'Now I wonder who had the middle watch,' said Number One.

Most of the commodores on the coastal convoys were either Commanders or Lieutenant Commanders in the Royal Naval

Reserve. In some ways they did not have so much freedom of action as the Ocean Commodores, because their ships were restricted to narrow corridors and the tails of the columns of their convoys were many miles astern, usually out of sight. Whereas the ocean commodore had sea room and could dispose his convoy over a wide front and exercise his charges before entering the danger zones, and had some chance to manoeuvre and take evasive action when attacked, the coastal convoy commodore had no such options. He had many other problems to deal with, problems that did not trouble the Ocean commodores.

The early convoy, FS 6, gives some idea of the challenges that were faced on a typical voyage. Commander C.C. Forrest RNR took the ten ships to sea on 11 October, 1940, setting off from Methil bound for Southend, escorted by the sloop HMS *Lowestoft*, the destroyer *Wolsey*, and two A/S trawlers. Three ships peeled off at the entrance to the Tyne and the Commodore transferred from *Folda* to *Marsden*; by the time the convoy had reached Middlesbrough the number of ships had increased to forty-six, which the escorting warships and the Commodore herded into their allocated places in two long, very long, columns. This was not a simple task because those destined for the earlier ports needed to be in the column next to the coast and those turning off first had to occupy the rear stations. This could result in the ships capable of the fastest speed being at the rear, and the sluggards in the van, conditions leading to a bunched-up convoy with the frustrated fast ships in the rear surging up alongside the leaders – or the reverse, which resulted in an uncontrollable convoy strung out for miles, with the leading ships racing to get in before the pubs closed. In FS 6 the job was made no easier by the absence of signalmen in the Vice-Commodore's ship and the consequent need to transfer his pendant to another ship.

Although these convoys had now been running for a year, one of the escorting ships reported that there were still several ships showing bright stern lights, and a sharp reminder from the Commodore was reinforced by the unwelcome appearance of two unidentified aircraft, suspected to be shadowers.

A stern wind from the north pushed the convoy along faster

than planned, putting it ahead of schedule at the point where five ships should have joined from Hull. They were not there, so *Wolsey* had to wait for them, leaving just one destroyer and two A/S trawlers to escort this unwieldy snake on the second night of its journey as it moved down the swept channel across the mouth of the Wash. Just before darkness fell on the second night the Commodore received a signal ordering him not to arrive at the Aldeburgh Light Vessel before 0630; after that point the buoys were not lit and the arrival of the convoy had to be synchronized with the progress of the minesweepers. So the night was spent with the ships creeping down the swept channel at 4¾ knots, with the wind up their sterns. The ships at times had to point up by as much as twenty degrees to counteract the strong set of the tide off the mouth of the Wash, sidling from buoy to buoy like crabs. This was a difficult bit of seamanship, made more so because many of the buoys marking the channel were unlit or out of position, a situation that was unremarkable because it happened frequently.

As daylight filtered through, the minesweepers formed up ahead. Ships had been mined in this area two days previously and one of the sweepers had run into a German device which blew up her starboard sweep, so that the pair of minesweepers were not able to sweep a broad enough channel to allow the safe passage of both columns. Mines were exploded one cable each side of the channel. The Commodore was well aware that ships in the middle of the snake often failed to repeat his signals, but, in spite of the danger that this manoeuvre would cause confusion at the rear end of the line where the ships were way out of sight, decided that he must merge the two columns into a single line. By dusk that evening the Commodore's charges had come safely home to Southend and the Senior Officer of the escorting ships reported that the Commodore had handled the convoy 'extremely well'. He had not been troubled by enemy attacks and the weather conditions were just normally unpleasant.

The slow and complicated progress of this convoy was typical of many and illustrates the difficulties of timing, navigation and handling of slow-moving ships in confined channels in winter conditions under constant threat from the air, from mines and from E-boats.

Commodore H.R. Wilkinson (Commander RNR), following with convoy FS 14 soon after, had much more to think about. His ship, the comfortable *Royal Fusilier*, didn't turn up and he had to hoist his pendant above *Fulham III*, a little collier, one of the coal-scuttle brigade which delivered their cargoes to the power stations up the Thames in Fulham. These ships were totally unsuited for use as a commodore's ship. There wasn't a master on the east coast, or a simple seaman, who didn't know that the Fulham ships were just basic seagoing trucks, built with hulls shaped to carry the maximum quantity of coal from Newcastle to the Thames, with some space reluctantly allocated to an engine to push the cargo along the coast to its destination. The space that remained, and there wasn't much, provided accommodation for the Master and crew. Had a commodore and signalmen been welcome, which they weren't, there would still have been no way in which they could have been given the most elementary comforts, even a bunk to sleep in. This was not too important as commodores didn't reckon to turn in at all on an east coast convoy; the navigation and care of their unruly flock required their constant attention even if the Germans didn't attack. But there were complications also about food and rations, lack of halyards for the signal flags, the quality of the coal, and communications with the engine room.

When the Commodore set off, half an hour late, he had no time to think about creature comforts because mines were already being sunk by the trawlers just ahead showing that a new crop had been laid since the previous convoy had passed that way a couple of days before.

Conditions were very poor as darkness fell on the second night. After 62D buoy off the Humber the convoy set off across the mouth of the Wash and visibility deteriorated so much that not a single buoy or its light was seen. After two and a half hours of blind steering, Commander Knapp, the SOE in HMS *Lowestoft*, a very experienced officer who had taken numberless convoys up and down the east coast wrote:

I considered that it was unsafe to continue without ascertaining the convoy's position . . . so I proceeded to the eastward as I felt fairly certain that the convoy had been swept to the westward

60

by the current. I found 59A buoy 4 miles to the eastward and got the convoy back into the channel again

There are two significant features in his report. The first is the use of the words 'considered' and 'felt'. He had only a compass to tell him his heading and a log to tell him how far he had been through the water; the lights on the buoys were not visible. In two and a half hours the tides and winds had carried the ships four miles off course. Had they been on course, the alteration to the east would have put them out of the swept channel perilously close to the British Mine Barrier QZ 152.

The second is the phrase 'got the convoy back into the channel again'. The Commodore and the SOE had first to find the channel; then they had to get messages to the leading ships, without lights and in lousy visibility; then they had to make sure that the rest of the ships followed and didn't lose touch; then they had to make sure that they weren't running into the north-bound convoy coming up on opposite course, which would have been experiencing the same problems of navigation.

The convoy was back in the channel but it had jumped right out of the frying pan into the fire. The leading ships of the convoy were already late for their rendezvous with the minesweepers and couldn't slow down. Meanwhile *Wolsey*, after a dark and confusing night at the rear of the convoy, had come up to report that the stragglers at the rear were now out of sight, 14½ miles astern and still dropping back. To add to the confusion, a floating mine was sighted to port and sunk by rifle fire. One of the minesweepers lost its sweep when it hit a German explosive anti-minesweeping float. Two bombs fell at the rear of the convoy. A further mine was brought to the surface right in the middle of the channel ahead of the ships and sunk by rifle fire. When these problems had been sorted out, the SOE suggested that the convoy might just get in before dark if it proceeded at maximum speed. The Commodore signalled nine knots, only to find that the collier in which he was flying his pendant could only make eight and a half, due to bad coal in its bunkers. So, since he had ordered his ships to do nine knots, they started to pass him, led by HMS *Lowestoft*, with the Vice-Commodore in *Houston City* close astern. At 1712, half a mile past the East Oaze Light Vessel and a few miles from home, there was a violent explosion and a large column of water was flung up abreast the port quarter of *Houston City*. She drifted slowly south across the path of the convoy, with her steering gear out of action. *Lowestoft* stood by her and the leading ships thought better of their dash for home, falling in dutifully behind the Commodore and giving him the honour of braving the next mine.

Lowestoft put an officer and some hands on board *Houston City* to bolster up morale and to provide help with wooden plugs to stop the holes in the engine room bulkhead, remaining with her until the tugs took over.[6]

The Commodore would have a day's rest, if he was lucky, before he picked up the next convoy going north. For *Lowestoft*, standing by *Houston City*, it was then too late to go into Sheerness and she waited for the next northbound convoy to come out. A fog came down, dense enough to cause the cancellation of the convoy already assembled off Southend and ready to go north.

Commander Wilkinson's next southbound convoy a month later was designated a slow convoy, but whoever had compiled the sailing orders did not allow for a strong northerly wind helping the ships on their way.

He arrived at the rendezvous two hours early, collected nine ships and pushed on. The convoy continued to creep ahead of schedule, because each time speed through the water was reduced the ships became unmanageable, yawing wildly either side of the course line and surging up on their next ahead as the wind caught them from astern. Off Flamborough Head no signal had been received about ships joining from Hull and the Commodore was in a dilemma. He was still two and a half hours ahead of time. If he went on, the ships from Hull would miss him. Worse, he would arrive at Aldeburgh while it was still dark, and from there on the buoys were not lit and he had somehow to rendezvous with the minesweepers who would be waiting to sweep ahead of him.

He turned the convoy back through 180 degrees at 0950. This was a nail-biting manoeuvre. It meant that his signalmen had to get the signal seen, acknowledged and repeated right down the line, and that each ship, in a narrow channel in a following sea, had to turn back 180 degrees on its tracks to the new course at exactly the right time – an essential but risky manoeuvre, but they did it and at noon he told them to do it again and they resumed their normal course, picking up two puzzled ships joining from the Humber.

At dusk an aircraft was spotted shadowing the convoy and at 1726 a Junkers 88 made three low-level bombing attacks and machine-gunned several ships who were slow to reply. But *Pitwines* reported that she had tried to fire her Holman Projector, one of the pieces of armament that was supplied to merchant ships to give the impression that they had a means of fighting back. The Official History describes it euphemistically as 'an extemporised weapon'. The projector used steam or compressed air to fire a Mills bomb in the general direction of an attacking aircraft, but on this occasion the grenade burst prematurely, killing one man in the *Pitwines* and wounding three others. HMS *Woolston* sent across her doctor to give medical assistance.

The convoy passed safely through the channels off the Wash, but next morning an enemy aircraft was seen to be shadowing the convoy, and at 1239 three Dornier 215s carried out a series of attacks lasting twenty minutes. Four single-seater RAF fighters were over the convoy at the time and could be seen clearly while the attacks were taking place. The pilots' visibility was so restricted, and communication from the ships to the aircraft so bad, that they were quite unaware that the other end of the convoy was being bombed and oblivious of the anti-aircraft fire of the escorting warships. Commander Knapp, the SOE, reported:

I have frequently had similar experiences before and such experiences are common to all escorts. While the very great difficulty of the single-seater fighters is fully appreciated, it is felt that the effectiveness of a fighter patrol over a convoy is greatly diminished on account of there being no means of communicating with them. . . . It is suggested that pending the provision of efficient communication arrangements between escorts and their fighter patrols, the following procedure might be of assistance:

> Fighter escorts to be ordered to patrol over the convoy and
> to remain in sight of the convoy the whole time. On sighting
> enemy aircraft, escort to make puffs of black smoke. These
> smoke puffs should be quickly sighted by the fighters if they
> are told to look out for them and it would at least warn them
> of the presence of enemy aircraft in their immediate vicinity.

This suggestion showed that Commander Knapp had at least
read and absorbed the contents of Confidential Book C.B.
MOSS/1940.[7]

The trials of FS 30 were not yet over. At 1412 *Baltrader*,
almost home and one and a half miles from the Barrow Deep
Light Vessel, hit a mine and sank clear of the channel with the
loss of two of her crew.

For crews in the water, the chances of survival on the coastal
convoys were greater than the ocean convoys for a number of
reasons. Ships could be mined or bombed, but the water was
often shallow enough to allow the damaged vessel to be beached
for temporary repairs or for the crew to remain on board until
rescued. If they did take to the boats or rafts, they had much less
distance to cover to get ashore; they were within range of aircraft
patrols and were unlikely to drift around for long without being
seen.

A major factor was the continuing life-saving activity of the
Royal National Lifeboat Institution. With its established string
of stations covering the whole of the coastline, with particular
strength along the east and south coasts where the main danger
lay. The RNLI carried out its work without interruption, with a
fleet of boats manned by coxswains and crew who knew
intimately every mile of the coast without any need for further
training. The knowledge they had could not be picked up on a
crash course; it was knowledge gained by a lifetime of operation
in all weather conditions over waters that were known to them
from years of experience, quite often handed down from father
to son, in boats designed to pick up shipwrecked seamen.

The slow south-bound convoy FS 69 was steaming in two
columns down E-boat alley off the Norfolk coast in very heavy
weather. The leading ships were nearing the Haisborough Sands,

well known to east coast mariners whether in peace or in war as a major hazard to all shipping. The Sands stretch for 9 miles in a bank a mile wide which at some points has only 2 foot of water over it at low water, and at the best 12 foot, nowhere enough to float a laden merchant ship surging up and down in a full gale.

That night the north-westerly gale was blowing the ships right across the narrow swept channel towards the shoals under their lee. In convoy at night the watch officer tends to tell his relief to, 'Follow that one ahead. See it? Got the weight? Then I'm off.'

So ships generally followed the next ahead in the blind belief that if the ship ahead was not aground, then there was enough water for the followers. In a gale, helped by a fierce cross-current, this could lead to a great sagging tail drifting down into the shoals. On 6 August, 1940, in the poor visibility of a wild grey daybreak, a leading ship followed the escort trawler HMS *Agate* straight on to the sands, followed by the whole column. Within minutes six ships and the trawler were aground on the sands, all in the space of a mile, with an ebbing tide. For four hours the escorts scurried around and pandemonium reigned, while the wind blew the ships higher and higher onto the bank. At 0800 it was clear that the ships wouldn't last much longer and that the crews' lives were in peril: to lose six ships was bad enough, but to lose their experienced crews as well would be a major tragedy.

Four hours were wasted before the RNLI was asked to help, but within eight minutes of the call the Cromer lifeboat was afloat and on its way to the scene. It had seventeen miles to go, arriving two hours later,[8] and followed by the second boat from Cromer and the Gorleston boat. The tide was ebbing and the seas were breaking over the decks of the ships. The escorts drew too much water to get near the grounded ships and in any case were quite unaccustomed to this type of rescue work.

RNLI Coxswain Herbert Bloggs took his lifeboat over the deck of the first ship and picked off sixteen members of the crew by driving the lifeboat into a crack in the hull of the wreck and holding her there for long enough for a man to scramble to safety. He repeated this manoeuvre sixteen times and came away with sixteen survivors. He then moved on to the second ship to take off another thirty-one, by which time his second lifeboat had come up. Bloggs transferred his second coxswain to her while he went on to the third wreck. Using the same technique he took off another nineteen men. Meanwhile the second Cromer boat took off the crew from the fourth wreck, while the lifeboat from Gorleston took off the crew of number five.

Which left the sixth. The tide had ebbed by now, leaving her high on the bank and Coxswain Bloggs' boat bounced on the bottom as he went in to collect another twenty-two exhausted crew members huddled on deck and swept by every breaking sea. As he tried to take his boat away she grounded along her full length, but came off on the next wave. This final effort brought his total up to eighty-eight men rescued, while the second Cromer and Gorleston boats took off another thirty-one.

In three hours these lifeboats and other ships present had rescued 119 men out of the 155 on board four British, one Estonian and one French ship at great risk to themselves. The Cromer boat was holed three times and had twenty feet of her fender and eight feet of her stem torn off. In the turmoil, the brass bolts securing her stem had been driven through eight inches of solid oak.

But the RNLI's rescues were not confined to the shallow waters of the North Sea. In December, 1940, a Dutch straggler coming in from the Atlantic, separated from her convoy by three days of gales and snow, lost her rudder off the west coast of Ireland and was driven ashore, becoming wedged hard and fast on the rocks on one of the islands off Bloody Foreland.

The great ocean rollers, nearing the end of their majestic journey across the Atlantic, stretched as far as the eye could see, 250 yards apart. These islands were the first obstructions to their progress. At first, as the shallowing water slowed them down, they towered up and then the crests began to curl over until they toppled and broke with all their fury before rolling in on the stranded ship.

The escorting destroyer went in as far as she could, until the seas were breaking and sweeping down her upper deck from end to end. When four foot of green water surged over her bows and took four of her crew to their death she could go no closer and had to abandon her attempts to take the crew off. The seamen clinging to the masts of the wreck launched their boat but all ten on board perished when it was picked up by a breaking wave and smashed in the cauldron of waves among the rocks.

The nearest lifeboat station was 25 miles away at Aran Island, to the south of the very top point of the north-west corner of Ireland where the wreck lay. When all else failed the lifeboat was launched with Coxswain John Boyle in charge. He took her up behind and to leeward of the wreck, still jammed between the rocks; there was no possibility of getting in to windward without being picked up by a monster wave and hurled on to the wreck. A vicious rip tide was boiling down the passage as he worked up through the islands to leeward and up tide; there he anchored and worked his engines to take some of the weight off his anchor cable. He and the lifeboat's crew had been at sea for nearly eight hours, exposed to the full fury of the gale when they started to pass a line across to the wreck. To do this the coxswain eased slowly down stern first on to the wreck by veering his anchor cable and steering with the help of his engines until he was close enough to fire across the line for the breeches buoy. Eighteen times the buoy was hauled across the cauldron of water, sometimes nearly 100 yards wide, and eighteen times it was hauled back with the weight of the survivor dragging in the tide. Twice the line parted and had to be renewed. After four hours of exhausting toil, stripped to the waist in spite of the snow and the cutting spray, the lifeboat men hauled the last man to safety. They cast off the line and set off on their seven-hour journey to the nearest sheltered harbour on the mainland where all of them, lifeboatmen and survivors alike, had to be lifted ashore exhausted, seventeen hours after the launch.

These are examples of the professional seamanship and gallantry of the lifeboat men who throughout the Second World War carried out their remit to save life at sea, irrespective of race or creed. In all they saved 6,741 lives. They are still saving life at an ever-increasing annual rate. Periodically it is suggested that the Royal National Lifeboat Institution, because of the national importance of its task, should seek or accept a subsidy from Government (subject to conditions of course) instead of relying on the generosity of the public, the hard work and dedication of the fundraisers and the huge courage and dedication of the

Lifeboat crews who provide this service. It is fortunate that this suggestion has been turned down flat, because just about every other naval reserve service, whether voluntary or subsidized, has been cut to the bone or closed down by successive Governments over the past twenty years, unlike the RNLI which has steadily and quietly, year by year, saved more and more people from the peril of drowning at sea, without any cost to the Exchequer.

In July, 1940, balloons were introduced to be flown from ships in the coastal convoys to discourage low-flying air attacks. They were handled by the Mobile Balloon Barrage Flotilla, manned by men drawn from a dozen nations. The balloons themselves, which seemed unaware of the disciplinary requirements of King's Regulations and Admiralty Instructions, proved difficult to handle at the best of times, even causing problems ashore. A Hull newspaper reported in March, 1941, that a balloon got loose and did as much damage as a minor air raid, dragging its cable around several streets, bringing down chimneys and finally dislodging the Guildhall Clock Tower. At sea on a wet and rolling deck in a violent gust of wind, they took on a vicious and unpredictable character of their own, fighting their handlers aggressively and resisting actively all efforts to bring them down to deck level for tethering.

HMS *Valorous* had been leading an FS convoy down the coast and into the Thames. She had been involved in an arduous journey, during which all hands had suffered from a thirty-six hour stint at Action Stations. The convoy ships, still flying their balloons, were just entering the Barrow Deep when, without warning, they were enveloped by a dense bank of fog. The Commodore ordered 'Anchor Instantly', a necessary but dreaded signal which could lead to extreme confusion in a fog. As the ships let go their anchors, a fresh batch of German bombers arrived, happy to aim at the ships' balloons flying above the fog bank and conveniently staking out their targets, permitting the bombers to take leisurely aim in the clear air above without the inconvenience of dodging flak. The ships themselves were wrapped from bow to stern in a cold wet blanket of water vapour, so thick that the bow wasn't visible from the bridge, deafened by the noise of anchor cables roaring out through the hawseholes as the anchors went down all around, and surrounded by the blasts of many sirens. The confusion was made bedlam by the crash of the bombs all around as the Germans completed their target practice. When the fog lifted there were ships everywhere, lying at all angles to the tides and winds, but strangely no collisions and no bomb damage.

After the tangle of ships had been sorted out and got under way *Valorous* arrived at her anchorage off Sheerness. Normally her ship's company could have expected a night's respite before turning round to take an FN convoy back up through E-boat Alley the next day, but due to the delays she was nearly twenty-four hours behind schedule. The men needed a break. After Hands to Dinner, her First Lieutenant ordered a make and mend.[9] The Officer of the Day checked the bearings to make sure that the anchor was holding, read the orders for the day in the log, walked round the ship to see that all was in order, told the Quartermaster and bosun's mate to keep a good lookout and went below for a cup of tea. He collapsed into an armchair in the wardroom. With the ship safe behind the Yantlet Gate, and no air-raid alerts to worry about, he put on the radiogram and played his favourite tune, the Inkspots singing 'I like coffee, I like tea . . .' and drifted off, dreaming of the Wren driver in his home port.

The next thing he remembered was the signalman shaking him.

'Captain would like to see you, sir.'

He pulled himself out of the armchair, grabbed his cap from the rack outside the wardroom and made his way to the Captain's cabin.

'Any signals or orders yet, sub? I was expecting our sailing orders by now, and one or two of the ships seem to be working their anchor cables.'

'Not a thing, sir.'

'Call away my boat. I'm going ashore to check up.'

An hour later a very upset Captain was back on board.

'Tell the First Lieutenant that we're weighing anchor immediately, and ask him to pipe Hands to Stations for Leaving Harbour. And tell the Yeoman to bring me the signal log.'

There in the signal log, as plain as day, was the Officer of the Watch's signature for a confidential signal at 1630 that afternoon. The exhausted officer had signed for the envelope containing the sailing orders, stuffed them into his pocket, but fallen immediately back to sleep and completely forgotten all about them.

In the first four months of the phoney war the commodores on the east coast were already involved in a shooting battle, on the outcome of which depended a vital sector of the distribution system in Britain, including the whole of the activity of the Port of London. Commodores were under fire in uncomfortable ships that couldn't fire back; their ships were bombed by Junkers 87s and Messerschmitt 109s, mined, deprived of normal navigational aids, and torpedoed by E-boats. They had to bring their slow, unwieldy convoys down channels that were not properly swept, escorted by a quite inadequate force of warships. When not harassed by the enemy, they had to exercise their skills as seamen to cope with the dangers of collision, grounding, tempest, fog and snow in one of the worst winters on record.

There was no glamour in the coastal convoys. The departure and arrival ports were very much in the war-afflicted areas. For the commodore, the officers and men, in warships and merchant ships alike, there was no comfortable overseas port of arrival. It was not unusual for them to be bombed as they left Scotland, attacked each day and night on the journey along the coast, bombed again on arrival in Southend, and then run into an air raid on return to their home port.

The coastal convoys ran right through the duration of the war and mines of one sort or another remained a menace until long after the end of the war.

In 1940 509,889 tons (201 ships) were lost to mines. But after the first year the coasters had accepted the need for the delays, discipline and inconvenience imposed by convoys, and between February and September, 1940, the number of minesweepers increased from 400 to 698, and in the next twelve months from 698 to 971, of which 42% were able to deal with acoustic and magnetic mines. These were being built all over the world, in Australia, New Zealand, India, Canada and Portugal, and the US had started building wooden all-purpose minesweepers. Greater use was made of surface forces to keep the E-boats at bay and there was better cooperation between aircraft and ships.

By the first half of 1941 the worst was over: 16½ million tons of shipping passed safely up and down the east coast, and in the full year 36 million tons entered and left the Thames estuary with losses reduced to less than 1½%.

Of the early days, of the coastal convoys the Official Historian says:

> A big unanswerable question still hangs in the mind. If Hitler, instead of attacking Russia, had concentrated the full weight of his airpower against our commercial ports, our docks and dock-yards, our unloading and storage facilities, our coastal shipping and river estuaries, and had he kept the might of the Luftwaffe so directed for months on end if the need were, could this country have survived?

Ralph Roxborough, a convoy Yeoman of Signals, had extensive sea experience in all areas of the European War from the Arctic across the North Atlantic, through the Straits of Gibraltar to Alexandria. He was sunk three times, rescued, went back, and survived the war. It is not surprising that he, and others with the same breadth and depth of experience, will say that the hardest times they experienced were the days and nights on the east coast convoys.

This was a major battle won, for which no special medal was awarded, but the coastal convoy commodores' worries and responsibilities for the long unwieldy convoys in the narrow channels started on the first day and never ceased until the last day of hostilities.

While the convoys were plodding steadily up and down the coast, the ports that they served were also suffering. All were bombed at one time or another. The 'Baedeker' raids on the Cathedral cities and the long-drawn-out tribulations of London have been fully described in numerous publications, but less has been said about the suffering and damage done to some of the east coast ports by air attacks. After inner London, Lowestoft and Yarmouth were the most heavily bombed boroughs in England in proportion to their populations. Another of the worst hit was Hull, a comparatively small city with a population then

71

of 320,000. It was an attractive target. It had been bombed, and no doubt mapped in detail, by the slow-moving Zeppelins in the First World War. It was on the route for German bombers flying to and from raids on the industrial cities of the Midlands, within range of bombers based in Germany as well as in the occupied countries along the facing coasts of Europe, easy to locate, just inland of the intersection of the coastline and the estuary of the River Humber and already identified in March, 1939, as a selected victim. Ten priority targets were marked on the Luftwaffe's maps of Hull: one was the oil refinery, three were clustered together in the north of the city at Stoneferry – the power station, the gas works and the water works. The others were the six important docks, which occupied the north bank of the river and behind which were the terraces of houses in which lived the people who worked in the docks and on the ships. These targets provided concentrated objectives of great strategic importance and they were all hit, some several times. The attacks started in the middle of 1940, but did not reach their full intensity until the spring of 1941. From March onwards they grew more and more ferocious, reaching their climax in May, in contrast to the rest of the country where the air raids declined as the German invasion of Russia claimed priority. They continued spasmodically until March, 1945.

In the 1940s, Harwich was still a small fishing port, so Hull was the closest large port to the maze of channels that thread their way between the sandbanks to seaward of the Wash. Her fishing boats and trawlers became minesweepers and her fishermen the captains and crews that manned them, totally involved in keeping the channels free of mines in all their varieties. The year 1941, when the raids were at their worst, was a crucial period because the docks in the west coast ports were swamped with shipping and some of the large ocean-going cargo carriers joined the convoys that came round the north of Scotland through the Pentland Firth or the Fair Island channel between the Orkneys and the Shetlands to join the regular east coast convoys that discharged their cargoes in the east coast ports. The main burden of keeping these routes free fell on the minesweepers based in Hull. Of the 1258 ground mines swept by the Nore command in that year, 725 were accounted for by

Hull's ships, led by the aptly named *Rolls-Royce* which managed to sweep its hundredth mine on Christmas Eve.

From Hull sailed the blockade-busting flotilla, *Gay Corsair*, *Gay Viking*, *Hopewell*, *Master Standfast* and *Nonsuch*, under the command of Commander Sir George Binney, who was commodore of these five specially equipped Motor Gun Boats (sailing under the Red Ensign), and completed several return journeys to bring back from Gothenburg 348 tons of cargo of special value, as well as sixty-seven Norwegian refugees.

The City of Hull paid heavily for its major contributions to the war effort, but received little recognition: on only four occasions did the BBC News mention Hull in connection with air raids. If a citizen of Hull didn't read his local newspapers and wasn't personally involved, he might have thought that nothing much was going on. But the records show that, over four years, air raids damaged 186,722 (97%) of its 192,660 houses and at one time or another rendered homeless 152,000 (48%) of its population.

In the 'double blitz' in May, 1941, thirty bombers struck during the first night and fifty during the second. The heaviest casualties occurred in the crowded streets behind the dock areas; whole streets of houses were evacuated and each day 25,000 meals were served by the municipal kitchens to the displaced and homeless, estimated to number 40,000. A mass funeral for the 400 killed during these two raids was held and they were buried in a communal grave amid scenes of terrible distress.

In spite of these horrors and the widespread emotional impact of this mass burial, the City staggered unsteadily to its feet and a week later Ministry of Information Bulletin No 7 dated 15 May, 1941, called on all unemployed dock workers to report the next morning as it was essential that all ships requiring to be loaded should be turned round quickly. The same bulletin announced that electrical kettles, at 2/6d and hot plates, at 5/- were available on loan 'until normal conditions were restored' and gave the good news that the Public Library Services would reopen the following day.

The lack of national coverage was a great cause of anxiety for servicemen and seamen away on duty, who were left guessing by the vague mention of 'an east coast town under air attack'. They,

73

or their mate, might return to base to find their house a heap of rubble, with their family missing, evacuated or on the casualty list. To add to this personal suffering, there was a sense of frustration among the fire crews, air-raid wardens and other inhabitants who had been involved in clearing up the mess and looking after the survivors of the raids when they heard on the BBC news about the doughty deeds performed by the citizens of other cities, but found that their city received no national recognition, although the details of damage and casualties were not secret but were recorded in the local papers and the City Records where they could be read, and can still be read, by anyone interested.

The trials that Hull survived are fully documented, but time and developers have erased the scars. The author quoted these figures to a friend who was a young man living and working there during these times, but he would not believe them.

Chapter Six

THE ATTACK ON CONVOY SC 7

As we have seen, the ocean commodores were involved in what Churchill christened the Battle of the Atlantic from the first day of the war, when Leutnant Lemp,[1] against orders, sunk the passenger liner *Athenia* with the loss of 112 lives of whom twenty-eight were American. Admiral Raeder, the Commander-in-Chief of the German Navy, is reported to have said on 22 July, 1939, after an inspection of Dönitz's U-boat flotillas that 'a war with England would mean Finis Germania'. When he learnt on 3 September, 1939, that the uncoded signal 'Total Germany' (declaration of war on Germany by Britain) had gone out to the ships of the Royal Navy, Raeder recorded that the Kriegsmarine was 'in no way prepared for the great battle and could only show that it understood how to die with honour'.

Dönitz was made of sterner stuff. He had already deployed his fifty-seven U-boats at strategic points around the coasts of Britain. No one can doubt the courage and morale of the U-boat officers and crews who fought at the start of the war and went back to sea time and again, even when it became clear that their battle was lost. It is true that a few did so at pistol point, and some more because of the psychological pressure put upon any man who made it known that he had had enough. But the casualty figures show that, even if they had doubts, the morale of the great majority remained unbroken until they were ordered to surrender. This was largely due to the superb leadership of Dönitz who believed that the only hope for Germany lay through the U-boat arm, and that, if called upon, the men who manned them must be sacrificed to save their country. He was convinced

75

that, if priority was given to building, training and operating U-boats, the British could be beaten. He was nearly right, but he was never given the priorities for which he fought.

It has been argued that if he had, the balance would have swung Germany's way before the withdrawal of the U-boats from the Atlantic in 1943. Nor is there much doubt that the new generation of U-boats would have cut communications with the USA if the boats had been operational a few months earlier. When the European War ended, 120 Type XXI U-boats, capable of speeds of 16/17 knots, with a range of 15,500 miles, and sixty-one smaller Type XXIII U-boats, capable of 12½ knots and with a range of 4,300 miles, were in commission and working up.

But others would argue that he lost the battle by his insistence on central control of the U-boat fleet and day-to-day reporting home to base. This wireless traffic was continuously monitored by a ring of shore-based direction-finding stations, and then augmented by direction-finding equipment fitted in the escorts, fleet oilers and rescue ships. The distant stations could give the general pattern of the U-boats' dispositions, and the ship-borne equipment could give more accurate bearings of individual U-boats as they manoeuvred into position to attack the convoys. But when the codes were broken the Admiralty began to re-route convoys to avoid concentrations of U-boats and to divert Support Groups to strike at U-boat rendezvous.

In the first year there were few pack attacks on convoys because there were rarely more than a dozen operational boats at sea. One of the first successful pack attacks came the autumn of October, 1940. On 5 October, thirty-five ships making up convoy SC 7 had gathered in the anchorage of Sydney, Cape Breton, under the command of Commodore MacKinnon (Vice-Admiral Lachlan MacKinnon CB CVO RN Retired). This officer had a record of forty-two years in the Royal Navy. He was the son of a parson and went to HMS *Britannia* as a cadet at the age of thirteen. He rose to be the gunnery officer of the battleship *Indomitable* at the Battle of Jutland, and then the first Commander of the battle-cruiser *Hood*. He was made a Companion of the Victorian Order by King George V for his part in organizing the Jubilee Review of the Fleet in 1935. His career on the active list ended after he commanded the 2nd Battle

Squadron in 1938, and he was placed on the retired list in November of that year. He played hard and worked hard, and though a disciplinarian was popular at all levels. He had a reputation for getting things right. On his Service Record Admiral Hood comments that, after inspecting the battleship *Barham*, he 'had never inspected a ship before in such a highly excellent condition in every way'.

Within a year, in October, 1939, he was back in harness as a convoy commodore and was one of the first to put to sea. In the first year he had completed no less than eleven ocean convoys and was coming up to his fifty-seventh birthday when he was sent to take charge of convoy SC 7.

For this convoy, the NCSO had chosen SS *Assyrian*, carrying grain, as the Commodore's ship. *Assyrian* was not the fastest, smartest, most comfortable or most modern ship in the convoy – indeed quite the opposite. She was built for the Germans in Hamburg in 1914 and handed over to Britain at the end of the First World War, since when she had been tramping around the world from her base in Liverpool. She had dropped out of her previous convoy because she couldn't keep up with the convoy speed of nine knots. She had no refrigerator and the icebox had shattered when she tested out her ancient First World War four-pounder gun. Her Master, Captain Reginald Kearton, was a cheerful young man from a seafaring family; her Chief Officer was almost double his age. Both were Irishmen, in charge of an English and Welsh crew!

Assyrian had two things going for her: she was a well-loved happy ship and she had four double cabins. The Commodore took with him his team of five: his Yeoman of Signals, two telegraphists and two young bunting tossers. At sea the Commodore would share the Master's sea cabin and the others would fit into the four double cabins with three Frenchmen who were taking passage back to Britain to join the Free French. Two to a cabin – luxury, but quite a contrast to the pomp and splendour of command of the 2nd Battle Squadron. He would have to do without his day cabin, his Admiral's barge, his Secretary, his Flag Lieutenant, his personal steward and the rest of the perks to which he had been accustomed.

He looked at the list of the ships that the NCSO had

assembled. For the past several weeks they had been collecting their cargoes from ports on the east coast of Canada and the USA, as far inland as Quebec and as far south as New Orleans. They had loaded grain, aluminium, copper, iron ore, steel, scrap, timber, paper pulp and railway lines, with crated aircraft on deck. There were eighteen British ships, six Norwegians (including *Thoroy* built in 1893), four Greeks, three Swedish, two Dutch and one Danish, and one large French tanker, a beautiful new modern ship. They included three 'Lakers', small flat boats under 2,000 tons with 100 hp engines, designed for trade on the Great Lakes and quite unsuitable for Atlantic seas in October.

The Commodore went ashore from his 'flagship' to carry out the last job before sailing, the convoy conference, which was not a very happy affair. The assembled masters were not encouraged by the news that, for most of their journey across the Atlantic, their escort would consist of a single sloop, HMS *Scarborough*. They all knew that the first of this series of transatlantic convoys, SC 1, had been escorted by the sloop *Penzance* and that the escort herself had been sunk after eight days while still with the convoy. How could a single ship possibly protect a convoy six columns wide with five or six ships in each column? They also knew that the SC series of convoys had originally been planned to end with the summer and they only had to look through the porthole to know that the Atlantic winter was upon them. The Master of the *Fiscus* had a premonition of doom and made no secret of it. Fortunately they didn't know that *Scarborough* wasn't even fitted with Asdics, relying only on hydrophones for the detection of the U-boats and the accuracy of her attacks. How desperate the authorities must have been to send such ill-protected and unsuitable ships on these early Atlantic convoys!

After the briefing and after sailing orders had been handed out to the masters, the Commodore returned on board. He and the Chief Steward had something more immediate and basic to think about. The convoy was due to sail in an hour's time at noon and the stores hadn't yet arrived. There was not enough food on board for the passage. Ships started to weigh anchor and *Assyrian* started to move. As she moved, dead slow, away from her mooring, a fleet of tenders arrived and hurled across bags of flour and other essentials. Not until the last package was on board did she pick up speed to lead the convoy to sea. Now at least they wouldn't starve.

The weather favoured them as the ships took up station. Once clear of the land the six leaders formed up on either beam of the Commodore, then their columns fell in behind them and before dusk fell they were on course and up to speed. The night passed without incident, but when morning came one of the Lakers had turned back and her place had been taken by *Sneland 1* a Norwegian which had arrived late and been sent on to catch up. Later in the day, the *Shekatika*, a Norwegian that had straggled from a previous convoy, tagged on.

From now on communication would depend on flag and sound signals, and, in extreme emergency, signal lights at night. There were no radio telephones and the use of W/T was discouraged. The Commodore took every opportunity of exercising emergency turns. Not only did the Norwegian have language problems, but she had no papers, code books or signal books because the NCSO had run out when she tried to collect her set. The station keeping was quite good, but the coal burners, *Assyrian* included, were making too much smoke, due to inferior coal. This was bad: visibility from a U-boat was normally very restricted because it was so low in the water, but smoke from a convoy on a clear day could sometimes be seen 50 miles away. The masters prayed for the weather to break: the visibility was too good and the sea too smooth for their liking. But the fine weather continued, and so did the Commodore's exercises in manoeuvring and signalling by sound and by flag.

On the evening of Thursday 10 October the wind and sea got up. By Friday it was blowing a full gale and the ships had lost their tight formation and were beginning to straggle. At dawn the daily count showed that four were missing – the two other Lakers and two more. But the miles were rolling away and by Wednesday 16 October the ships were beginning to think about the meeting with the Western Approach escorts coming out to meet them and even counting the days before the run into home ports.

79

In the afternoon the sloop *Fowey* and the corvette *Bluebell* made contact at the rendezvous point and took up station on the starboard side and astern of the convoy. Neither of them could match the speed of a U-boat on the surface, but they were a comforting sight to the thirty-one remaining merchant ships as they settled down for the last leg of the journey home.

But Dönitz had other plans for their future. One of his great strengths was to vary his points of pressure and achieve his results by concentrating his own strength against the weakest points of the overstretched Royal Navy and the convoy system. He had fourteen U-boats available in the Western Approaches, two on weather-reporting duties.

That night *U-48* reported contact with a homeward-bound convoy. *U-46, 47, 100, 101* and *99* were immediately ordered to form a patrol line across the convoy's approach to the North Channel, while *U-48* went in for an attack on the convoy's port bow where *Scarborough* and the ships in the convoy were silhouetted against the moon.

Just before 0400 *U-48* fired three torpedoes at a range of 1500 yards, aimed at three overlapping ships. The first hit the French tanker *Languedoc* and the second hit *Scoresby*, the Vice-Commodore's ship. Commodore MacKinnon ordered an immediate emergency turn to starboard away from the attack and *Fowey* and *Bluebell* came round to join *Scarborough* in a sweep up the side of the convoy, but found nothing. They then went back to look for the survivors, the crews of both ships having got away in their lifeboats. First they located *Languedoc*'s crew and got them on board. There was no sign of *Scoresby*, instead an enormous log jam of pit props in the water in the middle of which sat her whole crew in their lifeboats surrounded by a tangled mass of timber and wire, which formed an effective barrier to *Bluebell* who did not dare come closer in the darkness because of the risk of damaging her propellers. At first light they brought them out safely and went back to *Languedoc* which was still afloat. The Master and some of his officers and crew rowed across to inspect her but found too much damage to the engines and hull to give her any chance of survival. *Bluebell* sank her by gunfire and set off to catch up with the convoy which had disappeared over the horizon escorted only by *Scarborough*. Somewhere astern and out of sight *Fowey* was continuing the search for the attacker.

A Sunderland appeared, called up *Scarborough* by signal lamp and reported a U-boat on the surface ahead. Now *Scarborough* also set off at full speed in that direction, leaving Commodore MacKinnon bereft of his escort and the ships of SC 7 undefended. *Scarborough* continued this unsuccessful search all through the night, until, in the morning, with the convoy long since committed to the ambush lying ahead, *U-48* surfaced some distance away and showed her a clean pair of heels on the surface, whereupon she gave up and chased after the convoy. She took no further part in the actions which were to follow.

There is no record of the Commodore's feelings or those of his flock at this time. He knew that his convoy was on its own but had no knowledge of what lay ahead. Three of his ships (two Lakers and *Aenos*) were missing, two had been torpedoed (*Languedoc* and *Scoresby*), and his three escorts had disappeared.

Unknown to the Commodore and the SOE (Commander Norman Dickinson DSC, RN) in *Scarborough*, *U-38*, patrolling ahead of the convoy, had picked up and sunk by torpedo and gunfire the errant *Aenos* early on the morning of 17 October. The U-boat Commander did not report until the evening that he had seen a convoy the previous night. As a result of this report, the U-boats' line of interception was immediately shifted and the five U-boats made off at full speed to the north.

Otto Kretschmer's War Diary of 18 October makes it sound as if the sea ahead and around SC 7 was now full of U-boats on the surface: during the day he recorded sighting six U-boats on the surface making for the convoy, and that night they were swarming round this weakly defended slow convoy of ancient ships. Their main concern was not to collide with each other and not to be rammed by a seven-knot merchant ship. No wonder the U-boat commanders at this time described this period of the war as their 'happy time'.

Unaware of the trap closing round them, the convoy was cheered by the arrival just after midnight of two (but only two!) fresh escorts, the sloop *Leith*, which took over as SOE, and the corvette *Heartsease*. *Leith* stationed herself astern where she could best attempt to control any events.

U-38 came in from the port bow, which was guarded by *Bluebell*. *Bluebell*'s decks were already so crowded with survivors that her ship's company of fifty-nine had difficulty in getting to their action stations. *U-38* waited until *Bluebell* was at the extreme limit of her zigzag to starboard and, thirty-five minutes later, before the newcomers had time to settle into their stations round the convoy, opened the attack with a hit on *Carsbreck*, third ship in the outside port column. Her deck cargo of pitprops was flung into the air and some caught fire, descending like blazing cabers into the sea around her and silhouetting the ships in the convoy. She provided a terrifying spectacle as she was blown round through 180 degrees by the explosion, but she did not sink and had no casualties. Her next astern, *Shekatika*, managed to avoid her and the flying pitprops, and moved up into the gap that she had left in the port wing column.

U-38 was one of eight large, 1032-ton, U-boats built in 1938/39, with a maximum sustained speed on the surface of over 18 knots. Using this speed to advantage, the U-boat made off for the head of the column, got into position and fired another salvo. The old Commodore, who had had little chance to enjoy his shared cabin for the last two nights, was the first to see the track of a torpedo crossing his bow. He went hard a'starboard, and he, his two Irish friends and the Yeoman and the signalman watched the track of the torpedo as it crossed the bow of the gallant old *Assyrian* as she lurched round to comb the torpedo's track, followed by the rest of the flock.

U-38 scored no hits and does not appear again in this battle. Her reports would soon bring in the main pack and this was the end of the U-boats' assaults for the night.

The four escorts had made no contact with the enemy and were left with the problem of *Carsbreck*. After the explosion one of the lifeboats had pulled away, but had returned and she now had her full crew back on board and was limping along astern. The SOE was faced with a dilemma, whether to leave an escort to look after a damaged merchantman and denude the convoy's thin screen, or to try to protect the main body against possible further attacks and leave the crippled merchantman to its own devices. Commander Roland Allen RN detailed *Heartsease* to look after *Carsbreck* and her crew, leaving his own ship *Leith*, *Fowey* and *Bluebell* to protect the convoy.

All thoughts of a smooth run home for the last few hundred miles had been blasted out of the minds of the 1500 seamen on board the remaining ships and escorting warships of convoy SC 7, now already seven short of the original number. This would be the crucial night.

The Commodore had no need now to warn ships about smoke and straggling: the warning had come in its most telling form when *Leith* picked up nineteen survivors from the Estonian ship *Nora* from the previous convoy. These men had been adrift for five days and nights, hanging on to life-rafts in the freezing waters off Rockall. They were the lucky ones. The rest had perished.

The day passed with many signal hoists from the Commodore to the merchantmen. *Leith* took station immediately behind the convoy. *Fowey* left the port beam to do a search five miles astern and *Bluebell* took over her station. Even farther astern and making only six knots *Carsbreck* struggled to rejoin, escorted by *Heartsease*.

At 1745, in a calm sea and light south-easterly wind, Kretschmer in *U-99* was two or three miles to the south of *U-101*. It was a clear moonlit night with little sea running, just the usual long Atlantic swells that seldom rest. Patches of cloud drifted across the moon from time to time, but *U-101* could see the shadows of the convoy ships as she lifted on the crest of the swells. She was close enough to risk a shaded light signal to *U-99*.

Kretschmer, one of the U-boat Fleet's most determined and skilful commanders, dodged *Bluebell* and manoeuvred *U-99* into position on the port bow of the convoy. At 1749 he sighted a warship.

Searoom to manoeuvre would run out as the convoy approached the North Channel, but Commodore MacKinnon had warned his ships that at 2000 the convoy would take a sharp forty degree jig to starboard for three and a half hours and then back again in an attempt to avoid any U-boat ambush ahead.

But it was too late. The ships, by now quite well drilled by the Commodore's frequent daytime exercises, put their helms over and set off on their new course.

This suited Endrass, another U-boat ace, in *U-46*, bringing the Swedish ship *Convallaria* right into his sights. He nipped in ahead of *U-99* and put the first torpedo into her port side. She remained afloat for twenty minutes. The crew, only too ready for this disaster, got away smartly in their lifeboats and watched disconsolately as her bow rose up to the sky and her stern disappeared. Held afloat by the cargo of paper pulp in her holds, it was twenty minutes before she slid under the waves.

Beatus now spotted a U-boat close to port on the surface and sent out the alarm. The message was cut short by an enormous explosion from a torpedo which hit her between Nos 2 and 4 holds. She took forty minutes to sink and her crew pulled away in the life-boats. The Dutchman *Boekelo* slowed down and hove to to pick them up. This was a gallant action beyond any doubt, but strictly against orders and fatal. Before even one of *Beatus'* survivors was safely on board *Boekelo* herself was torpedoed. Immediately astern of these two stricken wrecks was *Shekatika*, who had pulled out of line to avoid collision, and she was the next to be torpedoed, again on the port side.

The U-boats kept at it, *U-99* commanded with great *élan* and skill by Kretschmer, went in on the surface just after 2200, dealing out short-range death in the bright moonlight. His War Diary reads:

2206 Fire stern torpedo . . . At 700 metres, hit forward of amidships. Vessel of some 6,000 tons sinks within 20 seconds.
  I now proceed head on into the convoy. All ships are zigzagging independently.
  Boat is soon sighted by a ship which fires a white star and turns towards us at full speed. I have to make off with engines full out.

An hour later he was back on the surface in the middle of the convoy. During the night, using both his bow and his stern tubes, Kretschmer fired eleven torpedoes and claimed six hits at ranges of 690 to 975 metres.

The slaughter continued. *Creecirk* went down with all thirty-six crew. The fast *Empire Miniver*, leading the starboard column, decided to make a run for it, but a torpedo aimed at *Clintonia* (which she dodged) went on to catch her before she got clear. *Fiscus* also decided to use her full speed and pushed on at her maximum ten knots, but she also was caught and went down like a stone, taking her captain and all but one of her crew with her, so fulfilling her Welsh Master's premonition. *Gunborg* was torpedoed, but took a long time to sink; all her crew got away in the lifeboats and a young seaman, adrift for the second time in a year of war, even had time to go back to collect his dog. They refused an offer of rescue from the Greek *Niritos*, which was hit in any case ten minutes later with only fourteen survivors.

There was nothing that the Commodore could do. Before the attack started, SC 7 was once more down to a single escort, a corvette this time instead of a sloop, and she was already loaded to capacity with survivors. *Leith* and *Fowey* were both off astern. In the first few minutes of that dreadful night he had lost three of his port column of ships. In the next two hours another six were hit. Among the burning oil from the sunken tanker, the timber and the log jam of pit props from the deck cargoes, the sea was littered with lifeboats and life-rafts. Above the devastation, the smoke from the burning ships and the fires on the waters, there was a moon and starshell from the escorts, as men drowned, choked and died from the burning oil in which they struggled. It was a scene from The Inferno.

Bluebell stayed for over three hours in the area, slowly moving among the litter and picking up boatload after boatload of survivors, herself stopped or moving slowly, an easy target for any U-boat that might be around.

At 0315 *Fowey* was carrying 150 survivors and *Bluebell* 140 more, including the masters of three ships. She stayed to complete the job while *Leith* and *Fowey* did their fourteen-knot best to rejoin what was left of the convoy.

Leith was off on a sweep astern for the attacker, but was unable to contact *Fowey*, also astern, and by this time had closed *Shekatika* to bring her survivors on board. She had no sooner completed this task than she came on *Boekelo*'s two lifeboats of survivors.

We have read Kretschmer's account of being sighted on the surface. The ship which sighted her and gave chase was *Leith*. It was a long chance, *U-99* was two miles dead ahead and capable of bursts of seventeen knots or more on the surface. *Leith*'s best speed was fourteen knots. It would have been pure luck if she had hit the tiny hull of a U-boat, beam 20.47 feet, at 4000 yards at night, by the light of intermittent starshells. The U-boat crept ahead, found a patch of darkness, dived and disappeared.

The odds against success, at much closer quarters, didn't deter Commodore MacKinnon. Suddenly, amidst the confusion, a U-boat appeared 100 yards ahead. The Commodore went full ahead and set course to ram. Captain Kearton called up the second engineer from below, pointed out the target and called for every ounce of speed. The Commodore made the signal: 'U-boat ahead on the surface,' and ordered all ships to open fire. In the engine room they pushed the revs up from their normal maximum 106 to 110 and *Assyrian* for the first and last time in her life made ten knots. She had no guns that would bear forward of the beam.[2] Her only effective weapon was her blunt bow, and for forty minutes, with the stokers going crazy, she had the U-boat running away with no time to dive. But slowly the U-boat drew away and a cloud came over the moon. The enemy was gone. *Assyrian*'s moment of glory was past and she dropped back to resume her sedate leadership at the head of the centre column, laying a smoke screen as she went. Everybody on board felt a lot better, even though they knew now for certain that they were the prime target of at least one submarine ahead of them with no escort up there to deal with it.

They were right. Almost immediately two torpedoes missed *Assyrian*, passing ahead, and then two more passed astern. At 0030 the fifth caught her on the starboard side, just forward of the engine room. A minute later another hit *Empire Brigade* and then another hit *Soesterberg* as she turned away from the danger point.

The explosion smashed *Assyrian*'s starboard lifeboat, killed five men in the engine room and blew three more over the side. The engines stopped and the lights went out. The roar of steam

1. 'Few officers could look back on such a distinguished career '(p18). Admiral Sir Fredric Dreyer *(Imperial War Museum)*.

2. 'I hate my job like poison. My life is so dull' (p.32). Vice Admiral Sir Malcolm Goldsmith *(National Portrait Gallery)*.

3. 'A specialist navigator, an admirable background for the job of a convoy commodore' (p.33). Rear Admiral Sir Kenelm Creighton *(National Portrait Gallery)*.

4. 'Admiral Horton (right) took over as C-in-C Western Approaches' (p36). With him is Commodore Dowding of the Royal Naval Reserve (see p.204) *(Imperial War Museum)*.

5. 'Leutnant Lemp, against orders, sank the passenger liner *Athenia* with the loss of 112 lives' (p.75). She is seen here leaving the River Clyde *(Imperial War Museum)*.

6. 'HMS *Valorous*, one of the renowned V and W destroyers that played such a significant part in the Second World War' (p56) *(Imperial War Museum)*.

7. ' He played hard and worked hard, and though a disciplinarian was popular at all levels' (p.77). Vice Admiral Lachlan MacKinnon *(National Portrait Gallery)*.

8. Rear Admiral Bonham - Carter (see p.200), on the right, had five ships sunk under him *(Imperial War Museum)*.

escaping at high pressure added to the chaos of this ghastly night. The crew started to man the port lifeboat, but this too had been holed and sank to its gunwales as it drifted away. *Assyrian* started to go down by the bow and took a list to port. The remaining crew set about releasing and launching the life-rafts. The hulk of *Soesterberg* drifted down upon them and crashed into their stern before rearing up and sliding down on her last dive. As she went, her cargo of pit props burst from her holds into the air and crashed on to *Assyrian*'s decks, shattering all the rafts and sinking the raft on which the second engineer, Venable, and one of the convoy signalmen had just got clear. They swam back, to be offered a gnarled hand by the Commodore and hoisted in.

A small group, including the Master, Chief Officer, the Commodore and one of his signalmen were now stranded on board. Both boats and all the life-rafts were either smashed to bits or had drifted away. The sea around offered the triple choice of death by drowning, hypothermia or being crushed among the churning pitprops. A lifeboat passed in the distance, full to over-flowing. Another from *Soesterberg*, pulled up to windward and let go a raft in the hope that it would drift down to *Assyrian*. The smashed starboard boat was cut away and floated upside down amid the debris around the hull. A gang of half-a-dozen, including the commodore, then set to, building a raft out of anything they could find, supervised by Captain Kearton and Chief Officer King.

Assyrian shuddered and started to go. They launched the makeshift unfinished raft and it fell to bits as it hit the water. *Assyrian* went with a rush, sucking men, drifting cargo bales and debris with her. Second Mate Frank Bellas and Radio Officer Stracy held the Commodore afloat until he had recovered his strength. The Master lashed his old Chief Officer to a spar. Someone started to sing 'Roll out the Barrel'. Men called from one to another as they clung on. The periscope of a U-boat slipped through the mess and went on its way.

The moon was obscured by clouds as the night wore on. The autumn cold and the loneliness of the vast Atlantic silenced the men in the water as they began to despair and to retreat into their own private worlds. The Commodore drifted up to a raft with six men on it, but there was no room for another. Clutching a plank he hung on for a while and then drifted off again on his own.

In the distance, through the turmoil in the waters around him, he could sometimes hear and see the flashes as the carnage continued. He knew that his Vice-Commodore in *Scoresby* had already gone down. The Germans were now finishing off the defenceless remainder. It took three torpedoes to hit and sink *Blairspey*. *Snefield* went next, followed by *Sedgepool*. The Greek *Thalia* went down with all hands. A third torpedo was needed to finish off *Shekatika*. Finally the *Clintonia* lost her desperate and unequal battle with *U-99*. The first torpedo missed, the second fired at a range of 690 metres hit, and she was sunk by gunfire from *U-123*.[3]

When *Leith* came through the scene of destruction there was no sign of any ships remaining, just an area in the ocean littered with the debris from the wrecks of *Assyrian*, *Soesterberg* and *Empire Brigade* and a few survivors clinging on to anything that would float. She went into the area which she knew for certain had very recently been swarming with U-boats on and under the surface and carried out a systematic search. She knew very well that any U-boat at periscope depth more than 2,000 yards away could watch her unscathed and outside asdic range. She had two alternatives: to obey standing orders and do her best to ensure 'the safe and timely arrival' of the remnants of the convoy, or to stop where she was in the danger area and save life. She chose the latter, setting about her long and very dangerous mission of mercy. She formed a perfect sitting target as she moved slowly through the wreckage, searching and stopping as sailors from her ship's company climbed down the scrambling nets to help the exhausted survivors, most of whom no longer had the strength to clamber on board. Their rescuers knew the risk, which was very real.

As the Commodore waited alone in the water, hanging on to his plank, hoping that he too would be hauled out, he saw the track of a torpedo going straight for *Leith*, his last hope of rescue. It did not explode, but when they found Jock MacKinnon, he had lost all his strength. He could no longer swim and he could not grasp the rope they threw him. They had

88

to hoist the Admiral aboard in a net like a bundle of discarded cotton waste.

When he came round he found the ship packed with survivors, presenting a fine illustration of what was described impersonally in official documents as D.B.S. – Distressed British Seamen. Many were badly burnt, some had swallowed oil, all were exhausted and shattered. He learnt that half of *Assyrian*'s crew were missing, including the Chief Officer, who had been lashed to a spar by the Master, but had died of exposure. One of his signalmen was missing and his Yeoman was seriously ill.

Food was very short on all the escorts as they made for port. They carried enough provisions for their own patrols, but they had between them 500 additional heads to feed. *Bluebell*, in addition to her normal ship's company, had on board 203 survivors, *Leith* 140, *Fowey* 157. Although the food was short and rations went as low as a small part of one ship's biscuit per man at the last meal, it is just as well that it was free, because at that stage in the war the seamen's contracts of employment ceased the moment that their ship went down and they had no money coming in.[4]

Merchant seamen survivors, indeed, from my memory, prisoners from sunken U-boats, were always treated very well when they were picked up by HM Ships, but it was a very different story when they got ashore, without any uniform, dressed in whatever clothes were available, and recognized only in their own local pubs. The survivors from *Shekatika* were not allowed into the dining room of the hotel where they were billeted because they were wearing the same clothes as they had worn when they went to the lifeboats and these did not include a collar and tie!

Commodore Lachlan MacKinnon, now on board *Leith*, was still hanging on to life. He had already recovered enough to make a lousy patient. *Leith*'s Commanding Officer had to be summoned to order him to use the one available bunk in his cabin. The young doctor had to deal with a patient who was in a fever, had pneumonia in one lung, was near to death, was in a medical sense steadily getting worse, but was still very strong-willed. On the following night a full gale blew up. Every time

Leith pounded on a sea the Commodore thought he was back on the bridge and that it was another torpedo.

Many young doctors in the escorts came straight to sea after qualifying with nothing to do except decypher signals and look after the daily trivial complaints of their little ship's community. Perhaps only once in their naval careers were they faced with horrific situations of battle casualties of which they had no previous experience. In this case Surgeon Lieutenant Robertson found himself responsible for 140 very shocked and frightened half-dressed patients without adequate beds or bedding, not enough food, seasick, in a full gale, in a tiny 1000-ton ship. *Bluebell* was even worse off, with no medical help at all and nearly twice as many sick people in a smaller ship.

The next day the Yeoman of Signals, Petty Officer Ronald Guy Parke, the Commodore's right-hand man, and another seaman from *Assyrian* died and were buried with full honours. Outside in the black storm a remnant of his convoy, five ships including the damaged *Carsbreck* and her escort *Heartsease*, came together for a while before the filthy weather split them apart once again during the night. Fog followed the storm as they felt their way towards land and came into soundings without sight of sun or stars for many days and nights. *Leith* went direct to Liverpool and made fast to Prince's Pier at 0830 on Monday 21 October, sixteen days out of Sydney.

Doc Robertson had brought MacKinnon through somehow and he was now well enough to sit up. His wife and daughter had tracked him down through the grapevine and when they walked into his sick bay he was sitting up dictating a letter to them. Three weeks later he felt fit enough to besiege the Admiralty for another convoy, but they put him on the retired list and he never went back to sea. He survived the war, dying just before his sixty-sixth birthday in 1948. He does not appear on the list of Convoy Commodores who lost their lives due to enemy action, and neither he nor Yeoman Parke nor any of his staff of convoy signalmen received any recognition – not even a mention in despatches.

Convoy SC 7

Ships Sunk	**Came Home**	**Turned Back**
Languedoc	*Corinthic*	*Winona* (Laker)
Scoresby (Vice-Commodore)	*Botusk*	
Convallaria	*Dioni*	
Beatus	*Valparaiso*	
Shekatika	*Karlander*	
Boekelo	*Inger Elisabeth*	
Creecirk	*Sneland* 1 (late joiner)	
Empire Miniver	*Thoroy*	
Fiscus	*Havorn*	
Gunborg	*Flynderborg*	
Niritos	*Trident*	
Assyrian (Commodore)	*Somersby* (Acting Commodore)	
Empire Brigade	*Eaglescliffe Hall* (Independent – Laker)	
Soesterberg	*Blairspey* (Towed by *Salvonia*)	
Sneland	*Carsbreck* (Badly Damaged)	
Sedgepool		
Thalia		
Clintonia		
Aenos		
Trevisa (Laker)		
TOTALS Twenty Sunk	Fifteen Home	One Turned Back

91

Chapter Seven

THE MERCHANT SEAMEN'S LOT

The nature of the difficulties experienced by the convoy commodores and the ships under their command changed continually throughout the war. The main characteristics of the years 1939 and 1940 were the acute shortages of escort warships, the many monotonous unmolested convoys, and occasional slaughters when B-Dienst accurately plotted the track of vulnerable convoys and wolf packs descended upon them.

The effectiveness of the few escort vessels available for convoy work was diminished by dividing their strength between escort groups whose primary duty it was to defend the ships of the convoys, and fighting groups to locate and destroy U-boats. As long as the threat of invasion continued, this too was awarded priority over the need to protect the merchant ships.

The escort vessels available lacked speed and endurance, few of them were fitted with high-angle guns for use against aircraft and their depth-charges were not able to reach the depths to which the U-boats could dive. Their commanding officers lacked training in the task of mustering, manoeuvring and protecting merchant ships in convoy. The escort ships were not trained together in groups: commanding officers and the senior officers of each escort group had been given little opportunity to develop cohesion and understanding. Convoys were only escorted for three or four hundred miles to the west of Ireland. Approaches to and departure routes from the ports of the British Isles were dotted with contact and acoustic mines to which the Admiralty at first had no answer. The impact of aircraft on the struggle to establish maritime supremacy and on the conduct of convoys had received little attention, and priority was given to bombing land targets.[1]

The merchant ships and their masters, officers and crews were also faced with great problems. Many of the ships had reached or were already past the end of their normal useful life and had been pressed back into service only because of the extreme need imposed by the war. The seamen and their officers had no experience of the frequent alterations of course and speed required for sailing in close company in convoy. Some of the ships were not even equipped for the accurate control of their speed through the water which was vital for close manoeuvring, passing 'requests' by hand between the bridge and the engine room, where the hard-pressed engineer timed the revolutions with the aid of a stopwatch.[2] Few of the merchant ships had any form of armament. They were not even issued with such basic necessities as fog buoys.

The commodores themselves were not much better off. They had no experience and very little training in the handling of ill-matched and cumbersome merchant ships and none had any practical experience of running a convoy, not a single exercise having been carried out in the years between the wars. They were sent to sea without the basic tools for their job, supported by a small staff of which the majority were lads straight from school. Their signalmen, on whom they relied completely for all communications with the escorting warships and the merchant ships, were new recruits with a few weeks' training at a shore establishment, strengthened by a Yeoman of Signals recalled from retirement. Frequently even the halyards on which their signals were hoisted were wrongly sited and the flags proved to be invisible to other ships. Too often the commodores were sent to sea in ships with inadequate or no accommodation, fitted with magnetic compasses which are notoriously unreliable in the high latitudes of the Norwegian Sea, belching clouds of black smoke from bad coal.

Although the number of operational U-boats did not reach thirty until March, 1941, it shot up thereafter: sixty-eight by the end of the year, 138 by July and 204 by the end of 1942, as did the number of Allied merchant ships sunk by U-boats, by bombing, by mines and by raider. In 1942 the Germans began to sink merchant ships faster than they were being built and put into service. This frightening trend, presented on charts to the War Cabinet at each of their meetings in their underground Cabinet Room in Whitehall, is summarized in the table below.

Allied Shipping Losses from all Causes
1939–1940

Year	Atlantic	United Kingdom	Total
1939	249,195 (47)	455,953 (165)	705,148 (212)
1940	1,805,494 (349)	1,793,748 (650)	3,599,242 (999)
1941	2,421,700 (496)	740,293 (350)	3,161,993 (846)
1942	5,471,222 (1,006)	214,885 (91)	5,686,107 (1,097)

In 1939 four merchant ships were sunk every week. 1940 and 1941 were bad years, but 1942 was the worst year when, on average, *three or four merchant ships were sunk every day of the year*, and many more damaged and docked. By the end of 1942 seventeen convoy commodores had lost their lives, while many of their problems remained the same: the endless discomfort, the vile weather, the loss of lifelong friends and shipmates and the continuous stress and advancing years.

But things were beginning to change. Merchant ships were now being armed and gunners trained. That formidable officer, Admiral Dreyer, had been brought in from his task as a convoy commodore. After a spell on anti-invasion duties, on 27 February, 1941, he reverted to his proper rank of Admiral and was appointed 'Inspector of Merchant Navy Gunnery', reporting to an Assistant Chief of Naval Staff. His first innovation was to speed the appointment of 2,500 Army gunners to merchant ships, with their guns and ammunition. Two days later he was personally trying out all available anti-aircraft guns on Whale Island's range and six days after that he had written a pamphlet entitled 'Notes on Close-range Bombing Attacks on Merchant Ships' which went out from the Admiralty on 5 March. Then 3,000 coasters were equipped with four machine guns and trained service gunners, and 300 Bofors guns, powerful 40mm weapons capable of firing one hundred rounds per minute, were supplied to selected merchant ships, with Royal Artillery gunners to man them. He then introduced the Dome Teacher, a mobile anti-aircraft firing teacher, which was taken round the main ports in double-decker buses.

By the middle of 1942 40,100 Merchant Navy officers and men had gone through a two-day anti-aircraft firing course. These first steps in weapons training of the men in the merchant service, and the establishment of DEMS (Defensively Equipped Merchant Ships) gunners on board their ships, had done much for the morale of the merchant seamen and enabled them to fire back at their tormentors.[3]

The number of escorts had increased and the first of the Support Groups, under Commander F.J. Walker, which included the escort aircraft carrier *Audacity*, had come into action, with enough ships to form an outer screen and to pursue a U-boat to its final destruction without seriously weakening the screen of anti-submarine escorts. The establishment of fuelling bases in Northern Ireland, in St John's, Newfoundland, and in Iceland had increased the effective range of the escorts, which in turn allowed some evasive routeing. Convoy escorts, Hunt class destroyers, sloops and corvettes built under the War Emergency Programmes of 1939, 1940 and 1941, were now at sea after proper training at HMS *Western Isles*. The rapid expansion of the Royal Canadian Navy and the cooperation of the Americans now made it possible for convoys to be escorted right across the Atlantic. The airborne and seaborne radar was greatly superior to the equipment available to the Germans. The threat and power of aircraft attack had at last been understood and a few long-range reconnaissance Liberators had been allocated, albeit tardily and grudgingly, to convoy protection.

To offset these improvements, the convoy commodores had other worries. The entry of the United States into the war, rather than improving the availability of escorts, increased the load. The U-boats experienced their second 'happy time' picking off tankers on the east coast of the American mainland. The arrival of U-boat milch cows, large supply U-boats which could accompany wolf packs and replenish their fuel, torpedoes and other vital supplies without the necessity of returning to base, increased their time on station several fold. The demand for shipping to carry the troops of our new Allies, their equipment and their fuel to Europe and Africa rocketed and could only be met by larger convoys, which presented communication problems when forming up the ships for their several destinations and controlling their manoeuvres when at sea. The congestion in the convoy assembly areas and ports increased. In New York and its anchorages the congestion threatened to become unmanageable.

The need to find officers and crews for the Liberty Ships pouring out of the new American yards placed another load on manpower resources. There were not enough experienced American seamen to officer and man the explosive expansion of their newly built merchant ships. As a result, in the new ships the officers and crews were young and inexperienced; even the masters themselves were sometimes still in their twenties.

This led to a conflict of interests. The Americans needed officers and men to crew their new ships. As in the First World War, the Americans were offering much higher rates of pay than the British shipping lines, and the British officers and men were influenced by their rotten treatment during the interwar years.

To appreciate their feelings, particularly those of the seamen and firemen, the history of their treatment in the first forty years of the century is relevant. At the start of the century the conditions of merchant seamen were controlled by the Merchant Shipping Act which dated from 1896. This Act had been modified by twenty statutes and incorporated into the Merchant Shipping Act of 1906, which extended the Plimsoll Line regulations to coastal ships and gave powers to detain unsafe foreign ships entering British ports. It laid down a requirement for a knowledge of the English language for foreign crews on British ships, and insisted on a minimum of 120 cubic feet (a space just under 6½ft long × 6½ft high × 3ft wide) for each crew member (but excepted Lascars from both these provisions). It reduced the qualifying period for an able seaman to three years(!). It laid down a scale of food, demanded tougher inspection and stipulated that a certified cook should be carried. Even these provisions were strongly opposed by the shipowners. Nothing further had been achieved to better merchant seamen's conditions when the First World War began in 1914.

The master of the ship retained, in theory, absolute authority on board his ship, and all on board were legally bound to obey his orders: no one, passenger or crew, could refuse an order. They had to do what they were told and complain afterwards. Transgressions were criminal rather than civil offences and the master was held responsible for enforcing the law. The men had little respect for their Union, and no way of representing their views with any strength since they were usually away at sea. They had seen inflation soar and freight rates rocket, to the benefit of the shipowners, but had great difficulty in getting any rise in their own meagre wages.

Nevertheless a great wave of patriotism, the strength of which it is difficult to appreciate today, swept through the country and was powerful enough to sustain the merchant seamen and inspire them to accept their lot in spite of their conditions of service and the awful destruction of their ships and colleagues by the U-boats. Their horror of the Germans which resulted from the U-boats' unrestricted warfare had introduced an unparalleled level of hatred into the battle at sea, some of which carried through into the Second World War.

During the First World War the Admiralty had tried to take all merchant service crews into the Royal Naval Reserve, so that they would be subject to naval discipline and penalties. Although this proposal was taken to Cabinet level and a lot of pressure was applied, the Admiralty was not successful. A seaman's wages ended the moment that his ship was lost, a terribly unfair condition that men in the British merchant service never forgot and the injustice of which is still remembered.[4] The shipowners fought with great tenacity and success against control of their empires: they looked after their shareholders well as freight rates continued to go up and profits reached record levels.

Further problems arose when the United States entered the war on 6 April, 1917, and set the American seaman's rate of pay at £18 per month, roughly twice the rate that British seamen and firemen were getting and three times the rates for the Chinese crews. The American Shipping Act of 1915 had already established a right to quit for foreign seamen in American ports. As a

97

result large numbers of British crews were deserting in America, and by July, 1917, one third of the seamen had illegally signed on in American ships. However, when their ships entered UK ports, they were liable to arrest. They were all fined; some were sentenced to hard labour and some taken into the Royal Navy for the duration. It is not clear which penalty was considered the most severe.

By the end of 1919 the battle at sea in which the merchant seamen had responded so gallantly to their country's urgent need had been won, but few believed that they had been fairly treated.

In the years between the two World Wars the merchant seamen's and firemen's bargaining powers, never used to their full effect, were weakened by the world slump in the shipping industry and the steady rise in the employment of cheap foreign labour in British ships. Their disputes with the Shipowners' Federation, and with their own union, bubbled on.

At the start of 1931 the number of British seamen on the ocean routes had fallen from 133,600 to 109,000. 57% of the firemen on the north-east and South Wales coalers were now Arabs or coloured men and freight rates were already down 16% and would be down 28% by 1935. Wage cuts followed. After sixteen years of peace, this was the British merchant seamen's reward for their sacrifices in war.

On 23 August, 1939, the Admiralty took control of all British shipping by requisition, charter or buying. This was the start of another bonanza for ship owners and incredible hardship and suffering for the many officers and crew who went to sea in their ships. In the struggle to replace the ships destroyed or lost through other reasons, ancient and unseaworthy ships, laid up for years, put to sea, sometimes in waters for which they were never intended.

In the first years of the Second World War when a merchant ship went down over 60% of her crew went with her; in the later years, when the specialized Rescue Ships travelled with the convoys, things improved and they had a better chance of avoiding death by drowning, hypothermia or burning, but it was still only an even chance. These, of course, were average figures. If your ship was a tanker carrying 100 octane fuel, you had no chance at all of surviving the ball of fire that erupted 600 feet in the air when the torpedo struck, consuming you and your ship. If rescued, the penniless survivors from merchant ships were then classified as 'Distressed British Seamen', (DBS). This was a good definition, since from that moment not only did they receive no money but also they were frequently not even recognized when they came ashore. If they were lucky enough to get back home, they had no uniform to sport in the local pub and were often accused of avoiding the call-up. Conscientious objectors found jobs as stretcher bearers, or worked in factories, but few of them fancied the job of the merchant seaman at sea.

The prospects were no better for the neutral ships, the sinking of *Athenia* making it clear that Hitler's Navy had no intention of observing the rights of neutrals. If neutral ships travelled in an Allied convoy they faced the same risks as British ships. If they travelled independently their chances of survival were even lower. Their seamen carried the additional burden of total separation from their families for the duration, and if they put into any home port they would be grabbed. When Norway fell, all Norwegian ships were ordered back to their home ports, but not a single ship conformed, although they all knew that they would be isolated from their families from that day on. Britain and the whole Allied efforts would have been crippled without the Norwegian tankers and their crews. Forty-five Norwegian tankers were sunk by the Germans, but they carried millions of tons of fuel before the U-boats got them.

Many of the ships on the transatlantic trade convoys were manned by Indian, African and Lascar crews, more accustomed to the peacetime tropical routes from the Middle and Far East to the UK, civilians who had not gone to sea to face North Atlantic and possibly Arctic conditions and certainly not to be exposed to the risk of being torpedoed, mined or bombed. Others, for example the tankers of The Anglo-Saxon Petroleum Company, were manned by Chinese crews, owing no allegiance to the British, except as employers.

Until Hitler declared war on the United States on 9 December, 1941, seamen of all nationalities could come and go with minimum constraints in American ports. It could be made difficult for them to get ashore if their ships were at anchor offshore, but they had to come alongside to load and offload, to pick up fuel and to carry out repairs. Few seamen, even today, get very far from the dockside pubs and clubs in foreign ports. Before America entered the war these pubs and clubs were well patronized by German agents with true stories of Allied losses at sea and offers of better paid jobs ashore. The docks were full of survivors waiting for new ships and crews shipped over from Britain to take new ships to sea. The seamen's clubs ashore were also infiltrated by German agents in many disguises, intent on suborning seamen away from the sea. The Greeks, with their large populations ashore, particularly in Montreal, were beset by wellwishers and helpers whenever they entered port. All these seamen had one thing in common: they were short of cash and cash could be earned in safe jobs ashore at American rates of pay which were much higher than a seaman's wage. There were enough survivors among them to tell horrific true stories of survival and death in lifeboats and on life-rafts, and few of them had not lost friends and relations at sea. The Germans in the dockside clubs were all too ready to repeat and embellish these stories.

As soon as Hitler and Dönitz realized that the war was not to be brought to a rapid conclusion by the invasion or surrender of Britain, they set about the alternative, which was to starve Britain to death by cutting off all supplies. One way was to eliminate the ships that carried the cargoes, a job where the main weapons were the U-boats and the bombers; another was to eliminate the crews who sailed the ships. So U-boat captains were verbally discouraged from picking up survivors from ships that they had sunk.[5]

It might be thought that the commodores were running great fleets of splendid ships full of hardy seamen inspired by a common desire to defeat the Boche. And indeed there were many hundreds of ships which sailed for the great and well-established British shipping lines, whose officers and crews were well looked after and stayed with them for the whole of their working lives. These ships could be easily identified by their appearance and by the atmosphere on board. On some the commodores and their staff were treated with respect and well looked after, but in many hundreds of others, the picture was very different and is exemplified by the poem written in September, 1941, by R.H.O.S. Collier, the Third Mate of *Everleigh*:

Ode to the *Everleigh*[6]

Atlantic Convoys

Oh shapeless mass of iron and rust
Wandering the seven seas for lust
Of money. Spend your life
Filling the coffers of Cardiff swine
A hundred times.

Oh miracle of infamy,
Of dirt and inefficiency,
How can we be proud to be
of you? Spending our lives
Working our guts out
Starving our wives –
For *Everleigh*.

I joined you in April,
I leave in September,
But the months in between
I shall always remember
–For you stink!

Now at last my task is done.
Yet ne'er forget I am but one
Of those who live in shame for thee
Oh *Everleigh*.

It is not surprising that there was a repetition of the desertions and mutinies that had occurred in the First World War. Crew trouble, as it was euphemistically described, became a major problem very early on, aboard British and Allied ships alongside in United States and Canadian ports. Some was spontaneous, ignited by conditions on board and the risks of an unpleasant death which had been thrust upon peaceable civilian seafarers. Some was ignited by agents ashore or planted on board, and

101

assisted in half the cases by booze and, in the early years, by the attractions of an America still uninvolved in the war.

President Roosevelt, whatever his personal inclinations, needed to handle this problem with great care. To bundle all seamen deserters into American jails could have been politically disastrous. A memorandum dated 30/9/41 states that 3,402 Allied seamen (including 664 from Great Britain and 847 from Norway) had deserted their ships in American ports since the outbreak of war, not including survivors brought to the USA and still ashore. Allowing forty men per ship, this meant that the experienced crews of about eighty-five ships had disappeared from Allied merchant ships. It would have taken a long time and cost many German lives to sink eighty-five ships by bombs or torpedoes.

The entry of the USA into the war made the position more difficult because it created a serious general shortage of labour in the United States, not only to man the warships and merchant ships but to work in essential war industries. The position deteriorated further as the Liberty Ship programme turned from a trickle to a flood. It became even more attractive to the Americans to recruit any experienced seamen of whatever nationality for their merchant ships. The obvious largest single source of such manpower was the British merchant fleet, a plum ready for the picking. Three organizations[7] in Britain put forward strong recommendations to prevent further desertions. They pointed out that the existing American law was not being fully enforced and asked for legal action to be taken in the United States. They asked that:

– The law forbidding Allied seamen from taking jobs ashore should be enforced. (However, it was not unusual for a British officer or seaman to take a job ashore while waiting for his ship to be repaired or made ready because he hadn't got enough money to live ashore otherwise.)

– Allied seamen should not be signed on in the USA except to ships of their own nationality.

– No seaman should be allowed to break his contract of employment in a US port.

– There should be compulsory registration of all foreign seamen ashore in the USA.

– These arrangements should apply also to Danish and Swedish seamen, as far as possible.

The same problems occurred in the main Canadian convoy assembly ports such as Halifax, Nova Scotia, Chatham, New Brunswick, and St John's, Newfoundland. The Canadians dealt with them with great subtlety. The Naval Control Service had the responsibility of certifying that each ship was in 'all respects ready for sea'. Part of their duty was to board ships before they sailed to make sure that German agents had not planted 'contraband', particularly delayed fuse explosives, on board in the ships' holds.

Under the remarkable Commander Oland,[8] Royal Canadian Navy, they expanded their terms of reference quite logically, to include 'crew troubles', arguing that a ship was not ready for sea if the crew was not up to strength or if they were mutinous or even if their morale and discipline were low. They set about making themselves welcome confidants and helpers to the ships they boarded by including as part of their routine the delivery of comforts to the crews, in the form of foul weather clothing and magazines. The boarding crews got among the crews of the merchant ships and developed a 'feel' for crew morale; they were able to report on, and provide solutions, for the great majority of causes of crew trouble with the minimum of fuss and force before they became serious. Some of the grievances were genuine, justified and remediable: they had perhaps been promised some sort of armament to bring to bear on surfaced U-boats, or they had been promised gas masks before sailing to Britain, or their sleeping quarters leaked and were uninhabitable.

However, the problems created by desertions became unmanageable as casualties mounted and more and more ships were prevented from sailing by shortage of crew. A general strike in Greek ships in the autumn of 1940 brought matters to a head and the Canadian Government issued Order in Council PC 4571, enabling the immigration authorities to detain any crews refusing duty. Later this was replaced by the Merchant Seaman Order which gave powers to imprison seamen who were not prepared to sail. These regulations might have been a useful threat, but they didn't always get the ships to sea because some survivors reckoned that it was more comfortable and infinitely safer to go to jail than to go to sea. In any case, to put a deserter in jail did nothing to help a ship to go to sea unless he could be replaced.

From the Canadians' experience was born the Naval Boarding Service, which boarded and saw to sea over 50,000 ships. The Canadian methods and techniques of gentle persuasion, backed later by disciplinary powers, formed a model for practices adopted widely by the Admiralty.

In New York the size of the problem and the difficulties in dealing with large numbers of deserters were made more difficult by the size of its humming port and the mixed nationalities that made up its population. Seamen arriving in New York from occupied European countries, such as Denmark, France, Holland and Norway, had no homes to return to and found colonies of compatriots ashore, still experiencing conditions in which their day-to-day lives ashore were not much affected by war. It was true that they had been uprooted from their homelands, but there was no threat of bombing and no shortage of food or of luxuries for those who had the money. There were plenty of jobs and no secret police.

The position became critical after the National Maritime Union Convention in July, 1941, in Cleveland, Ohio, when it was decided to open an employment office for foreign seamen, to agree to a fourfold increase in employment of foreign seamen on American ships (from 5% to 20%), to authorize the employment of foreign seamen ashore in American ports and to employ them in American tugs. The British Minister of War Transport, Norman Guttery, referred to these proceedings in a telegram to the Minister in New York on 12 November, 1941, and used the most emphatic language. This forthright civil servant telegraphed:

> The effect [of these actions] would be to permit British officers and crews to serve on American vessels. . . . This would create a very unpleasant situation in view of the tremendous difference in wages and war bonuses between British, other Allied and American ships. . . . All these orders and resolutions will increase the temptation for Allied seamen to desert their ships or . . . to

try to find employment on American controlled vessels. . . . Position will become most difficult, if not impossible, should desertions continue. . . . Cannot over-estimate the importance of this matter and hope you will impress on U.S. Authorities that it is vital. General war effort must be weakened if U.S. Authorities do not put end to desertions even if those deserting help to man ships under U.S. flag. . . . All control and all powers of compulsion will then cease to be effective.

He certainly made sure that his views were widely known: there were thirty-two addressees who received copies of this telegram, including T.T. Scott in the British Merchant Shipping Mission in Washington, DC. If B-Dienst ever saw this document it will certainly have confirmed Hitler's and Dönitz's conviction that the manning of the merchant ships was the Allies' Achilles heel, which should be attacked as a very high priority.

In the first five months of 1942 1767 seamen deserted in New York Harbour alone and thirty ships' sailings were consequently delayed, a major setback to vital imports. As a result the Americans formed the Recruitment and Manning Organization (RMO) under its director, Marshall A. Dymock, whose terms of reference were to cooperate with Allied Governments to secure adequate personnel to man their ships.

Between April and July, 1942, 889 foreign seamen were arrested to be deported. A number decided to return to sea, but the Chinese presented the greatest problem because they crewed many British and Dutch ships and because, once they were in the USA, they would rather stay in jail than ship back to sea or go home. So those who didn't go back to sea were retained in custody, which cost a lot of money and did no good to anybody.

Efforts were made to solve the problem by holding monthly meetings from August onwards and special attention was given to Chinese crews. Although there were no Chinese ships, representatives from China were invited to join because of the many Chinese employed in British ships and the large number deserting. For this reason Chinese crews were not allowed ashore (or only under armed guard), because if they got ashore many were never seen again. They were adept at disappearing into the large Chinese communities in United States ports.

In June, 1942, a meeting of the Joint Maritime Commission of the International Labour Organization had resolved that there should be no unfavourable comparison between the treatment of Chinese, Indian and other seamen from Asia, Africa, and the West and East Indies.

The Chinese felt that they were discriminated against, and agreement was reached to increase their pay in line with British seamen and to define their entitlement to leave, overtime, back wages, and compensation to them or their widows for disability or death from war action. (The Agreement also dealt with the important question of Tea Money.⁹)

The basic gross wage of a British seaman in the Anglo-Saxon Petroleum Company which employed nearly two-thirds of the Chinese seamen on British ships at this time was £12 12s 6d per month plus another £10 per month War Risk. Since the Chinese paid no income tax, and the British did, the Chinese then became better paid than their British opposite numbers. Meanwhile the Greek owners, to get their ships to sea, were paying $210 per month to their seamen which was a sevenfold increase. The long-suffering British seaman didn't do very well out of these deals and had good cause to feel resentful.

But even these improvements didn't do the trick. In another attempt to stem the desertions, more concessions were given to Chinese seamen arriving in New York and the ban on shore leave was lifted. This didn't work either. By December, 1942, one third of all Chinese seamen entering the port of New York had deserted, representing in some ships as much as half or three-quarters of the crew. Desertions took place on every ship granting shore leave and ship after ship was delayed.

In December the arrest of Chinese seamen entering the United States illegally and not shipping out was resumed. But there was still no improvement. In 1943, of 187 ships with 7171 Chinese crewmen on board 1774 (25%) deserted when given shore leave.

In contrast, when shore leave was not granted, on fifty-six ships with 1853 Chinese crewmen on board, only four deserted. It paid to be tough, although the atmosphere on board must have been explosive and force had to be used.

So the commodores put to sea in whatever ships they were given. Sometimes they were fine, well-found ships, manned by efficient crews with great traditions; sometimes they were old ships, with men from a score of nations as masters and crews, many ready to desert at the first opportunity. In the same way, Nelson's ships went to sea shorthanded with crews from the prisons, and made up the numbers by pressing crews of many nationalities from East Indiamen homeward bound off the Scilly Islands.

Chapter Eight

THE LIBERTY SHIPS

'Neither is it very desirable that commodores themselves should
be subjected to any unnecessary hardships as they have all done
their apprenticeship.'

There is no doubt that the results achieved by the Americans in
the creation of their great fleet of cargo carriers with such
amazing speed was one of the major achievements that enabled
Britain to survive. Their achievement is that much more amazing
when it is remembered that they started from a very small base.

Between 1922 and 1937 they had suffered from a surplus of
ships laid up and kept in reserve after the First World War.
Commercial shipbuilding came to a halt for fifteen years,
producing only thirty-one cargo liners and a few tankers in that
time. In 1936 the ships which had been put into reserve were
rotting at their moorings and had reached the end of their useful
life, highlighting a need for replacement by an efficient modern
merchant service to meet commercial and military needs. The
Americans recognized this need and plans were made for new
ships to be built in America, owned and operated by Americans
and sailing under the American flag. In some important respects
the Americans were in the same position as the British in 1996.
American operating costs were 50% higher and construction
costs 100% higher than foreign competition. However, instead
of sitting back and doing nothing about it – the British solution – they tackled the problem head-on by introducing and
passing the Merchant Marine Act of 1936 which provided for
appropriate subsidies.

The disastrous failure of successive British Governments in the second half of the twentieth century to take similar bold action has led to the disappearance of the British Merchant Service, previously one of the country's main employers and revenue earners.

In 1939 the British were forced to accept the essential statistic on which the Battle of the Atlantic, and so the timing of the end of the European part of the Second World War, would be decided. Quite simply, if the Germans sunk cargo carriers faster than the Allies could replace them the battle was lost and the British, like the rest of the European continent, would go under. The Americans had accepted this analysis five years before they were attacked by the Japanese and the Germans.

In that year they not only acknowledged the need but devised answers and took the necessary action to meet the need. The United States Maritime Commission was established and a programme to build 500 ships (4 million grt) was approved to take place over the next ten years. Thus, before the outbreak of the Second World War, the Americans had already taken the first positive steps to meet the need for a modern efficient merchant service.

In 1939 the speed of the construction programme was doubled from fifty to 100 ships per annum, and then doubled again in 1940 to 200.

Nevertheless, they had a lot of ground to make up. Their apathy up to 1936 led to over 90% of the 1442 US merchant ships in 1940 being over twenty years old, relics of the previous conflict, and when the Americans came into the Second World War, U-boats were still sinking ships faster than they could be replaced by the British building and repair yards.

In September, 1940, a British Shipbuilding Mission went to the USA, to enlist, at a cost, the American industrial might to build sixty cargo ships. They took with them plans derived from a ship designed and built by the Sunderland yard of J.L. Thompson and Sons, the *Dorington Court*, 7,176 gross register tons, able to carry 10,500 tons of fuel, stores and cargo at eleven knots. This British design was based on traditional methods of manufacture with a riveted hull, whereas the American hulls were welded. Initially the British approach was not received with great enthusiasm by Admiral Land, Chairman of the US Maritime Commission, who was influenced by a strong body of opinion in the USA and the rest of the world, which predicted that Britain would go under quite soon, following the pattern established by the rest of the European powers. It required some tough negotiation before a deal was struck for the Americans to build and the British to buy sixty ships, based on the Sunderland designs and engines, but with welded hulls. These were named the Ocean ships.

The approach to, and the execution of, this contract demonstrated dramatically the ingenuity, determination and huge productive power of the Americans. Two new yards were created from scratch, run by a syndicate of the Todd and Henry J. Kaiser yards. Unlike the bosses in the yards in Britain and Northern Ireland, Henry J. Kaiser had no shipbuilding experience or background whatsoever. His approach was completely untrammelled by irrelevant practices and traditions in shipbuilding, which clogged the minds of the European shipbuilders and their work forces. He started his working life as the owner of a photographic shop, went into the sand and gravel business and then moved into the construction of massive projects such as the Grand Coulee Dam and the San Francisco bridge. Although he was to control many of the new yards that were to spring up in the USA and Canada, 'less than 1 in every 200 of his shipyard workers had ever seen a shipyard, and 25% had not even seen the sea'. It would be hard to imagine an approach that differed more from the traditional shipbuilders and unions in the British yards.

In January, 1941, nine new emergency yards, two to build the Oceans and seven to build 200 American-owned ships, based on a modification of the same design, were started. These were the first of the Liberty Ships, described by President Roosevelt as 'dreadful looking objects', built for the emergency and planned realistically to give a useful life of only five years.[1]

Admiral Land, once the decision was made, threw himself into the project with the enthusiasm of a convert. With much National publicity he announced the birth of the Liberty Fleet by naming 27 September, 1941, LIBERTY FLEET DAY, ten weeks before the Germans declared war on the United States. On that

110

day the first Liberty Ship, the *Patrick Henry*, and fourteen others, were launched.

This first Liberty Ship had taken 245 days to complete. This soon came down to fifty-eight days and within a year the best time from start to finish had been reduced to fifteen; the final record time was four days, fifteen and a half hours. Ninety-three ships were completed each month. The Americans had expanded their shipbuilding capacity sixfold in five years by a fundamental insistence on welded hulls, standardization and prefabrication.

As rumours of these extraordinary achievements – a million tons being added to the Allies' carrying capacity every month – filtered through to Dönitz, he redoubled his efforts to get first priority for all aspects of the U-boat campaign, from steel to manpower to the U-boat building yards and bomb-proof bunkers, to the recruitment and training of the crews, to the provision of adequate air support. He never succeeded in getting all that he sought, but he didn't give up. His U-boats were re-armed and, for a disastrous three months, tried unsuccessfully to fight their way in and out of the Biscay ports on the surface, against ferocious and unremitting low-level attacks by Coastal Command.

By December, 1941, the Americans had increased their ship-building plans again and set a new target of 24 million grt – 3148 ships. They actually built 2710 Liberty Ships (approximately 20,500,000 grt) in all under the emergency programmes. The magnitude of their achievements and the huge contribution to victory in Europe can be judged by the fact that the tonnage they built was equivalent to the sum of all the Allied and neutral wartime losses, 21,570,720 tons, and to the total of all British merchant ships in 1939.

The long-term effect of the Liberty Ships programme was to accelerate the disappearance of the Red Duster from the oceans of the world except in small yachts. Over half the wartime merchant ship losses were British, but, by agreement with the Americans, the British yards concentrated on building warships, a dead market after 1945. This was disastrous for the specialist union-ridden and hidebound yards in Britain, where even the desperation of war had not loosened the grip of the cold hand of tradition. The Liberty Ships built under an emergency programme for a five-year life flooded the shipping market at knockdown prices for the next twenty years.

Nevertheless, there is no doubt that the volume of American production of ships, particularly of Liberty Ships, was a key factor, if not *the* key factor, in the European War.

But there was a price to pay and it would be the men of all the Allies' nations in the merchant service who would be called upon to pay it. The frantic pace at which these ships were built and the lack of previous testing and experience of welding as a method of ship construction led to a lot of trouble under the severe ocean conditions of the North Atlantic in winter, and particularly for the ships that had the misfortune to be sent on to Russia through the Norwegian Sea.

Commodore Cresswell's report on the experiences of Convoy ON 223 illustrates some of the weaknesses of these ships. He sailed from Liverpool with fifty-seven ships bound for Halifax, Nova Scotia. His ship was the Liberty Ship *Edward L. Godkin* on her maiden voyage. This was a mid-winter convoy in the North Atlantic, which suffered some very severe weather conditions. The Commodore discussed several times with the Master the possibility of heaving to, since many were Liberty Ships in ballast. The design made these very 'stiff' when not carrying a full cargo. The weight was concentrated low down so that the ship tended to come back upright very sharply after a roll, so sharply that the masts could be dislodged and any loosely stowed gear could break its lashings and run wild. On this voyage the savage movement of the ship frequently put the gyro compass out of action, even though the standard precaution of loading 1500 tons of sand as ballast had been taken. If speed was reduced to fifty-six revolutions, equivalent to five knots, the ship would lie with her head forty degrees off the wind, but if the revolutions fell any lower, even to fifty-four, the ship would cease to answer her helm and blow helplessly sideways. When she pitched over the crest of a wave the propeller came out of the water and the revolutions raced up to seventy, only to drop back to forty when the stern settled back into the trough of the wave. There was no mechanical governor to control these variations and produce a steady speed.

112

The ships roll at a speed which slings gear about, they are so light that they race their screws excessively, and have so much windage forward that they are liable to fall off the wind up to 70 degrees and require full speed to bring them back. If they pound, each pound is followed by 60 terrible oscillations: the deck seems stretched like a tympanum.

The position fixing depended on sextant sights taken from the upper bridge where the movement was worst, and the signalling was carried out in all weathers from this same totally exposed station. The one means of telling the distance run, the patent log which was towed over the stern, had been cut on the journey out and its replacement was out of order on the way back. The only method to calculate the speed of the ship was to use a Dutchman's log, which entails throwing something over the bow and timing how long it takes to get to the stern – very unscientific and inaccurate, particularly in a full gale.

The Commodore, with impeccable politeness, congratulated the Master of the ship, Captain Zepp 'for the efforts that he and his first and second mate made in the navigation of the voyage and overcoming the troubles of a new ship, new gear and a very inexperienced crew,' but added, 'I do not recommend that any ship should carry a commodore on her maiden voyage, as many uncertainties are bound to arise.'

One week later Commodore Smithwick sailed in a large convoy ON 224 with eighty-one ships. His language was more direct, listing the following defects on the *John N. Robins*:

No gyro compass and the magnetic compass unreliable.
No depth recorder.
D/F fitted but broke down.
Patent log 'quite useless'.
Relationship between speed and revolutions not known.
No method available to count revolutions automatically.
When light, difficult to keep on a steady course, even in the slightest seaway.
Officers rather inexperienced. The Master has been in command for six months and is only 28. Officers rather lacking in experience and had only the dimmest ideas about Mersigs.
Signal flags too close together and hard to read.

113

Flags obscured over important areas.
The signal lamp situated on a slippery deck in a completely exposed position.
No working wireless available.

He gives credit to

the Master, G.D. MacCallister [who] very nobly surrendered his nice-looking but somewhat uncomfortable bunk to me and made do with a makeshift bunk alongside the helmsman! He used the chart house to sit in (when rolling permitted). With very little forethought vastly better arrangements could have been made at negligible expense and in very short time. . . . As the Commodore and his staff are in convoys for the purpose of controlling the ships in the convoy, it would seem that they should be in the best ship that can carry them. . . . This is not achieved by exposure to the weather, violent motion, etc. In fact a complete breakdown after a few days can be anticipated. We were incredibly lucky. Even so there were a couple of days when lifelines were required and no signal could be written down until cover was reached on the deck below. . . .

Neither is it very desirable that commodores themselves should be subjected to any unnecessary hardships as they have all done their apprenticeship.

With regard to seaworthiness, loading and ballasting, if the one half of what I am told even approximates to the truth then the state of affairs is serious. Ships are loaded with no regard to seaworthiness, and the ships' officers appear powerless to get the cargoes correctly distributed to keep the metacentric height within reason.

It seems pretty obvious that a ship with a [roll] period of only 4 seconds is going to be bad in the North Atlantic and with a very big metacentric height is going to be so stiff as to cause very serious strains through the violent jerkiness of her movements.

Walking about and sleeping [are] very difficult. The shuddering which follows the mildest of pitches is also startling and lasts from five seconds upwards in decreasing wavelets, and must have a very serious straining effect through the hull, leading at least to undue wear and tear and hence repairs, even if not actual cracking athwartships.

Goggles of US Navy pattern [should] be supplied to

114

commodore and signalmen. The low temperature and lack of dodgers makes face protection essential.

On another convoy, Commodore Smithwick's daily reports of the convoy's position show that wind and sea conditions were so bad that they only made good four miles in one twenty-four-hours period in February, 1944. He judged that 'this ship is quite unsuitable as at present arranged and fitted out for the purpose of Commodore's ship. Further I do not think that any Liberty Ship should be selected as such in the N. Atlantic in winter weather unless loading, ballasting and general seaworthiness are greatly improved.'[2]

These problems were not confined to the new untried Liberty Ships. Commodore Brownrigg (Admiral Sir H.J.S. Brownrigg KBE CB DSO), the most senior officer to lose his life on active service in the Second World War, was lost when *Ville de Tamatave*, a French ship built in 1931 and chosen to lead the convoy, capsized and went down with all hands in heavy weather on 24 January, 1943. She was carrying seventeen passengers and a crew of seventy-one, including the Commodore's Yeoman of Signals and all his convoy signalmen.

Chapter Nine

THE BAIT CONVOY – SL 125

At the end of July, 1942, although the sinkings of Allied ships were at a very high level and Stalin was hectoring Churchill for more Russian convoys, the decision was made to invade French North Africa. In the autumn the planning was finalized and the huge military convoys got ready to carry the 70,000 American and British troops to the target ports of Casablanca, Algiers and Oran. The operation, under the command of General Eisenhower, was code-named 'Torch'. These massive and complicated movements involved some 334 British and American warships, three battleships, including the *Rodney*, aircraft carriers, cruisers, destroyers and fleet oilers in fifteen special (military) convoys, timed to converge at predetermined intervals at the landing points. The force that set out from Britain steamed in a great arc, setting off from Britain's west coast ports, curving out into the Atlantic Ocean, turning south and then south-east and east to converge on Gibraltar. The Rock was the hub of all activities inside the Mediterranean as the Allied forces moved on to the landings. Everything passed through the Straits except troops and supplies for the American landings at Casablanca, planned to coincide with the Mediterranean landings, which sailed in convoys direct from the United States to the landing beaches.

Torch made it necessary to suspend temporarily the Russian and South Atlantic convoys (352 ships monthly), in order to release many of the escorts. The seven available escort carriers were diverted to Torch, as well as the newly formed Support Groups, including five sloops and thirteen corvettes. Many trade convoys were rerouted. They continued to run but with even fewer escorts than before and a great increase in journey times, leading to a serious fall in imports to Britain. The risk of running the faster merchant ships independently without escort was taken and it didn't always pay off. Many of them were sunk.

The Germans had 360 U-boats in commission in October, 1942. 180 were operational, of which 161 were in the Atlantic.[1] Although the north and south shores of the Straits, and movements to and from Gibraltar's harbour and moorings, were in full view of German agents, who could and did report daily movements of shipping, German intelligence failed entirely to appreciate the imminence of the landings in North Africa, one of their greatest failures.

By chance, however, there was a group of six to eight U-boats, code-named Streitax, further south off Freetown looking for the Sierra Leone convoys. During the first three weeks of October these boats had little success and, by chance, nine boats were on their way to relieve them.[2] German Intelligence, although working at full strength, failed again to reveal that the ocean in the area off the south-west of Ireland was black with the ships of the Torch convoys, then making sedate and undetected progress at the start of their journey to Gibraltar unthreatened and unmolested. In these critical days, when so much had been staked on this first offensive movement of the combined British and American forces, B-Dienst had missed the largest invasion fleet ever to sail.

To avoid the sea equivalent of traffic jams and the dangers inherent in one convoy sailing through another at right angles, the Sierra Leone–United Kingdom convoys were suspended from October, 1942, until March, 1943, but not in time to stop SL 125, the last of the series. Off the Canary Islands and well south of the Torch routes from the UK to Gibraltar, these homeward-bound ships ran straight into Group Streitax' patrol line. From then on this wolf pack was totally involved in a long and determined attack on the convoy which absorbed their whole attention, fortunately for the Torch invasion fleets.

The ships of SL 125 were led by Commodore Reyne (Vice Admiral Sir Cecil Reyne KBE, RN). His ship was *Nagpore*, one of the smallest in the convoy, leading the sixth column with a load of scrap iron in her holds. The Vice-Commodore was Commodore Garstin (Captain R.H. Garstin CBE Royal Indian Navy), leading the ninth column in *Stentor* with his small staff of a leading signalman, three signalmen and a telegraphist, under Yeoman of Signals Geoffrey (Nobby) Clarke. She was carrying 125 passengers and a crew of 122.

Stentor had a history behind her. She was built in Dundee in 1935, designed for the Far East passenger and cargo trade and capable of thirteen and a half knots. She had sailed in one of the first westbound convoys in September, 1939. In that convoy she was leading one of the columns on the night of 16 September, 1939, when the convoy encountered a single ship ahead on opposite course sailing independently. The Commodore, in *Dilwara*, leading the next column to starboard, ordered an emergency forty degrees turn to port. *Stentor* did not get the signal and she altered course initially to starboard. Almost immediately *Dilwara* loomed up through the night, converging on a collision course. By putting her wheel hard a'port she avoided major damage to both ships as they collided gently beam to beam. In Jeddah on 3 April, 1941, she was bombed and machine-gunned by a British aircraft, but only slightly damaged.

After these first shocks she survived the grind of the convoy routes without major incident until SL 125 sailed from Freetown at 1100 on 16 October, 1942. This was the last month of a very bad ten-month period, when Bletchley Park was losing the decyphering battle. B-Dienst had changed their code book in early 1942 and at the same time they had increased the number of wheels in Enigma from three to four, and Bletchley Park had not yet solved this problem. As a result the Admiralty were operating blind, while the Germans were continuing to decypher the Admiralty Convoy Code.[3]

There were forty-one ships escorted only by four corvettes, HMS *Petunia* (SOE), *Cowslip*, *Woodruff*, *Crocus*, and two trawlers. Once clear of land they deployed into eleven columns. The cargo they carried was a mixed lot, including scrap iron, frozen meat, tea and general cargo; two ships were in ballast. The ships immediately ran into heavy weather, which always caused grave problems if it occurred at the start of a convoy

9. 'Henry J. Kaiser had no shipbuilding experience whatsoever' (p.110) *(Popperfoto)*.

10. Described by President Roosevelt as 'dreadful looking objects' (p.110), a Liberty Ship unloading in North Africa *(Imperial War Museum)*.

11. *Tirpitz*, 'probably the most powerful warship afloat in the European conflict' (p.204) *(Imperial War Museum)*.

12. The aircraft carrier *Victorious* with Albacores (see p.209) *(Imperial War Museum)*.

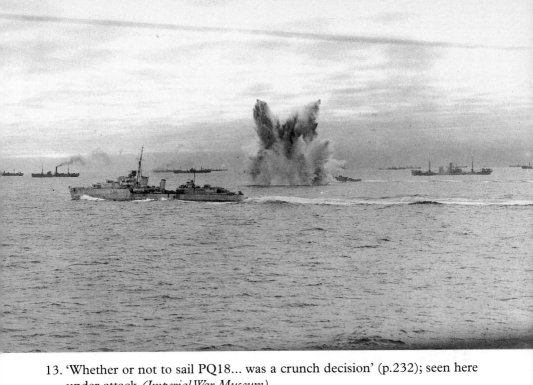

13. 'Whether or not to sail PQ18... was a crunch decision' (p.232); seen here under attack *(Imperial War Museum)*.

14. Illusory calm. A North Atlantic convoy in 1940 *(Popperfoto)*.

15. & 16. Extreme conditions on an Arctic convoy. The photograph below was taken on board HMS *Scylla* (see p.230) *(Imperial War Museum)*.

before the ships had had enough time to settle down. On this occasion the problems were more acute than usual because the Commodore's ship could not make good more than seven knots and this regulated the speed of all the ships. As the weather deteriorated, the Commodore's speed of advance continued to deteriorate until he was making good no more than five knots. The larger ships, particularly the two in ballast, were extremely difficult and sometimes impossible to handle at that speed. They needed more speed to stop their heads paying off in a gale of wind, and the old *Nagpore* was holding them back. The wrong choice of commodore's ship had jeopardized the whole fleet's ability to keep in a compact and manageable formation.

On 27 October, the luck of Vice-Commodore Garstin's ship, *Stentor*, finally ran out. Destruction hit her in a particularly unpleasant form. A torpedo struck her in number two hold where she was carrying a cargo of palm oil in a deep tank. The oil ignited and the flames shot 200 feet in the air and blew back over the bridge. More flaming oil covered the upper decks and poured into the passengers' accommodation.

Fifty years later, Nobby Clarke, the Commodore's Yeoman of Signals remembers:

I had gone up on the bridge. It was dark, between seven and half-past in the evening. I hadn't been there very long and there was a sort of thump. Contrary to what one might think, there wasn't an almighty explosion and a great big fount of sparks and things. There was just a thump as if we had bumped into something, and the effect wasn't immediate. It seemed to be a short while afterwards before eventually the forward hatch seemed to erupt, because the ship was not a tanker but she simply had a deep tank in the No 2 hold which was just forward of the bridge.

This hold was full of palm oil, not aviation spirit or fuel oil: it was palm oil which we had been told was almost non-inflammable, but it turned out not to be the case because it simply erupted into a huge fountain that shot straight up into the air and fanned out when it got high in the air. It was on fire when it came back down, so it was raining fire on everything and raining an oily fire. My immediate job was two-fold. One of them was to sound off on the ship's siren a succession of S's which was the signal to let everyone know that we had been attacked by a

119

submarine and torpedoed. That was the first thing that I had to do, so I did that, and of course in order to do that I had to go out into the open and pull on the lanyard which operated the thing and all the while it's raining fire.

My next job was to get hold of the confidential books. Those were all the code books which were kept in a bag which was zipped up and weighted with lead so that this could be heaved over the side to make sure the enemy didn't get hold of them: that was my next responsibility. Now that bag was kept in the chart-house which was just behind the wheelhouse. I was on the port side of the bridge, the torpedo had struck on the starboard side, the other side, and the wind was blowing from the starboard side to the port side.

I opened the door of the chartroom because I knew that the confidential books were in their bag just inside the door on the floor. I went to get them, stepped inside the chart room door to pick them up, and somebody on the other side of the bridge opened the chartroom door on the other side as the chart room had a door on each side.

Because the wind was blowing and because everything was blazing, a sheet of flame just shot straight through the chart room at me just as I was bending down to get hold of the confidential books, and I couldn't get hold of them so I just had to get out.

I got out and I didn't get them. I didn't do my job in other words. I couldn't get the confidential books out, but I'm quite happy in my own mind that they never got into enemy hands. From there I went out onto the bridge.

I saw that the Commodore had been blinded because he had made the mistake of looking up into the sky, and he was being taken along the boat deck by one of the merchant ship's company. I had a look to see if I could see my signalman and he wasn't there. I wasn't sure what to do and I could see that the ship by then was settling down, was going down by the head. I thought well I've got to get off if I can.[4]

Vice-Commodore Garstin on the shattered bridge had looked up into the sky. The towering flames were the last thing that he ever saw as a flame licked back into his face. Major Turner, his hands very badly burnt, led him back along the upper deck and Commodore Garstin was heard to say, 'I am blind'.

R. Borrer, Stentor's radio officer, remembers:

The whole of the bridge structure and Nos 1 and 2 lifeboats on the Captain's deck were ablaze. Topping this awesome picture, on the monkey island, surrounded and illuminated by the flames, were the third and fourth mates (Mr C.R. Hearne and Mr G.D. Lewis) busily throwing overboard live ammunition from the Oerlikon gun locker, regardless of the imminent fate of the ship. . . . I reached the ship's side by the boat which was being bumped to and fro by the swell, so I jumped into the water just astern of the boat and pulled myself to its outboard side by the grablines. . . . Just as I was about to climb into the after end of the boat . . . the ship upended as though on an axis; the stern rose high in the air and I could see the funnel horizontal against the darkening sky. The ship seemed to hang in this position for a few seconds before starting to slide slowly beneath the sea. I was pawing on the ship's side as she was sinking when something caught in the shoulder of my lifejacket dragging me under. It seemed that my time had come but, surprisingly, in no time I found myself on the surface again. . . . All this had happened so quickly that the ships that had been in line astern of the *Stentor* in the convoy were still passing us in the water at the spot where she had been sunk.[5]

Stentor sank at 1943, eight minutes after she was hit. The senior surviving officer, Staff Captain W.B. Blair, reported:

The Ship's Doctor behaved with extreme gallantry. He calmly continued to dress the Commodore's burns, although the ship was sinking rapidly, sending his assistant away to his boat station while he himself was seen taking the Commodore up to the boat deck. Both Doctor Chisholm and the Commodore are amongst those missing and there is no doubt that the doctor's very gallant action cost him his life.

The sinking of *Stentor* at the head of column nine was followed by the sinking of *Pacific Star* heading the adjacent column eight to port. The same U-boat, *U-409*, had worked into a position ahead of the convoy before darkness, had penetrated the screen and surfaced between the columns of the convoy, in the tradition of the famous Kretschmer, firing successively from bow and stern tubes on the surface and then submerging and disappearing

121

in the utter confusion of burning ships, wreckage and near collisions.

The U-boats in Group Streitax were commanded by a bunch of Dönitz's best officers, trained in the techniques of the wolf-pack attack. Their tactics were to shadow on the surface below the horizon, far enough to be invisible from the bridges of the convoy and its escorts, and to work their way ahead into an attacking position before nightfall. After dusk they would dodge the slow corvettes, get in among the columns of ships, surface and attack at close range. While confusion reigned, they would submerge, disappear and repeat the operation the following day and night.

U-203 shadowed the convoy and brought back *U-409* the next morning for an abortive attempt, and then again for another attack on the evening of 28 October. The weather by this time had turned nasty, with big seas running and all the ships again finding it difficult to keep station.

At 1900 *U-409* came into the convoy for the second time, torpedoing the Commodore's ship *Nagpore*, leading column six. Two of her four boats were smashed by the explosion. It was a pitch black night as, in quick succession, the emergency rockets and snowflakes around *Nagpore*'s superstructure ignited and flew horizontally round the bridge and along the boatdeck, adding to the confusion of wind and spray, the hiss of steam and the noises of the ship breaking up. One of the remaining boats was lowered and rowed away by thirty Lascars who abandoned ship without orders and were never seen again. There was just time to release some rafts and lower another lifeboat with forty Lascars on board, which was taken away by the Chief Officer, Mr E.J. Spurling, before *Nagpore* broke in two. She folded amidships, her two masts coming together as her cargo of iron dragged her down. She sank ten minutes after being hit, leaving many struggling in the darkness.

Among them was Commodore Reyne. While he was still in the water, he was struck by some wreckage and hauled out of the water unconscious on to a raft by Mr S.W. Walter, the Third Officer. The rest of the convoy had steamed past and disappeared into the darkness and the violence of the storm. Their orders were not to stop to pick up survivors. An hour later, another explosion signalled the sinking of *Hope Castle*, lying second in column seven.

Conditions on the raft were appalling. It was bitterly cold and there was no protection from the seas, which were flooding over the raft and tossing it and its occupants about in every direction. There was still no sign of any rescue, but the Third Officer held on to the Commodore. For two hours he was unconscious; then he came to and suffered intense agony with every movement of the raft. Another hour and a half went by before the corvette *Crocus* found them. They had been nearly four hours in the water as the corvette manoeuvred to haul them on board, but a moment after she reached them, she sheered off in hot pursuit of another U-boat. This was the last straw and the occupants of the raft felt that their end had come. But *Crocus* came back and found them again, hoisting them on board at 2340, exhausted almost to the point of death after four hours and forty minutes in the water. The Master, Captain Williams, four officers, thirty-four crew, and Convoy Signalman Bannam were missing.

Thus, on the second day of the attack, four ships had gone down including the Commodore's and Vice-Commodore's ships, and the wolf pack was still very much in touch. *U-134* continued the shadowing and after darkness on 29 October the pack sank *Brittany*, *Corinaldo* and the tanker *Bullmouth*, which blew up in a sheet of flame. *U-604* kept contact and on 30 October the group sank the 11,898-ton ship *President Doumer*, with a casualty list of 260, *Baron Vern*, *Tasmania* and *Silverwillow*. *Alaska* was also torpedoed, but made it to Lisbon with forty-eight survivors rescued from the other ships. On 31 October the U-boats were still in contact but finally broke off contact as the convoy came within range of air cover from Gibraltar. Captain W.A. Haddock, the Master of *Empire Cougan*, had taken over as Commodore. His language and descriptions of events are less restrained than most convoy commodores:

The speed of the convoy was 7 knots when first attacked – the speed of the Commodore's ship. This made the big ships sitting targets, and I estimate that fifteen ships were hit and they were all the best vessels.[6] When the Commodore's ship was sunk I was appointed Commodore. . . . The behaviour of the men was exemplary, but it was unfair to the men and placed their lives in extra peril for a 7-knot ship to have been appointed pacemaker in the circumstances.

Survivors from sunken ships in the North Atlantic rarely came out of the clutches of sea into warm arms and loving care and attention. The Royal Navy without exception did what they could and did it wholeheartedly and unsparingly, but the corvettes had no doctor on board. All escorts with their normal ships' companies were overcrowded in wartime: more weapons, depth charges and electronics replaced bunks and hammock hooks. They were often short of food, fuel and even water.

The survivors of SL 125 still had many trials to endure. The crew of *Anglo Maersk* were landed in Hierro Island in the Canaries and were immediately jailed by the Spanish. The corvette *Woodruff* (complement 85) had over 200 survivors on board for six days. Even after she had offloaded half to HMS *Ramsay*, a destroyer that came to the convoy's assistance on 31 October when it was all over, she still had to fight the ship and look after a hundred very badly shaken men until they reached home on 9 November. They were all mentally and physically shaken and many of them seriously ill.

What do we mean by 'seriously ill'? Nobby Clarke describes his ordeal:

When I came out of the wheelhouse [of *Stentor*], I sort of had a look at myself and saw that I was in a bit of a mess. . . . I was wearing a short-sleeved shirt and my arms had been covered pretty well with burning oil. You see, this palm oil was almost like lubricating oil. It's fairly thick and the skin on my forearms was hanging down in strips, and there were puddles of this oil on the deck. I was wearing gym shoes and the ship was listing and going down a bit and I had difficulty in finding my feet and I kept falling down in these puddles of blazing oil, so I was pretty uncomfortable. . . . In the end I persuaded myself that the only thing I could do was to jump in, which I did. . . . There were people in the water, people screaming for help, and the horror of the thing was the fact that we couldn't help them. The boat we were in was built for thirty-five people and we had fifty-five in

124

it. She was almost gunwales under. If we'd have picked up any more, we would all have gone. . . . The flames eventually disappeared and the night gradually became black again. . . . A lot of them were lost.

We were picked up by a frigate called *Woodruff*. We went alongside and they threw a scrambling net, which is a rope net, over the sides of the corvette and we managed to manoeuvre the lifeboat alongside, and we were told to scramble up onto this thing, you see. Well, for my part, the last thing I wanted to do with my hands being in the state they were was to grab hold of a rough hemp rope and haul myself up. . . . I was the last one in it and I was trying to pluck up courage to do a bit of a leap and grab and haul myself up. Then suddenly I heard, from the bridge of the ship, the corvette, which is only a small vessel, 'Contact Ahead'. I heard the Captain call out 'Full Ahead' in order to attack the submarine and I knew I was going to be left behind if I didn't get out, so I did the flying leap, just as I didn't want, but I had to, and I scrambled my way up and got onto the deck and promptly passed out. . . .

I was put on top of a locker which ran along the side of the ship, I believe. I had to lie face down because my back was in a bit of a mess. I stayed there for the rest of the trip home, which took ten days. I had to lie face down with my arms on either side. I was obviously stripped off, stripped to the waist at any rate, and there were no doctors on board the corvette . . . there were many others like me with burns. . . . The poor sick berth attendant came to see me and his method of treating me was to put on gentian violet . . . just spread it all over the burn areas and covered it with a . . . gauze and that was all he could do.

One of the things which was terribly painful was the fact that once a day he would change the dressing and, of course, inevitably the dressings would be stuck to the wounds and he had, literally, to tear them off. By the time three or four days were up I got to the stage where I was almost hysterical when I knew he was going to do it, because it was exceedingly painful. . . .

One of the signalmen on my staff was with me. He was a wonderful chap called Jim Brady and he looked after me all those ten days. He fed me because I couldn't feed myself, just lying face down, and he fed me and kept me alive. By the time I got to hospital they said that I was just rotten from head to foot with septicaemia, in other words all the wounds that I had had gone septic and my chances of survival were quite limited.

On this disastrous convoy the Commodore, R.H. Garstin, had died, thirteen ships, their cargoes and many of their crew and passengers had been lost. Among those who survived was Commodore Reyne who owed his life to Third Officer Walter. He went back to sea to complete thirty-nine ocean convoys, including HXM 301 of 133 ships. He was appointed a Knight of the Order of the British Empire on 1 January, 1944. He was placed on the retired list on 4 September, 1945, at the age of sixty-four, some fifty years after he had entered the Navy as a cadet.

Another to survive was Yeoman of Signals Geoffrey (Nobby) Clarke. He didn't stay ashore to become a barracks stanchion, as he deserved, but went back to sea to serve for the rest of the war. He tells the story of his visit to collect a replacement set of kit from Liver Buildings in Liverpool after he came out of hospital. The Wren in charge asked him what he had lost, and he answered,

'Everything – the lot.'
'But you can't have lost everything. What did you come ashore in?'
'A pair of socks,' I said.
'Oh,' she said 'In that case you can have a full kit, less one pair of socks.'
I didn't dare object. She gave me a look which meant 'Don't you know there's a war on?'

He was a boy when he joined, but those years made him a man and today he carries his years and his scars well, without bitterness. He does not boast or bear the laurels which are his due, but only remembers his mates who suffered as he did, but didn't survive.

The Naval Historian, S.W. Roskill, says, 'The ocean passages [of the Torch convoys] were made in almost complete safety, not least because the only [U-boat] Group in the approaches to Gibraltar had been fortuitously attracted to a Sierra Leone convoy, which was passing to the east and north of the invasion fleet between the 27th and 30th of October.'

Others have suggested that SL 125 was used as a 'bait' convoy to draw the U-boats away from the Torch fleets. However, the convoy, when first attacked, was 140 miles south of Madeira. The last torpedo struck home five days before the American force arrived on their direct path to Casablanca. It is clear that it was only by mischance that Group Streitax was on passage south at the time. The Germans had no knowledge whatsoever of the Torch fleets and this patrolling group of U-boats was encountered by SL 125 when a long way south of the point at which it could have interfered with Torch. Roskill's map (*War At Sea*, Vol II, p. 317, No 32), shows it to have been several hundred miles south of the invasion forces that had set out from Britain. It would also have been extremely unlikely, (and quite unnecessary) to include the 11,898-ton passenger ship *President Doumer*, and *Stentor*, also carrying hundreds of passengers, in a convoy knowingly routed straight into a U-boat concentration.

It would, in any case, have been difficult to send convoy SL 125 on any other course. An alteration to port (west) would have led the shadowing U-boat pack close to the path of the American convoys making for Casablanca. An alteration to starboard (east) would have brought the convoy too close to the Canary Islands, leaving them little sea-room to manoeuvre and drawing the U-boats closer to the American landing areas.

Chapter Ten

THE OIL CRISIS – WINTER 1942/43

Torch, and the impetus that followed America's entry into the war, imposed further strains on the merchant service fleets and the oil tankers in particular. Every winter had seen an oil crisis, but this was the most crucial, because the demand shot up at a time when sinkings were at their worst.

Throughout the war the British public imagined that the Americans were still living in peacetime conditions, unaffected by the rationing and hardships that were being experienced in the UK. In fact at the time of this oil crisis it was the Americans who came to the rescue, this time at the expense of their own citizens' comfort and way of life, particularly in the states on the north-east seaboard. Mr Ralph Davies, the United States Petroleum Coordinator, diverted supplies of fuel going north for American domestic supplies by rail, to the New York Navy Pool in New York, whence it could be loaded and shipped much faster and with less risk into the Atlantic convoy tankers. This, of course, was done at the expense of the Americans in that part of the country.

Floods had stopped transport by rail, the Great Lakes froze up and stopped all shipping movements. In March the petrol ration was halved, a measure that brought real hardship to a country that relied largely on private and commercial motor transport. The severity of the winters in New England and the impact of this decision on the Americans who lived there can best be gauged by the fact that a plan was prepared to evacuate private citizens from their Boston homes into communal buildings, where the oil available for heating could be used more efficiently.

These were hardships that were difficult for an American to bear, living in a country remote from the war area that had only just entered the battle.

The effect of that hard winter was also felt at sea, particularly in the North Atlantic, where conditions were among the most severe on record, slowing down the speed of the convoys and causing devastating weather damage to old, slow and inadequately maintained ships, many of which had already been subjected to merciless flogging during the two previous North Atlantic winters.

In the event, although the American public suffered grave discomfort and privations, Mr Davies' action only served to shift the bottleneck. As his actions built up the stocks in New York the port became congested as ships queued up to load and the onward passage of the oil across the Atlantic slowed down.

In Britain the series of oil crises that had always worried the War Cabinet reached a climax in the closing days of 1942. There were three main reasons. The first was that oil supplies were not reaching the UK as fast as they were being used and there was a steady decline in stocks throughout the year. The second was the enormous extra demand for fuel and for shipping for the North African landings and for the maintenance and reinforcement of the Allied armies once landed. The North African landings began on 8 November, 1942, and were dependent on seaborne supplies of fuel. When this operation started, all the British Forces' fuel supplies, between 300,000 and 400,000 tons, were provided from stocks held in Britain, and many tankers normally supplying the UK were diverted from the Atlantic supply routes to the Torch landings. After the landings the demand continued to rise from day to day.

The third and most important factor was the appalling shipping losses inflicted by the U-boats in October, November and the first half of December, 1942. The convoy escorts were already overstretched, at a time when Dönitz' U-boat fleet had reached the highest level so far, and was still increasing. U-boats sank 619,417 tons (94 ships) in October, 729,160 tons (119 ships) in November and 330,816 (60 ships) in December, nearly all in the first half of the month.[1] When these ships went down their carrying capacity was lost, many experienced officers and crew were killed and the oil in their bunkers went with them.

By the end of November, 1942, oil stocks for all purposes in the UK had fallen 30% below the minimum safe level set by the Oil Control Board (and agreed, somewhat reluctantly, by the Americans). This minimum was around four million tons or sixteen weeks' supply. It took a long time for the oil to travel from the oilfields to the storage tanks in Britain. A disastrous event, such as the almost total annihilation of a tanker convoy, could cause serious unforeseen imbalances in the types of fuel available. Even if immediate steps were taken, it took weeks or months for the effects to be felt by the user in Britain.[2]

The commercial stocks situation was absolutely critical. The U-boats' dramatic successes, particularly in the Caribbean, the Gulf of Mexico and all along the east coast of America, had slowed up shipments and reduced the commercial stock of oil fuel in Britain to ten weeks' supply. Any further deterioration would result in a need to draw on the Navy's emergency reserves, in order to fuel the merchant ships, at the risk of immobilizing warships. By mid-December stocks were down to 300,000 tons, against a monthly consumption of 130,000 tons.

Churchill minuted, 'This does not look at all good.' It would have been even worse if it hadn't been for the undemanding friendship of the Norwegians.

Since April, 1940, when the Germans invaded Norway, a great deal had depended on the Norwegians. At the time there had been more than 1,000 Norwegian merchant ships at sea, so the Nazis sent out a fake signal ordering them all to return home or put into neutral or German-controlled ports. Not one of them complied. They made for British or Allied ports, making themselves available for charter. To offer their ships to the British was not to the financial benefit of the shipowners, to whom the German's offered huge bribes in their efforts to get control of the Norwegian ships. The income from her shipping industry dominated Norway's economy and the Norwegians badly needed hard currency, which they could have earned either by accepting the German bribes or by chartering to the Americans, not yet in the war, and other oil-rich areas where the freight rates were much better than those of the British.

This practical help, one of the most altruistic gestures by any nation in the Second World War, would not have been possible without the support of their merchant service officers and men. The seamen faced exile from their country and separation from their wives and families until the end of hostilities. They faced reprisals from the Germans if Britain fell and their ships were grabbed by the enemy. The decision to accept these risks was taken at a time when almost every country in Europe had fallen to Hitler, and most of the world believed that it was only a matter of time before the British went under.

Without the support given by the Norwegian shipowners and the officers and men who manned their ships, it is quite possible that supplies of fuel and reserve stocks in Britain would have run out.

An obituary in *The Times* on 17 October, 1996, half a century later, reminds us of our debt to that nation:

> In a contribution to the British war effort which was out of proportion to Norway's tiny population, Birger Lunde was one of thousands of his country's seamen who helped to keep supply lines open throughout the Battle of the Atlantic. It is not generally recognized what epic sacrifices were made by the Norwegian merchant fleet between 1940 and 1945, nor what a massive difference Norwegian ships made to the supply situation in Britain's most desperate hours. When the Germans invaded Norway in 1940, more than 1,000 Norwegian ships were at sea. They sailed without hesitation to British ports to place themselves at the disposal of their ally on charter, in spite of huge financial inducements by Germany to become part of its merchant marine. Britain thus acquired at a stroke the services of the world's fourth biggest merchant navy.
>
> In fact the apparent hyperbole probably underestimated the situation. Throughout the entire war Norwegian merchant ships carried 40 per cent of all the oil brought in to Britain plus similarly great amounts of ammunition, food and other vital supplies.

Churchill wrote:

> Getting the Norwegian ships during the darkest days of the war was the equivalent of getting in England a trained and equipped army of one million men.

131

But the Norwegians paid heavily. One fifth of the crews perished over the five years from May, 1940: many men survived only with nerves shattered beyond repair.

In spite of this addition to the fleet, tankers were taking much too long to complete their journey cycles. In the autumn of 1941 the round-voyage time of tankers from the Caribbean ports to the UK west coast was 63½ days, of which no less than 50% was spent loading, sailing and waiting in United States waters. By 1942 these delays were much worse: the round-voyage time had increased to eighty-two days and the time hanging around in United States waters to 55%. The American fleet of fast 15,000-ton 'Greyhound tankers' was withdrawn from the ponderous Atlantic convoys, which at the best achieved eight knots and at the worst in really bad sea and wind conditions might make good only fifty miles in a day. The Greyhounds could in a given period lift double the tonnage carried by a slow tanker in convoy. But they were extremely difficult to handle at normal Atlantic convoy speeds, since they had been designed to operate at fourteen knots or faster. In bad weather they represented a marine hazard in a convoy of slower ships and four Greyhound tankers were lost in a single month. Now that an effective convoy system had been introduced from the Caribbean to New York, it was safer to use these fast tankers on the American east coast shuttle where they could carry great tonnages in special fast convoys to the New York Navy Pool for onward shipment across the Atlantic to the UK.

To supply the Allied Armies' needs in North Africa was a long, dangerous and roundabout trail: to send the oil up to New York from the Caribbean, carry it in convoy across the North Atlantic during one of its worst winters, and then down past the Bay of Biscay and the marauding Condors, which was a course that led straight across the U-boats' normal routes to and from their Biscay bases.

The planners reckoned that the North African landings would need another 900,000 tons from the UK stocks; even after allowing for deliveries, this would bring the level down further to below half the 'minimum danger level'. A member of the Naval Staff said, 'Our shipping position has never been tighter.'

In the closing days of the year, impatient with the withdrawal

132

of the Greyhounds and pressed by the needs to supply Torch, the Admiralty took unusual risks and despatched an important tanker convoy, TM 1, with a weak and slow escort, direct from the Caribbean to Gibraltar.[3]

The need was urgent but it could not have come at a worse time. Bletchley Park had still not caught up with its backlog and the Admiralty was still operating blind. B-Dienst, on the other hand, had been deciphering the Admiralty Convoy Code for a long time. The Monthly Anti-Submarine Report of January, 1943, which was widely circulated among the Western Approach escorts, warned that 'the potentially annihilating superiority that the enemy . . . might [now] bring to bear on a convoy unlucky enough to be caught early on a homeward-bound journey cannot be appreciated by reference to any past experiences,' a long-winded way of wrapping up a warning that a disaster was likely to happen at any moment, without suggesting any solution.[4]

On 26 December, 1942, the German U-boat 'Delphin' Group, *U-571, 620, 575, 381, 436* and *442*, accompanied by the milch-cow *U-463*, was deployed west of the Azores and about to make a sweep right across the Atlantic towards the Brazilian coast.

On 28 December the Masters of eight of the nine tankers assembled ashore at Port of Spain in Trinidad for the convoy conference. The Master of the ninth tanker, *Empire Lytton*, had been nominated as Commodore of this convoy, but he failed to turn up, because he was busy sorting out some engine-room problems in his new ship. So Captain Laddle, in *Oltenia II*, took over at a moment's notice, with the Master of *British Vigilance*, Captain Evans, as Vice-Commodore. It is odd that no experienced commodore with his own Yeoman of Signals and small but battle-hardened staff of convoy signalmen was to take charge of this large and very valuable cargo of fuel so urgently needed by the Allied armies in Tunisia. The Germans were aware of the impending departure of the convoy and of its destination through SIGINT and through agents in Trinidad, who will have had no difficulty in observing and reporting the tankers as they left Port of Spain. About the only things that the Germans didn't know about this convoy were the course ordered, which was distributed to masters on board their ships just before sailing and

133

after contact with the land was broken, and the convoy speed, which was easy enough to guess.

As we have seen, the number and quality of the escorts allocated to Atlantic convoys had been much diluted to meet the needs of Torch. Convoy TM 1 consisted of nine tankers, but, in spite of the value of its ships and cargo, was to be escorted only by the B5 Group, consisting of one destroyer, *Havelock* (SOE), and the three corvettes *Saxifrage, Godetia* and *Pimpernel.* Air cover would be provided by the Americans for the first twenty-four hours, but thereafter the ships would be on their own until they came within range of aircraft from Gibraltar.

Seven tankers sailed in convoy that afternoon. *Empire Lytton, Vanja* and the corvette *Godetia* were suffering from engine troubles and needed time to complete their repairs, so they followed behind. Six hours out the Catalina sweeping ahead of these latecomers spotted *U-124* on the surface seven miles ahead. *Godetia*, still with only one boiler serviceable, set off along the bearing reported at the best speed she could make on one boiler, but found nothing. This is not surprising since her best speed with both boilers was only fourteen knots against the U-boat's seventeen knots on the surface.

The OIC Summary on this date noted that 'Special Intelligence during the past week has been fragmentary. The enemy's main effort is still concentrated on the North Atlantic convoy routes. . . . A group of six U-boats . . . is proceeding to a patrol line, the exact position of which is uncertain. It is possible that this line is west of Madeira and is designed to intercept American Casablanca convoys.' The Summary estimated that 169 U-boats, the greatest number ever, were operating in the North Atlantic.

By dawn on 29 December the three late starters had caught up and the convoy was deployed and steaming in five columns, with *British Vigilance* leading the centre column, followed by *Empire Lytton*, a ship new from the Teesside yard of the Furness Shipping Company and now the pride of the fleet.

By 1 January, 1943, *Godetia* had completed her engine repairs, but the next day her radar had burnt out and she had no spares.

On the same day the U-boat Group Delphin, 'acting on Radio Intelligence', shaped course to patrol the direct route from the

Azores to New York, (north of TM 1's direct route) and started sweeping westwards.

At this point, and quite by chance, *U-514*, on its way home, sighted the convoy and was ordered to shadow with *U-125*, which happened to be 250 miles to the eastward. As a result of *U-514*'s report, Group Delphin was given a course to steer to intercept TM 1, 900 miles away.

Clearly B-Dienst now knew where the convoy was and had a fair idea where it was going. If the tankers were to reach Gibraltar, they must pass through the 200-mile gap between Bermuda and the Canary Islands. In the afternoon the convoy was ordered to make a substantial alteration to the south of their planned route and to execute this alteration of course (to 085°) just after dark. The course ordered would have taken TM 1 120 miles south of the southern end of the U-boats' patrol line.

U-514, with orders to shadow and permission to attack, torpedoed *British Vigilance* at nightfall on 3 January. This was a bold attack carried out on the surface, approaching from ahead and going down between the columns. *British Vigilance* went up in a ball of flame. The U-boat carried on down the side of the blazing tanker and met *Empire Lytton* as she pulled over to starboard to avoid the blazing *British Vigilance*. Captain Andrews saw the U-boat ahead on the port bow and set course to ram, missing the U-boat's stern by some 20 yards as it set off at speed on the surface. The continuous stream of fire hitting *U-514*'s conning tower from all ships and particularly from *Empire Lytton*'s oerlikon, manned by apprentice Basil King, backed up by *Norvik's* four-inch gunfire, made it too hot for the U-boat, which crash-dived as soon as it got clear. At this point *U-514*'s wireless went out of action, which is understandable since Captain Andrews claimed 200 hits with oerlikon shells on the U-boat's conning tower and superstructure.

U-125 had never made contact and now Dönitz had no communication with the convoy. Both *U-514* and *U-215* tried for several days to relocate the convoy but were not successful and neither took any further part in the action. In contrast, after pursuing *U-514*, it took *Empire Lytton* just two hours to get back into the convoy, where she resumed station at the head of the centre column.

All could have been well for the remaining eight tankers as they plodded on with their cargo of tens of thousands of tons of fuel, but the escorts, particularly *Havelock*, were themselves running out of fuel. During 3 January *Havelock* had been trying to take on fuel from *Norvik*, but the weather and faulty gear made this impossible. *Norvik*'s fuelling gear was worn and the second set was too light. *Havelock* should anyhow have been refuelling from *Cliona*, which was properly equipped for the task, but she didn't know this.

Looking for better weather to facilitate fuelling, the SOE, in spite of the course diversion order, altered the convoy back to the north (055°). When he reported the sinking of *British Vigilance* and his new course, this alerted the Admiralty to the fact that the diversion that had been ordered had been discontinued. The order to take a more southerly course was repeated, and this time the alteration was carried out, but only until 1008 on the morning of 4 January, when the SOE informed the Admiralty that he couldn't take the convoy on the course ordered and again turned the convoy back to the north. This was the second time in as many days that a course diversion ordered had not been carried out.

It is difficult to understand the SOE's conviction that he would find better weather further north. The wind and sea conditions around the convoy as recorded by the ships at that time are set out in the Table below:

Date	Wind Force	Sea/Swell
3/1/43	Force 4	34
4/1/43	Force 3	23
5/1/43	Force 2	12
6/1/43	Light Airs	02

Nobody could wish for better conditions in the Atlantic Ocean in midwinter.

The resumption of this course would take the convoy straight into the middle of the patrol line of Group Delphin, but if the convoy had stuck to the diversion to the south as ordered it would have avoided the line of patrolling U-boats.

There was no direct evidence of this because Bletchley Park

had not yet overcome the backlog of signals accumulated during their blind period. But from the shore stations' HF/DF fixes and the volume of W/T traffic, the OIC knew that there were a lot of U-boats in the area, and their report for the situation on 28 December showed a very significant increase of fifteen U-boats in the Azores to Cape Verde area, the area through which any convoy from the USA to Gibraltar must pass.

The analysis of the U-boat situation was one of the outputs of Bletchley Park, based partly on the decryption of the German U-boat W/T traffic and partly on the Submarine Tracking Room's analysis of these decrypts. It was a highly confidential document, marked: 'MOST SECRET: FOR THE PERSONAL USE OF THE ADDRESSEE ONLY'.

Only four copies were circulated, to the First Sea Lord, two Assistant Chiefs of Naval Staff and the C-in-C Home Fleet, and only nine people had access to the contents. Not even the C-in-C Western Approaches was on the list of recipients. The interpretation and use made of the contents was a matter for the personal judgment of the recipients.

But it was too late now for a further diversion because this would have lengthened the convoy's journey time by a day, causing more fuel problems for the escorts and so exposing the remains of the convoy to total destruction.

The convoy steamed on, taking the direct course for Gibraltar. The ships did not zigzag because this would have delayed them further, and the fuel was urgently needed by the troops in Africa. In retrospect, maybe it would have been better to remember the old saying: 'It is better to arrive late than never to arrive at all.'

By 8 January Group Delphin was patrolling across the line of the eight tankers and their four escorts. Two of the escorts were 'blind', with defective radar sets. *Havelock* was the only ship fitted with HF/DF, and should certainly have gathered from the volume of U-boat signals ahead that they were running into severe trouble. The shore stations picked up the signals, but *Havelock*'s set operated only intermittently and sometimes not at all.

Dönitz had lost contact with TM 1 and was disgruntled. The OIC report of January, 1943, tells us that he 'had only the vaguest idea of the composition, whereabouts and course of the convoy. He subsequently expressed his displeasure at this state of affairs, and issued general instructions to all U-boats to avoid a repetition of such an incident.'

Things changed in an instant at 1503 on 8 January, when *U-318*, third U-boat from the northern end of the waiting line, sighted and reported the convoy. The meticulously trained U-boat commanders brought into action the well-oiled machinery of the wolf-pack attack. This was their chance and they took it. To reinforce the six boats in Group Delphin, *U-134* and *U-181*, short of fuel and homeward bound, and *U-522* and *U-511*, outward bound, were brought in.

The attack started at 1945 on 8 January when *U-436* fired three torpedoes, hitting the *Albert L. Ellsworth*. She did not sink or blow up, but presented another problem to the SOE. Should he leave one of his four ships to stand by her, or should she be left to her fate? He took the latter decision and he heard no more of her.[5]

The next to be hit was the Commodore's ship, *Oltenia II*, which sank like a stone. An aggressive counter-attack by *Havelock* drove off *U-436*, while *Pimpernel* drove off *U-571* and *Godetia* repulsed *U-575*. The SOE had to choose hourly whether to pick up survivors, to protect damaged ships or to look after the ships which were still in convoy. He could not do all three, but he tried and for most of that night only the corvette *Godetia* was in station to protect the convoy, while the other escorts carried out searches and attacks on the U-boats and picked up the survivors. With the U-boats charging around on the surface, the escorts carrying out their attacks and the merchant ships firing at the U-boats, there was complete confusion. In the course of the night *Pimpernel* was fired on by *Cliona*, *Saxifrage* had to go hard a'port to avoid *Havelock* in hot pursuit of a U-boat and four ships simultaneously opened fire on a surfaced U-boat. In the midst of this turmoil, after *Oltenia II* sank, Captain J.D. Millar in *British Dominion* was appointed Commodore and the escorts, by superhuman efforts, successfully held off the pack, now up to seven, until after midnight.

But the odds were too heavy for the lull to last. At the end of the middle watch on 9 January the U-boats got through again, hitting *Minister Wedel* and *Norvik* between 0315 and 0330.

Neither sank after the first hit, leaving as many crippled ships to be succoured as there were escorts.[6]

There was a short lull while the U-boats redeployed, but the next attack by *U-442* caught *Empire Lytton* in her forward fuel tank. Instead of immediately igniting her three million gallons of high octane in a fireball, the torpedo caught her in her forward fuel tank which did not catch fire, leaving her crippled but still afloat, an enormous explosive charge ready to go off at any moment. It was no place to be. Captain Andrews and thirty-one of his crew pulled away in two lifeboats, lay off until daylight, and then with great courage reboarded the ship and tried to get her under way again, but the damage was too great to permit them to continue. *Saxifrage* took off the survivors, of which there were thirty-one out of forty-seven. Fifteen were missing and one dead. The dead man was Chief Officer Baughn, who had been supported for two hours by an Estonian seaman, but died after swallowing quantities of oil fuel when boarding the lifeboat. Captain Andrews mentioned Greaser N. Murray and Fireman J. Reid who remained quietly at their posts in the engine room after the torpedo struck, shutting off fires and fuel valves. They stayed at their posts below decks, going about their duties quite calmly from the time that the ship was struck until the master rang down 'Finished With Main Engines'.[7]

During the day *U-181* and *U-134* were driven off. *U-134* was damaged by *Godetia* and *Harvester* and *Godetia* depth-charged *U-381*. When *Saxifrage* rejoined the convoy on the night of 9 January six of the nine tankers had been hit. There were now more than twice as many sunk or crippled ships as there were escorts.

Only *Cliona*, *Vanja* and *British Dominion* steamed on in a convoy of three. *British Dominion* (6983 tons) carried a crew of fifty-three and a cargo of 10,000 tons of benzene. Up to that time the ships had not been zigzagging, in order to save time. The tension aboard is difficult to imagine. They had seen six of their colleagues torpedoed and it was now flat calm. The wind had fallen to a light air that scarcely rippled the surface. The new acting Commodore, the fourth to bear the responsibility, started zigzagging during the middle watch.

The attacks went on as up to five U-boats continued to shadow the remaining ships on 9 and 10 January. At midnight on 10th/11th the convoy altered course and eleven minutes later *British Dominion* was hit by three torpedoes on her port side. *Vanja* saw the U-boat on the surface and opened fire with her 4-inch gun and her Colt machine gun. The escorts sighted another four U-boats trying to attack on the surface and drove them off, but obtained no asdic contacts.

Aboard *British Dominion* the Commodore received a blow on the head which knocked him out. When he came to, his face was badly burnt, his clothes were on fire and the ship was burning furiously. The Third Officer ran past him through the wheel-house and dived over the side. He was about to follow when he realized that the surface of the sea was covered in blazing benzene into which the Third Officer had dived head first and that the ship was still going ahead at four or five knots leaving a blazing trail behind. The first lifeboat that he found was useless as the rope to lower it had burnt through. He was helped into a boat and an hour later *Godetia* came to pick them up.

His hands were so badly burnt that when he summoned enough courage to grab hold of the scrambling net the pain was so great that he could not haul himself up. At that moment *Godetia* sighted another U-boat and set off in pursuit, not re-alizing that he was still hanging from the net. He was hauled on board. When the sick berth attendant opened his shirt and saw the ghastly-looking wound on his neck he uttered a cry of 'My God!', disappeared and was not seen again. In due course the doctor came over from *Havelock*.

He was carefully looked after by the Navy, but on arrival in Gibraltar was put straight into the Colonial Hospital in Gibraltar, where he remained until 2 February, remarking of that period: 'treated very badly – disgusting food – never hot or even warm – not fit for pigs. Medical attention very poor.'

Masters of tankers were brought up in a hard school and carried great responsibilities. It is sad to hear one of them finding it necessary to bring to the attention of the Admiralty the in-different treatment that even a man of his seniority in the merchant service received.

Of his crew of fifty-three, thirty-six were missing and seven of the survivors were injured. He finishes his report of the sinking of *British Dominion* with the words: 'All the crew behaved exceedingly well.'

The night continued with further alarms and when daylight came HMS *Quentin*, *Penstemon* and *Samphire* and a Catalina from Gibraltar arrived, to find *Cliona* and *Vanji* still unharmed. Dönitz ordered that 'The last two tankers must also fall'. Two U-boats were told to continue the pursuit, which they did until the evening, when they gave up in order to refuel from their milch cow.[8]

At 0930 on 14 January, the day that the Casablanca Conference opened, *Vanja* and *Cliona* limped into Gibraltar. Ultra intelligence reports were fed to Churchill during the Conference. If it achieved nothing else this disaster might have helped to emphasize the priority that must be enforced. At its final Plenary Session on 23 January it agreed that the first sentence should read: 'The defeat of the U-boat must remain a first charge on the resources of the United Nations.'

What an awful price to pay.

The loss of these seven tankers and their crews in one convoy and the 80,000 tons (tons, not gallons) of fuel destined for the troops in Africa was a severe blow, one of the major convoy disasters of the whole Battle of the Atlantic.

Further south eleven 'independents', or stragglers, were sunk. In a couple of weeks eighteen ships, including the seven tankers of TM 1, many of their crews and their contents had gone down at no cost to the enemy. As Churchill said at Casablanca, 'This doesn't look good'. As the contestants went into the ring for the next and decisive round of the Battle of the Atlantic, there was no doubt who had the bloodiest nose.

Apart from this, and in spite of the number of U-boats now deployed and the very heavy traffic which landed the troops and kept them supplied in the African landings, losses had been surprisingly small. The efficiency of the salvage tugs resulted in eight out of twelve damaged ships getting home. Nevertheless, this disaster was a timely reminder of the killing power of the U-boats and Dönitz' amazing resilience and ability to switch his attacks to areas of vulnerability and to take advantage of any overconfidence.

In the case of TM 1 several mistakes were made at all levels.

The command of each convoy was vested in the senior officer of the escort, when present. If not present, the command fell on the Commodore of the convoy. Several times the SOE was not with the convoy because of the need to counter-attack the pack of U-boats on every side, to answer cries for help from valuable crippled tankers, or to rescue survivors near to death in the burning waters. Several of the tankers, although badly damaged, did not sink when torpedoed and remained afloat as the convoy steamed on. Should he protect these damaged ships, which might still be brought home, should he abandon them to their fate or should he sink them in case their fuel might prove useful to the U-boats?

He also had a difficult decision to make when fuel ran short in *Havelock* and his corvettes, which caused him to fail to implement fully two evasive routeing signals, omissions which resulted in the almost total annihilation of his convoy. Six of the seven tankers sunk were lost after this failure.

Although there were many occasions, some mentioned in this book, when commodores followed the naval tradition of overriding orders from ashore or from the SOE when they, the men on the spot, thought it necessary, an experienced commodore would have been unlikely to disobey a convoy evasive routeing signal without very strong reasons.

Since the Ocean Commodores were all very senior and experienced officers, usually holding ranks higher than the SOE, their opinion was rarely ignored by the SOE. An experienced Ocean Commodore, with the rank of Admiral or Captain RNR, might well have offered strong resistance to orders from the SOE that twice ran contrary to a routeing signal to evade suspected concentrations of U-boats, particularly when the SOE's action was based on a guess at the type of weather that might be experienced elsewhere.

ERRORS MADE:

Sending a very valuable convoy carrying about thirty-five million gallons of fuel on the direct route.
A patently inadequate escort.
No adequate arrangements for refuelling the escorts.

Poor radar and HF/DF maintenance and availability of spares.
Failure to use effectively OIC's assessment of available information.
Failure to carry out Connav's evasive routeing instructions.
Ignoring the old saying, 'more haste less speed'.
Absence of an experienced Convoy Commodore and his staff.[9]

Chapter Eleven

CONVOY ONS 154

The ships for this convoy had been brought round in coastal convoys to Loch Ewe from London, Hull, Immingham, the Tyne and the Firth of Forth on the east, and from the Bristol Channel, Liverpool and the Clyde on the west coast. The escort planned for the convoy consisted of ships from the Royal Canadian Navy's Escort Group, C1, under a new SOE, Lieutenant-Commander G. Windeyer, who had just taken command of the destroyer HMCS *St Laurent*, and five Canadian corvettes, with the addition of the destroyer, HMS *Burwell*. The Royal Canadian Navy, overall, and particularly in the last two years of the transatlantic convoys, had made an extraordinary contribution to the Battle of the Atlantic, but it had its ups and downs and its rapid expansion, which might be described as an explosion, presented many challenges.

The RCN started the war with a strength of about 3500 officers and men, of which half were reservists, with a fleet of four minesweepers and seven destroyers. It finished the war with a strength just short of 100,000 and a fleet of 413 ships – twenty-eight destroyers, seventy frigates, 122 corvettes, seventy-three minesweepers, three Armed Merchant Cruisers, a depot ship and 116 small craft.[1]

The RCN expanded so fast that, by the end of 1942 and the first months of 1943, when the Battle of the Atlantic had reached its critical period, this infant navy was already playing a vital role both at sea in the front line, and in the work done by the Naval Control Service (NCS) assembling the ships and crews for the thousands of convoys from Halifax, the New Brunswick port of Sydney, and St John's, Newfoundland.[2]

The Canadians had many problems, all of which they tackled with tremendous energy and eventually mastered. The few ships that they possessed at the outbreak of the Second World War were unsuitable for North Atlantic convoy work. As Henry J. Kaiser had shown with the Liberty Ships, corvettes could be built quite quickly, but the RCN had no suitable shipyards for building anything bigger than a corvette. The yards on the Great Lakes, which had built a third of the corvettes, could not build bigger ships and the British Ministry of War Transport had tied up the other yards. Canadians had contributed little to the sea battles of the First World War (although a great deal to the Allied Armies, in numbers and in casualties) and had done nothing to build up a Canadian Navy in the interim years. Why should they? The feeling against war was even stronger than in Britain. Whereas the Royal Navy was able to recall pensioners and retired experienced key ratings to train the Hostilities Only ratings (HOs) and to form the backbone of the Royal Navy as it expanded to meet the needs of the conflict, Canada had no such experienced manpower reserves upon which it could call and no training establishments in which to train the flood of raw recruits. There were hard men from the fishing fleets of Newfoundland and New Brunswick and the Pacific coast, whose seamanship could not be bettered, but fishing was not the same as manning a warship and fighting the U-boat war. Officers, commanding officers and men were equally inexperienced.

When the first seventy Canadian-built corvettes were commissioned they were inadequate for ocean escort work, lacking flare forward, or a bridge and gun platform high enough to survive Atlantic conditions. They didn't carry enough fuel for the transatlantic convoys and their speed was several knots slower than a U-boat on the surface. By that time the Royal Navy had made extensive modifications to the forward sections of their corvettes and had re-armed them with modern weapons. The Canadians also needed the expertise of the British Admiralty Technical Mission but had neither the wealth nor the ruthless commercial drive that characterized the Americans. They took years to decide what they wanted and how their building

145

programme would affect their Navy after the war had ended. They were also fighting a hopeless battle for priority since the building of British frigates took first priority and the building of merchant ships next, both ahead of the RCN. As a result the thirty RCN frigates which were ordered and due to be in commission by March, 1943, were cut down to five. Meanwhile, little attention was given to the immediate need for corvettes to be modified to make them reasonably effective as ocean escorts. The Canadians havered, being unwilling to build ships to an already obsolescent design. Through lack of experience they had yet to learn that all warships are out of date or unsuitable by the time they become operational. The Canadians built too many, too short, corvettes because the west coast yards were too far away to take a big part and because the longer ships, the frigates, could not be built on the Great Lakes where the building yards were to be found, as they would not have been able to get through the locks on the St Lawrence River.

The ships that the RCN did commission lacked modern anti-submarine equipment. The asdic equipment used by the Royal Navy was never as good as it was expected to be, but when fitted in the RCN ships it did not even have the benefit of a gyro compass, which greatly reduced the overall efficiency of the ship, as well as its asdic capability. They lacked an efficient radar system adjacent to the bridge and communications between the bridge and the radar and anti-submarine operators. The short-comings were so pronounced that RCN corvettes were not considered good enough to work with Admiralty corvettes on a convoy screen.

When a tardy decision was taken to modernize the Canadian corvettes, the whole programme was held up pending stability trials. The modifications that had been found necessary for the RN corvettes, and had been approved and carried out, had now to go through the same rigmarole of testing and approval by the RCN in Halifax. It was a sorry story of delay and bureaucracy, the result of which was to delay the start of the modernization until January, 1943, too late to be of any benefit in the crisis months of the Battle of the Atlantic.

In a U-boat attack the warships involved were often working out of sight of each other and of the convoy, and the air was crackling with undesirable W/T traffic. Whether the escorts in a group were 'modern' or not, their commanding officers needed to be trained to work together with a minimum exchange of signals, a lesson learnt in the early days of the battle. Once trained, ships in a group needed to stay together when they started their convoy duties. A trained escort group of four or five ships was worth double the number of ships which had been thrown together just before their convoy set sail.

In 1942 the need for this group training had been recognized, but had not extended to all ships or to the Canadian groups. Escort Group C1 had been brought over to Britain for this training, but it had not taken place because of bad weather and defects in the submarine with which they were supposed to be exercising. In the case of convoy ONS 154 the SOE did not even call a conference of his commanding officers before they went to sea, pleading the absence of suitable boats to bring them on board in vile weather.

ONS 154 sailed at the critical time when the number of operational U-boats had almost reached its peak and the Germans were benefiting from the boost to their morale after the massive sinkings of shipping along the east coast of America. The U-boats' effective time in operational areas had been greatly improved by the use of milch cows, large MK IX U-boats stationed in mid-Atlantic to replenish operational U-boats with fuel, torpedoes and supplies, obviating the need to spend most of their time at sea travelling to and from their bases. The Germans had been positively helped in their attacks on the American east coast shipping by Admiral King's refusal to benefit from the lessons learnt in three hard years of continuous battle by the Royal Navy about the use of convoys. For several months after they entered the war, shipping, even the oil tankers, continued to sail independently up and down their old routes between lines of lighted buoys, silhouetted against the shore lights of the USA, which were still shining brightly. The U-boats had been picking them off with the greatest of ease and the minimum of risk. The winter of 1942/1943 was the worst for fifty years and full gales or storms were recorded on 116 days out of 140.

The Canadian-built corvettes which started to appear in the

spring of 1941 were even more basic than the British corvettes, which, it has been said, would 'roll on a wet lawn'. They were the smallest ships ever to brave the North Atlantic for long periods without a break. For the ships' companies, being at sea in a corvette was just plain exhausting. The clatter and crash of the ship working in a seaway, the banshee howl of the wind, the perpetual fight against the pitch and roll of the ship and the cold were enough trial for experienced seamen, but many of the recruits on board had never even seen the sea before. The design was seaworthy, but it was the endurance of the men who manned the ships that was the limiting factor.

The convoy conference for the Masters of the merchant ships in convoy ONS 154 took place on the morning of 18 December. The forty-five ships, which included a tanker, would be sailing in twelve columns with Commodore W. de M. Egerton, in *Empire Shackleton*, due to weigh anchor at 2100 that night. Commodore Egerton had completed eight ocean convoys of which HX 212 at the end of October had been the most eventful, with a loss of seven merchant ships. His personal diary shows him to have been a man of strong personality who would stand no nonsense from his charges:

> Fired gun at *Barnhull* to get her to take any notice of calls on lamps. . . . SOE made excessive use of R/T, scarcely ever silent. Had I been a commanding officer of one of the escorts my set would have had a bad breakdown.[3]

He brought with him his staff of six: his Yeoman of Signals, a leading signalman, and four convoy signalmen. Sailing in the convoy was HMS *Fidelity*, carrying two seaplanes and a motor torpedo boat fitted with anti-torpedo nets on deck. These had been fitted on several merchant ships but were found to be difficult to rig while at sea. They were not popular because of the additional work involved for crews already overworked with all their normal duties to perform, as well as extra lookouts while in convoy. *Fidelity* was manned by a French crew and carried two Commandos en route for the East.

Once clear of the land, the contingents took up station line abreast in twelve columns, three or four deep, with *Fidelity* and the rescue ship *Toward* in the rear. In reasonable weather the compact rectangle of ships would stretch over five or six miles in width and up to two miles in depth.

The escorting warships did not sail as planned because both destroyers, the escort's teeth, were in dock. *St Laurent* had collided with the oiler in Moville and was under repair in Belfast: she sailed nineteen hours late at speed to catch up the convoy, burning up fuel which she would need desperately in the coming days. There was something wrong with *Burwell* which was not unusual for one of the ex-American four-stackers; she never joined the convoy. Thus forty-five ships set off, escorted by five corvettes which had not completed their working up exercises, a very inadequate and slow escorting force for so many slow ships. Without destroyers, there was little chance of any offensive sorties to keep U-boats submerged if an attack developed because on the surface the U-boats were faster than the escorts. The five corvettes had been fitted with 271 radar, but it was new to them.

This was a bad start, and very frustrating for the Commodore and his signalmen who had the job of getting all these ships into their correct stations without a single escort with enough speed to bite at their heels.

The job was completed at dusk on 18 December and the ships cleared Bloody Foreland at eight and a quarter knots. *St Laurent* set off the following night at 2215 to catch up, without calibrating her HF/DF and without the officer responsible for its operation on board, and made contact with the Commodore at 1030 on 19/12. The convoy was otherwise without HF/DF except for the rescue ship *Toward*.

On 22 December the weather started to deteriorate. Two aircraft were seen, a Sunderland and another which was glimpsed through the low cloud but not identified. As the weather got worse so did the station-keeping. The merchant ships reacted in different ways. The most difficult to handle were those in ballast, outward-bound and carrying no cargoes, which rode high in the water and caught the fierce blasts of wind on their bows as they came up out of the troughs between the great Atlantic swells. If the speed of the convoy was reduced they

149

became unmanageable and impossible to steer: if they went too fast there were ships that could not keep up without damage to their structure or to deck cargo.

When darkness came on 23 December the main problem for the Masters and commanding officers was to avoid collision as the ships were carried this way and that by the huge grey seas in very low visibility. The prudent and seamanlike action was to keep as far away from any other ship as possible. As a result the convoy formation and its protective screen of warships slowly disintegrated.

The winds were cutting the tops off the seas at their crests and driving the salt spray across the surface as first light slowly broke through on 24 December, but it found the Commodore hove to with only one other ship in sight. So much for the lecture on keeping closed up at the convoy conference back in Liverpool.

The escorts were in no better shape. *St Laurent* and the five corvettes were also hove to and had lost touch, in spite of the radar newly fitted in three of the corvettes just before sailing. On board the flush-deck *St Laurent* the after-quarters were cut off from the bridge. Wire lizards were rigged from forward to aft, from which hung lanyards to hold on to if it was imperative to brave the journey along the upper deck. The galley was forward under the bridge and for those whose messes were aft there was no hot food.

When the seas moderated slightly and the visibility lifted the Commodore and the SOE set about relocating their charges. On board *St Laurent* in the after messes there were other more pressing priorities. It was Christmas Eve and there had been no hot food for two days. The most junior and expendable ordinary seaman was despatched on the perilous journey to rustle up something from the galley amidships. He negotiated the journey forward safely but got very wet, and was sent back carrying a great tray of bergoo, a sticky mess of gluey porridge with plenty of body in it, but not an easy thing to carry with one hand while clinging on with the other to the lanyard as seas swirled across the deck knee-high and the ship rolled and pitched. He made the journey back, ducked into the after superstructure with a sigh of relief and started down the vertical ladder to the messdeck. He was halfway down when a vicious sea caught *St Laurent* on the stern. She gave a sharp buck with her hind quarters and he fell flat on the deck with the tray of bergoo spread over him from head to foot.

At least the Commodore knew that these conditions made it impossible for U-boats to operate on the surface or even at periscope depth. Their commanders would have taken them down and be as snug as you could be in a submerged U-boat below the turmoil.

Chivvied by the busy corvettes, the cumbersome ships lumbered back into formation and by 1550 on 24 December were in station with *St Laurent* and two corvettes ahead and the other three astern. *St Laurent* was already concerned about her fuel and on Christmas Day fell back with the convoy oiler *Scottish Heather* to refuel at sea. Today refuelling at sea is a 'routine' task for warships. Then, it was a new technique with untested gear and no experience. On this occasion both ships hauled out of station, reduced speed and dropped astern. *St Laurent* came up parallel with the oiler and passed across a bow and stern line to steady her in position while the oil hose was hoisted up on a boom and passed across. Both ships were rolling with different rhythms; they required a degree of accuracy in the steering that was not possible at low speed in the sea conditions at that time. A wave roared down between them and threw their heads in opposite directions, parting the bow line. The hose carried away; the stern line was still made fast and was brought up taut; *St Laurent* fell beam on to the sea before the line could be released and she had to give up the attempt.

On Boxing Day the convoy had entered the area in mid-Atlantic which was out of range of regular air support from either Newfoundland, Iceland or Ireland, the area referred to as the Black Pit in which Dönitz' U-boats were able to manoeuvre at speed on the surface without fear of attack or observation from the air. *U-664* was now in touch six miles off the port quarter of the convoy, shadowing and signalling course and speed back to Headquarters and to the U-boats in Group Spitz. Well trimmed down, she could not be seen by the merchant ships or the escorts, but could comfortably monitor the ships' movements during the daylight hours. The wind had dropped to force 4 and *St Laurent* tried again to oil, this time successfully, taking

151

on board 100 tons before the securing wires and hose carried away again.

While Group Spitz of ten U-boats, and Group Urmgestum, with another seven, closed at maximum speed with orders to attack after darkness fell, *U-664*, bored and frustrated by this passive roll, settled down to do his job, but let his attention wander so that the range came down to four miles. *Toward* had got an accurate bearing of one of his W/T reports and an escort charged him and made him dive.

From the radio activity around him and from sightings it was clear to Commodore Egerton that he was in for a bad night. He could expect no more escorts to reinforce Group C1. The U-boats had had plenty of time to get into attacking positions. Warnings were flooding in from Admiralty of wolf packs in his vicinity. He already knew this because *Toward*, on the spot, was reporting strong HF/DF signals. His escort was weak in numbers and sadly lacking in speed and further warnings were of little consolation when they were not backed up by any hint of re-inforcement. He called up his charges, signalled 'Convoy Close Up', and ordered all ships to prepare for emergency turns to star-board at midnight.

The attack started at 2146 on 26 December when *Chediac*, now stationed ahead, reported a U-boat at full speed on the surface on the port bow. This was the first positive indication of the method of attack that would be used. In the interwar years Dönitz had made preparations for the U-boat war by intensive training for his future U-boat crews in high-speed Motor Torpedo Boats, teaching them the concept that the U-boat was just a submersible version of the MTB, attacking on the surface, penetrating right into the convoy, firing from bow and stern torpedo tubes and retreating on the surface, before disappearing underwater and leaving total confusion astern. He had used the inland waters of the Baltic to very good advantage for this purpose and here was a wonderful chance to use these years of preparation.[4] Neither the SOE nor the Commodore could do much about it with the only destroyer short of fuel and a great force of U-boats all round that had the legs of the corvettes. The only option for defence was to try to route the ships clear of the enemy.

At midnight the Commodore executed the first emergency turn to starboard, and the second twenty minutes later. A turn to port would have taken the convoy away from both wolf packs, but by bad luck these turns to starboard took his ships straight into the path of *U-356*, commanded by *Oberleutnant* Ruppelt, the boldest of the bold. The action started on a low key when *Norse King* dropped astern showing two red (not under control) lights, which made convenient markers for any U-boats which couldn't see the ships with their binoculars. Then *Chediac* dropped out of the screen to look after her. An hour later *Empire Union* was hit and the sedate progress of the convoy escalated into near panic with an immediate display of fireworks loosed off by all the ships, making quite sure that the convoy's location was clearly revealed and suitable targets silhouetted. Ten minutes later *Melrose Abbey* was hit, and then another of the escorting corvettes, *Napanee*, was detailed to stand by *Toward* as she went about her job of picking up survivors.

At this point the SOE had detached two of his six escorts to stand by three disabled ships and *Toward*, leaving only one destroyer and three corvettes, none with HF/DF, to protect the other forty-two ships in the convoy, known to be surrounded on all sides by U-boats. To make it worse, the escorts detached were so slow and already so short of fuel that they must take a long time to get back in station when they returned.

This was the old, recurring, agonizing decision that an SOE had to make, whether to pick up crews struggling in the water and leave undamaged ships unprotected, or to leave the men in the water to take their chances while carrying out the standard orders to ensure the 'safe and timely arrival' of the remainder.

At this point his decision appeared to be justified. Shortly after 0230 on 27 December *Empire Union* and *Melrose Abbey* went down, but *Toward* had picked up all but thirteen of their crews and *Norse King* and *Chediac* were hurrying to rejoin.

But a very heavy price had yet to be paid. *St Laurent* had fallen astern of the convoy to cover the gaps left by *Chediac* and *Napanee*. *U-356* reloaded and came in from the starboard beam through the gap left by *St Laurent*'s move, running up between columns eleven and twelve. His first torpedo hit *Soekaboemi*, with seventy on board. The usual fatal fireworks display started at once, conveniently illuminating the whole convoy once again and floodlighting the course that the U-boat had chosen through the convoy. *U-356* turned across the columns and five minutes later fired at *King Edward* which sank like a stone in three minutes taking twenty-three of her crew of forty-eight with her.

Ruppelt was running at full speed across the bows of the convoy when he sighted *Battleford* and turned back down the starboard side of the convoy on opposite course. As he reached the last ship in the column he was turning under full rudder to run up between the columns again when *St Laurent* picked him up on radar and shortly afterwards sighted him on the surface. *St Laurent* was hampered in her attempts to open fire by the proximity of the convoy ships, but obtained some hits and dropped two patterns of depth-charges. This was the end of Ruppelt, his crew and *U-356*, which had torpedoed four ships in less than two hours, all of which were eventually sunk.

Commodore Egerton's convoy plodded on, leaving a trail of slaughter, behind. Wrecks, lifeboats, rafts and debris littered the ocean for miles. The only good thing about the night was the work done by *Toward* picking up survivors. By 0450, still screened by *Napanee*, she had picked up ninety of the 103 people from the two casualties, *Empire Union* and *Melrose Abbey*, and was on her way to the scene of the sinking of *Soekaboemi* and *King Edward*. She was now getting near the limit of her capacity to feed all those on board. She now had three times her normal complement and, even with harsh rationing, she could run out of food and water before she reached harbour. She arrived in the area of search at 0730 to find *Soekaboemi* still afloat. So often there were serious casualties resulting from discipline breaking down and mistakes being made in lowering the lifeboats when those on board torpedoed ships were in a state of shock. Captain Haijo had a mixed crew, mainly Dutch, but including Chinese, Javanese, one British, RN, Dutch DEMS gunners and four passengers, but he and his officers had got all of them away safely in the lifeboats. Seeing that *Soekaboemi* was showing no further signs of sinking, he had even gathered enough volunteers to go back on board and join him in an effort to get the ship under way to attempt the journey back to Britain, provided an escort could be spared. Aware of the U-boats following the convoy and the impossible demands on his one destroyer and the corvettes, this plan was vetoed by the SOE and the seventy-four survivors from the two ships were transferred to *Toward*, now carrying 164 on board, and *Napanee*.[5] The two ships started off on the long haul to catch up with the convoy which was now thirty-five miles ahead. On their way they reported many U-boats trailing the convoy and manoeuvring into position for further attacks.

At 0900 the Commodore mustered his convoy. He had plenty to think about. Three of his escort of six were trailing along behind, while the U-boats closed the range from astern and others worked round the ends of his columns on the surface, but beyond visibility range, making ready for renewed attacks from the beam and from ahead. As the hours went by and the demands on the escorts required frequent forays and bursts of speed, the fuel shortage assumed major importance. At dusk the convoy oiler, *Scottish Heather*, dropped back behind the convoy to fuel *Chilliwack*, and *Kenogami* turned back to escort a straggler. *Toward* and *Napanee* were still catching up. The position was worse than it had been the night before because these ships all provided a trail to help the U-boats keep track of the convoy's course and position, and the SOE had only *St Laurent*, *Chediac* and *Battleford* to protect his eleven columns and thirty-seven ships.

Attempts were made to bluff the trailing pack by signalling to non-existent reinforcements and the convoy did an emergency turn to port during the afternoon.

Darkness came early in the winter afternoon of 27 December. At 1830 *Chediac* spotted and gave chase to *U-225*, but lost contact in the darkness. *Scottish Heather* was instructed to abandon her zigzag to hasten her return to station, which was convenient for *U-225*, her shadower, making it easier to deduce her course and the convoy's bearing. At 2047 *U-225* fired a torpedo which hit her. This crippling of the convoy and escorts' main oiler just when she was most needed was a severe blow. The U-boat avoided *Chilliwack*'s counter-attack, surfaced and continued at top speed to catch up with the convoy.

At midnight on 27 December things seemed a little better, *Napanee* and *Toward* were back in station after 22 hours of exhausting but very successful rescue work, and so was *Chilliwack*. On the other hand *Toward* was reporting heavy W/T traffic and strong HF/DF bearings which left no doubt that there were U-boats all round. No reinforcements could arrive before morning at the earliest and it seemed that only an Act of God, like fog or extreme weather, could now save ONS 154 from a massive attack.

At 0042 *St Laurent* drove off the first of the attackers. Two hours later she avoided what appeared to be an ambush, worked round the position of the U-boat that had lured her on and made a promising asdic attack.

Forty-five minutes later *Chilliwack* claimed a direct hit and reckoned to have another kill. With the news that two of the escorts reckoned to have sunk U-boats morale improved and the night passed without further loss.[6]

Unknown to the masters of the merchant ships, two reports from *Toward* had been received by the SOE and the Commodore. They contained further bad news. From her station astern of the convoy *Toward* reported that there was still massive W/T activity from U-boats astern, obviously still in touch. She also gave notice that although she was a specially fitted and provisioned rescue ship, she would run out of water and food to keep her crew and the 164 survivors alive before she reached harbour eleven days away. She was advised that some of her survivors would be taken off when reinforcements arrived in the morning of 28 December. (They didn't arrive until the 29th and then could only stay until midnight on the 31st.) From then on *Toward* ceased picking up survivors, concentrating on reporting the HF/DF intelligence that continued to pour in,[7] and the rearmost ship in each column was detailed to act as rescue ship – not much help if it was the rear ship that was torpedoed.

Bletchley Park had just come out of the blind period that followed the introduction of the fourth wheel in Enigma, but had an enormous backlog of signals to decypher and analyse. However, the air was once again hot with messages warning the convoy of U-boats around them.

At dusk that evening *Chediac* attempted to refuel from *S.G. Suebert*, using a different method. *Chediac* came up astern of the oiler which streamed a line astern to be picked up and hauled in

156

through the bullring. Hanging over the bow of *Chediac* and trying to catch the steadying line and haul it on board was very frustrating and required an expert fisherman to pick it up as it tossed from side to side in the bow wave. Once this line was secured, the oil hose was paid out and oiling could start. The method depended on taking the weight of any sudden lurch or pitch of the towed ship on the steadying line rather than on the hose, which could take no strain. Equilibrium had been reached with the oiler towing *Chediac* at four knots. The SOE, worried about the gap widening between the two ships and the convoy as night came on, ordered *Chediac* to cast off the steadying line and use her own engines. The line and hose carried away, the oiling was abandoned and *Chediac* now had the task of covering the tanker's return to the convoy at the rear of column seven.

She arrived back in station in time to beat off the first attack, just before the convoy made an emergency turn at 1800. The U-boat commanders and their controlling headquarters, aided by B-Dienst, were well used to the convoy escorts' routines by now. The convoys had followed the same route across the Atlantic for a long time, much to the outspoken fury of some commodores. At or after dusk, if they still had plenty of searoom, they would make an emergency turn of about forty-five degrees either to port or to starboard. If they were getting close to their destination, with little room to manoeuvre, they would probably go straight on. One boat of a shadowing wolf pack, given reasonable weather, could advise U-boat headquarters and his colleagues which alternative had been adopted.

At 1820 *Battleford*, leading the convoy from the starboard bow, sighted a U-boat and made to attack, but was immediately presented with a sight the like of which no other ship had ever seen, or was ever likely to see again – three more U-boats coming towards him, travelling in line ahead on the surface, exchanging light signals. He could expect no help from *Napanee* or *St Laurent*, who were dropping depth-charge patterns on contacts miles away on the starboard beam.

The situation in the convoy was very serious indeed and the SOE had recourse to desperate measures. Travelling in the convoy, destined for the Far East via Colombo, was HMS *Fidelity*, a very unusual ship. She was previously the French armed ship *Le Rhin*, 2455 tons and 270 feet overall, built in 1920. After France fell, Captain Claude-André Costa and a group of Free French volunteers took her to Gibraltar and offered their services to the British. Due to Captain Costa's bullying attitude half the crew changed their minds, went ashore for repatriation to France and were replaced by Belgians. In September, 1941, after complicated negotiations following Captain Costa's claim for prize money, *Le Rhin* was commissioned in the Royal Navy as HMS *Fidelity*, a Special Duty ship designed for amphibious operations. All the original crew changed their names, including the Captain, who became Commander Jack Langlais RN, bringing with him as his First Officer Madeleine Guesclin, who became First Officer Madeleine V. Barclay WRNS. She (the ship!) was extensively rearmed and her engines overhauled to give a speed of twelve knots. Her ship's company was increased to 334, including two Royal Marine Commandos.

The SOE, casting around for a way out of the trap in which he found himself, was particularly interested in the two Kingfisher seaplanes and the Motor Torpedo Boat which she carried on board which could be launched using the Jumbo fifty-ton derrick fitted for that purpose.

After *Battleford* and *St Laurent* had put down the first wave of attacks, the SOE steamed across the rear of the convoy to close *Fidelity* at the rear of the fifth column, to discuss the possibility of launching a seaplane, but on the way stumbled across another U-boat on the surface which crash-dived and which he depth-charged.

He then went on to *Fidelity*. Except in dire necessity, no seaman would think of trying to launch a seaplane from a derrick in mid-Atlantic, even in daylight, in anything but a flat calm. On the night of 28 December the sea was not flat, but there was a dire necessity. The seaplane was lifted out, but lurched around in the swell and dipped a wingtip as it tried to take off. On the second attempt it capsized, decanting its pilot and observer into the water, while the seaplane disappeared under the waves. *St Laurent* spent half an hour rescuing them both, but while everybody within sight, glad to have some distraction, was watching this unproductive activity astern of the convoy, *U-203* and

U-435, intent on destruction, entered through the unprotected starboard beam and both fired torpedoes. Having got that far, their commanders must have been furious when neither torpedo found a target. Their attack was illuminated by the usual fireworks display and the U-boats disappeared at speed out of sight some while before *Battleford*, at her full sixteen knots, appeared in the area. Meanwhile *U-591* came in and torpedoed the Norwegian *Norse King*, followed by *U-225* which fired two torpedoes, hitting the next astern, *Melrose Abbey*, then swinging round the victim's stern to fire two more, one of which hit *Ville de Rouen*, after which he belted off into the darkness.

Three ships had been hit in five minutes – it could have been four or five if *U-203*'s and *U-435*'s torpedoes had done better – leaving behind a sea covered in débris and survivors clutching on to anything that would float, singing defiantly at first and then slowing down as the cold of the Atlantic waters seeped through to their bones. *Toward* steamed on; she could take no more on board.

There was no end to this night. Almost immediately afterwards *St Laurent*, at twenty knots, sighted a U-boat 600 yards ahead, apparently on fire and a perfect target for ramming, but Lieutenant-Commander Windeyer, very much aware of his ship's responsibility for the surviving merchant ships, coolheadedly rejected this opportunity for ultimate satisfaction and instead opened fire at close range, joined by *Kenogami*. The U-boat dived and two patterns of depth-charges were fired, but *St Laurent*, in firm asdic contact, found her freedom of movement so restricted by the mass of wreckage from the three ships torpedoed in the starboard column that she had to slow down and abandon the attack. In his capacity as Commanding Officer of *St Laurent* and SOE C. 1 Group, Commander Windeyer was again faced with an agonizing dilemma, so often repeated in this bitter war – whether to let the U-boat go free or to drop depth-charges in a location that might seriously injure or even finish off survivors in the water.

Napanee meanwhile was trying to ram a U-boat on the starboard beam. Then there was a lull for a few minutes, broken by a dash on the surface by *U-260* which had for some time been shadowing *Empire Wagtail* leading column eleven, but had been put off the attack by the three hits from *U-356* which had demolished column twelve. *Empire Wagtail* was carrying an apparently innocuous cargo of coal and oil fuel, but the torpedo caused a massive and immediate explosion: the ship disintegrated and all her superstructure, boats and rafts were hurled in the air. She disappeared almost at once without a single survivor from the forty-four on board, an appalling sight that gave further cause for depression in the surviving ships.

Fidelity, which had fallen behind while trying to launch her seaplane, now reported that her engine had broken down and that she had an asdic contact. In the middle of this unequal battle, during which, on average, one ship would be torpedoed every fifteen minutes, *Chediac* was taken off her duties of protecting the ships in convoy to stand by *Fidelity* with her complement of 334.

U-203 attempted to attack the starboard columns again but was driven off and tried her luck on the two leading ships of the port column, turning into the convoy between columns two and three. Both her torpedoes missed, and she ran out to the port side. Meantime *U-406* had come in to attack with a FAT torpedo, which hit *Lynton Grange*, and then another which hit *Zarian* and then *Baron Cochrane*.

The convoy, before the attack, stretched about five miles from side to side. In the past 135 minutes, nine ships had been torpedoed, the attacks coming from all directions. At 2130, with the night still to come, neither the commodore nor the SOE knew which ships had been sunk, which were still afloat, or how many had survived undamaged. *Toward* had been unable to continue her rescue duties as she was full to overflowing.

The option of surrender in an impossible situation was not open to merchant seamen of whatever nationality in the U-boat war. The awful decision had now to be made by the master of each surviving merchant ship – to go against their training and nature and press on and save their ships and crews, or to follow the custom of the sea, stop and pick up survivors in the middle of a wolf-pack attack. The execution of the order to the rear ships in each column would have meant that several more merchant ships would have lain stopped – sitting targets among the wreckage that spread for sixteen miles astern and illuminated by the flickering glow of ships still on fire. The order for the rearmost ships in each column to act as rescue ships was impracticable and was ignored.

The confusion was as bad for the U-Boats dodging in and out of the columns of the convoy. Most were in a position to attack using the same method, entering between two leaders, going down the columns to the rear, firing as convenient, turning back up between the adjacent columns and departing at speed in the direction from which they had come. They were trained for these opportunities and the escorts had no answer, being short of warships, speed and training to work as a group. Neither the warships nor the merchant ships had many clear chances to engage the U-boats when they were attacking on the surface, because the range was foul and there were other merchant ships in the line of fire.

After 2130 there was a lull and the ships attempted to reform and put themselves in order. Commodore Egerton and his Yeoman tried to make sense of the huge volume of conflicting reports and signals which had flooded the air during the preceding hours and work out a plan for the night hours ahead.

U-225 was enjoying a run of successes. Three of *Oberleutnant* Leimkühler's torpedoes had struck home and now he set out for the prime target leading the centre column. He knew this would probably be one of the more valuable ships with an important cargo on board, carrying the Commodore and his staff. His plan was to enter between columns five and six, torpedo the Commodore, continue through the convoy, turn back 180 degrees and come through the adjacent columns, leaving at speed ahead of the ships.

The U-boats had now almost completely demolished one side of the convoy torpedoing seven of the twelve ships in the three starboard columns, including the leaders of each column. The Commodore's ship, the prime target, led from the middle of the front line in position 61. *Empire Shackleton* was a fine ship of 7087 grt, sailing light from Liverpool with only 200 tons of general cargo on board and 100 tons of ammunition. In addition to the Master, Captain Henry Ellington-Jones, and his crew of forty-eight, the Commodore and his staff of seven, including the wireless mechanic, she carried seven naval and four Army DEMS

161

gunners, a total of sixty-eight. Leimkühler now decided to go for the Commodore. On her starboard beam, only one ship remained in the front rank. On her port beam, there was a gap due to the absence of *Scottish Heather*, the oiler, torpedoed but not sunk and now 200 miles astern, making for home.

The ideal attack for a U-boat was the *Hundekurve*, in which the U-boat came in from ahead on the wing of the convoy, pointed continuously straight at the target, and followed it round as it approached. In this attack, by presenting the smallest silhouette, it ran the least risk of being seen by the target, but on the other hand, if its target was the Commodore leading the central column, it had to move right across the front of the other columns. It would then plan to fire torpedoes from its bow tubes at the very minimum safe range, about 400 metres, when the target reached a position beam on. With ships in station on either side, this method of attack was not possible, because the U-boat ran a great risk of being rammed by the leader of the adjacent column as it neared its firing position. But with the Commodore now unsupported on either beam, this was the bold attack planned by Leimkühler, after which he would turn hard a'port between columns five and six, round the stern of column six and make his way at full speed out of the convoy the way he had come in.

The manoeuvre required very fine judgement and nerves of steel. *U-225* came in on the opposite course to the broad front of the convoy with every man on board each remaining ship of the convoy at their action stations with their fingers on the triggers. As the ships loomed closer and closer, the bearing of his target changed faster and faster until the *Empire Shackleton* was beam on in his sights, range 300 metres.

At 2215 the Commodore's brief respite ended as *U-225*'s torpedo, fired at point-blank range, exploded in number one hold, so close that *U-225* itself was shaken by the force of the explosion. *Empire Shackleton* was badly damaged and the order was given to abandon ship. There was some confusion on board, but lifeboats and rafts were manned and lowered very smartly and pulled away from the ship. The Canadian *Calgary*, the only ship in the convoy to carry out the Commodore's order for the rear ship in each column to act as rescue ship, started to pick up

Empire Shackleton's survivors, a hazardous task that she kept up for an hour as the convoy plodded inexorably ahead, before being ordered to press on at her full speed of fifteen knots to rejoin.

Meanwhile the Belgian ship *President Franqui*, the next ship astern of the Commodore, had made a violent alteration of course to pull out of the line, but was caught a few minutes later when Leimkühler, having already torpedoed four ships, carried on with his planned attack, went round the stern of the column and torpedoed *President Franqui*, his fifth victim, on his way out of the convoy.

When they had time to assess the damage, the Master of *Empire Shackleton* and his officers decided that their ship still had a good chance of making port under her own power and limped off for the Azores. She did not last long. She ran straight into the U-boats following astern and forty minutes later, at 2215, she was sunk by simultaneous hits from *U-123* and *U-435*. One of her life-rafts and some survivors were picked up by *Chediac*, while her two lifeboats, with about fifty on board, including the Commodore, drifted astern.

President Franqui was the ninth ship to be torpedoed in two and a half hours. Although badly damaged she did not sink and her Master made the same decision to make for the Azores. She lasted only until early the next morning when she was hit by three more torpedoes and sank at 0930 on 29 December.

At midnight on 28 December the sea astern of the convoy was littered with crippled ships limping away for the nearest port, with wreckage from those that had sunk and with survivors in the freezing waters clinging desperately to anything that would float. There were all the hours of darkness until dawn to be endured.

There was no Commodore and no visible sign of any reinforcements. The sparse and exhausted escorting warships were packed to the gunwales with survivors and very short of fuel.

At about 2230 Egerton and the survivors from *Empire Shackleton* had taken to the two lifeboats as ordered by the Master. Fourteen ships in his convoy had been hit, of which nine had now gone down. Unknown to anyone at that time, the oiler

Scottish Heather, although hit once, had set off at seven knots for the Clyde, *Zarian*, *Norse King*, and *President Franqui* were lying disabled where they had been hit, attended by *Chediac*, but surrounded by U-boats.

There was one other ship undamaged but suffering from a dreadful sequence of mechanical breakdowns which had caused her to straggle and lose touch with the convoy. *Fidelity* had occupied the rear position in column five until she became involved in the unsuccessful attempt to launch one of her seaplanes. She dropped out on 28 December at the height of the battle and fell behind as the convoy continued on its way.

Fidelity, although a warship of the Royal Navy and fitted with radar, HF/DF, asdic and R/T, had been more of a liability than an asset to the Commodore and the SOE. She had been tagged on to the convoy as an afterthought and had remained at the rear of the fifth column without taking any positive role in the defence of the convoy. As we have seen, she responded to the SOE's request to launch one of her seaplanes, but in so doing took one of the escorting corvettes out of station for her sole protection. On the night of 28 December, at about 2050, she made her next contribution by reporting an asdic contact astern of the convoy; the same signal announced that her main engine had broken down. Although an old ship, she had twice been docked for extensive modifications and overhauls which included a lot of work on her engines. Again the corvette *Chediac* was detailed to stand by as she dropped further and further astern, leaving another large hole in the hopelessly inadequate screen around the convoy.

C-in-C Western Approaches, shortly after midnight, asked for the tug, *Eminent* to be sent from Gibraltar on a three-day, 1000-mile journey to her assistance, and at 0530 the destroyer *Milne*, on her way to spend a brief while as reinforcement to the convoy, picked her up on radar and reported that she was making two knots in the general direction of the Azores. *Milne* carried on to search for survivors and at 0815 reported *Fidelity*'s position, course and speed. She was now some thirty miles astern, still guarded by *Chediac* and still unable to say when or whether she would be able to complete her repairs. *Fidelity* was fitted with nets, which could be rigged over the side on booms to protect her from torpedoes. As we have seen, these nets were heavy and cumbersome to handle and not at all popular on the merchant ships on which they were fitted, not only because of the extra work involved but because dragging the nets through the water reduced the ship's speed and manoeuvrability. The rigging of the nets presented less of a problem to *Fidelity* than to merchant ships because she carried large numbers of Marine Commandos on board who badly needed something to do. She also had her own MTB on deck which could be launched to patrol and protect her, as well as two landing craft and the remaining seaplane.

After the sweep astern by *St Laurent* and *Kenogami* before midnight, *Chediac* was ordered to rejoin the convoy, passing through the areas where the ships had been sunk and picking up survivors to add to the many that she already carried. *Fidelity* was still out of action and unable to say when repairs to her engine would be completed. *Chediac* reached the search area at 0200 on 29 December and searched for three and a half hours. Among the survivors she picked up were seven on a liferaft from the stricken *Empire Shackleton*. *Chediac* was very short of fuel and still nearly forty miles astern, several hours steaming at maximum economical speed. The faster she went to catch up, the less fuel she would have remaining. She had so many extra hands on board that food and water were also very short. At 0600 she set off at twelve knots to rejoin, arriving back in station at 1300 after an absence of sixteen hours. Since there were no other rescue ships operating, this absence from her normal station was providential for the many survivors she had saved on her way back, but now *Fidelity* was left unsupported.

Vice Admiral Egerton was no longer with the convoy and no longer Commodore. His fate was now intertwined with *Fidelity*'s and we will return to her after the convoy has completed its journey through the valley of the shadow of death.

At 0900 on 29 December, the Vice-Commodore, Captain W. Evans, took over the duties of Commodore in *Fort Lamy*. He had just been through a night that was the climax of one of the worst disasters of the Atlantic convoys. In the past thirty hours thirteen ships had been sunk. In the early hours of the previous night U-boats had been blasting around at speed on the surface in the middle of the convoy, torpedoing ships apparently at will. In spite of the Herculean efforts of the hopelessly outnumbered Canadian escorts, the Germans had lost only one U-boat. There was a great deal of W/T traffic astern and *Toward* reported HF/DF fixes on several U-boats following astern.

After the first attacks the wolf pack had turned into a pack of hyenas, snapping at the heels of the convoy and finishing off the wrecks that they found littering the wake of the ill-fated ONS 154 as it plodded on. During the night the crippled ships *Empire Shackleton*, *Zarian*, *Lynton Grange*, *President Franqui* and *Baron Cochrane* were finished off.

At 0501 on 30 December C-in-C Western Approaches diverted two corvettes from convoy KMS 4, the destroyers *Viceroy* and *St Francis* were sent from Gibraltar and the destroyers *Milne* and *Meteor* made contact. *Fidelity* had reported that she would be under way shortly, and later cancelled her need for the tug *Eminent*. HM ships *Fame*, *Dallas*, *Cole*, *Arrowhead*, *Chicoutine* and *Digby* were to join.

The picture was still grim. *Battleford* and *Chediac* went off for fuel. (*Chediac* eventually ran dry on the morning of 31 December and was towed for the last forty miles by *Battleford*, who herself had very little to spare.) *Napanee*, *Milne* and *Meteor* were due to leave for the same reason later in the day. (*Milne* towed *Meteor* for the last five miles.) The SOE, who had had a basinful over four days, reported that 'the situation looked extremely black. . . . I considered that we were done for.'

The signals deploying these reinforcements were intercepted by B-Dienst and Dönitz called off the pack, of which only five were still engaged, the rest having left to refuel or to replenish torpedoes from the milch cow *U-117* which was close at hand.

Forty-five ships had sailed; thirteen had been sunk; *Fidelity* had disappeared. Of the ships torpedoed, only *Scottish Heather*, the convoy oiler, made it safely home to the Clyde unescorted. 161 merchant seamen, officers and DEMS gunners were lost. 374 were lost from *Fidelity*. The only U-boat lost was *U-356*, credited to HM Canadian Ships *Battleford*, *Chilliwack*, *Napanee* and *St Laurent*.

The slaughter of this convoy coincided with the withdrawal of the Canadian escorts from the North Atlantic at a critical time. Eighty per cent of the casualties over the past two months had been in convoys under their care. But it must be remembered that they were assigned the slow convoys when the U-boat strength was at its peak, and that in this convoy they had nineteen U-boats attacking a large slow convoy defended by one destroyer and five corvettes, all short of fuel.

After going through the concentrated training which was mandatory for the RN escorts, the Canadian ships were back in the battle within three months, carrying much of the weight. Within a year they had successfully taken over all the escort duties in the North Atlantic, with a fleet composed of new ships manned ninety per cent by men who had joined for 'Hostilities Only' – an amazing achievement.

We now return to *Fidelity*. She had dropped out of the convoy at about 2045/28 with her first engine defect when *Empire Wagtail* was torpedoed. *Chediac* was ordered to give her cover during the repairs and she continued on this duty, dropping further astern of the main body while more torpedoes slammed into *Baron Cochrane*, *Lynton Grange* and *Zarian*. There was nothing *Chediac* could do about it until she was ordered to return at 2215, picking up any survivors on her way, whether or not she had accommodation, food or water for any more.

Fidelity was now on her own and we will follow her progress as she battled with her engineering problems. She was in a terrible situation, wallowing in the area where U-boats were most likely to be as they pursued ONS 154. The large number of Commandos on board this small ship crowded the messdecks to capacity. The low freeboard amidships, cluttered decks and December cold would not have allowed them to stay on deck, although many might have preferred to do so as they saw ship after ship torpedoed ahead while the convoy was still in sight. The most eerie and nerve-racking sensation is a ship at sea stopped and without the steady throb of her main engines turning; the many false starts could not fail to impose a severe strain on the mixed and idle crew, in one of His Majesty's Ships under foreign command with a French lady as First Officer.

At 0500 on 29 December *Fidelity* tried out her engine again and set course to the south in the general direction of the Azores. She made little progress; even though the wind had dropped to a light force three and her revolutions were sufficient to give her three or four knots the torpedo nets slowed her to a sluggish crawl.

At 0545 contact was made by radio with the destroyers *Milne* and *Meteor* as they steamed across her wake to reinforce the convoy. Shortly afterwards her engine broke down again, but for an unexplained reason Langlais reported this to no one until 1015, when he signalled the SOE and C-in-C, giving her position and the information that she hoped to be under way in three hours' time.

It was then that she was sighted by *U-615*, *Kapitänleutnant* Kapitski, who inspected her carefully and with great suspicion through his periscope. She fitted very well the description of a U-boat trap as described in his handbook and he approached her with the necessary caution. *The Submarine Commander's Handbook* devotes two and a half pages to this subject.

Section VII B para 300/301: How to proceed when stopping steamers. . . . In war, it is a fundamental rule that every steamer is suspect. When stopping steamers, the commander must therefore behave with due caution in spite of his eagerness to use his boat for purpose of attack. . . .

Para 331 (a): Submarine traps must also be reckoned with in dealing with convoys. These have instructions to station themselves among the last steamers, and to fall behind, pretending that they have engine trouble, etc in order thus to attract attacking submarines, to lead them away from the convoy and to be able to attack them. Be cautious therefore, when attacking steamers sailing behind convoys. . . .

Section 395: If a final shot is necessary to sink the damaged ship, remember that the number of misses at a kill is proportionally greater than in firing during the attack.[8]

U-615 was very conscious of these dangers since *Fidelity* had dropped behind the convoy and was obviously experiencing, or faking, engine trouble. He could see that she carried landing craft and was operating intermittent air patrols that interrupted his ventures on the surface. He decided to take no chances and to trail her until dusk.

Between 1100 and 1200, *Fidelity* signalled that she was making for the Azores and launched her Kingfisher. At the same time she armed, provisioned and launched her MTB. Even in the light wind then blowing this was a difficult job, since the MTB, weighing nine tons and measuring forty-five feet, was difficult to control as the ship rolled gently in the swells. She had to be hoisted off the deck with a giant derrick and lowered over the side into the water. At 1230 the Kingfisher started its first patrol and was back within fifteen minutes to report two U-boats, one of which was on fire, and two lifeboats with fifty survivors on the surface over the horizon. Langlais sent off the MTB to investigate and signalled his intention to attempt to engage the U-boats with 'aircraft, motorboat and machine guns'. Unfortunately yet another engine breakdown, this time the MTB's main engine, caused him to delay this move and to resort to her auxiliary which gave her a maximum speed of seven knots. Langlais recalled her after half an hour and instead launched the two thirteen-knot landing craft towards the position of the lifeboats.

Fidelity's main engine then broke down again, the fourth engine failure since she dropped back from the convoy. In a signal timed 1300, without further explanation, *Fidelity* signalled: I AM HEADING FOR THE AZORES WITH SERIOUS ENGINE TROUBLE, I SHALL TRY TO ENSURE MY OWN PROTECTION WITH MY MOTOR BOAT AND AIRCRAFT, WILL FLY THE AXIS FLAG.

Among all the mass of trivia which was flying around the Admiralty at that moment, alarm bells started to sound, loud enough to provoke an immediate reply from Admiralty: *FIDELITY* MUST ON NO ACCOUNT FLY THE AXIS FLAG.[9]

At this time the SOE, HM Ships *Milne* and *Meteor*, the C-in-C and the Admiralty all knew where *Fidelity* was and where she was heading. They knew that she was experiencing bad engine trouble and that she was in the middle of a nest of U-boats.

Even so, things at last seemed to be going a little better and at 1530 she was under way again at five knots, making for the position of the lifeboats. Her patrolling Kingfisher did not spot *U-615*, but still made its task more difficult, causing it to dive several times until the aircraft was hoisted back on board as darkness approached. At the same time the landing craft sighted the lifeboats, which were carrying about fifty survivors from *Empire Shackleton*, including the Commodore and his staff, who had been adrift for about eighteen hours. At 1950 on 29 December, Langlais was able to signal that they were on board *Fidelity*. Apart from communications with the MTB, this was the last signal ever received from *Fidelity*.

U-615 shadowed all day, observing these activities and diving to avoid detection or attack by the Kingfisher. As night fell he closed the range. It was a very dark night with no moon and no glimmer of light filtering through from the stars in a cloud-covered sky. He fired four torpedoes in two attacks but registered no hits. He turned away and fired another from his stern tube. This time, after a long delay, an explosion was heard and he surfaced to find his target still moving on the same course with no apparent damage and the MTB lying astern, which was a shock and caused him to crash dive. At 2010 *Fidelity* made an asdic contact and dropped a pattern at 2029.

A few minutes later the MTB, which had been following astern of *Fidelity*, saw a U-boat on the surface which immediately dived. Another pattern was dropped at 2130, after which the MTB's engine overheated and she lost contact astern at 2300.

She kept watch during the night but her batteries were failing and at daylight there was no sign of *Fidelity* except some very faint indecipherable R/T transmissions at 0900 on 29 December.

At 0930 the MTB's engines overheated again and stopped. (This was the sixth occasion on which *Fidelity* and her tenders had been seriously endangered by engine defects since they straggled from the convoy. They stripped both engines down but abandoned any hope of repair.) Since the remaining petrol would only take them fifty miles and it was a beat to windward to the Azores, 230 miles away, they sewed blankets together, rigged a lee-board and set sail towards the UK, 900 miles downwind.

To come back to *Fidelity* and her trials: by chance *U-615* sighted her again next day, not far from her previous position, but having already fired five torpedoes at this sitting target with no success Kapitsky pushed off disgruntled.

The luck could not last. At 1300 on 30 December Strelow in *U-435*, ordered to disengage from the attacks on ONS 154 and looking for other targets, sighted smoke and, after an hour's steaming at speed, raised *Fidelity*'s mastheads. After a thorough look he too suspected a trap. He was an experienced U-boat Commander only recently involved in the Arctic convoy PQ 8 when he had attacked and sunk HM Minesweeper *Leda* and the merchant ship *Bellingham* on 22 September. After a cautious approach, he fired and hit *Fidelity* with two torpedoes at 1938. Either his aim was better or he had a better batch of torpedoes than *U-615*. They hit and exploded one after the other, eight seconds apart, shattering the ship. Two more big explosions followed, probably caused by *Fidelity*'s own depth-charges as she went down.

After watching for thirty minutes to make sure that there were no escorts around, *U-435* came up. There were no lifeboats, but he found a mass of human flotsam covering the surface, on rafts, on scraps of wreckage and in lifebelts.

Twenty minutes later, at 1848, he reported the sinking and 'hundreds of survivors'.

At 1952, only four minutes later, BdU replied: STRELOW TO REPORT IF SURVIVORS IN (BOATS) OR WHETHER THEIR DESTRUC-TION IN THE WEATHER PREVAILING CAN BE COUNTED UPON.

Strelow replied at 0007/31, over four hours later, without specifically answering the BdU's signal: 3–400 SURVIVORS ON RAFTS LAUNCHED, AND DRIFTING IN WATER. NO BOATS, PRESUM-ABLY STEAMER CREWS AMONGST THEM.

But he did not reply directly to the order to report whether the destruction of the survivors could or could not be counted upon.

His signal did, however, make clear that there were hundreds of survivors either in the water or on rafts. At daylight, some eight hours later, Strelow revisited the scene of the sinking and on 12 January, in an interview after he returned to St Nazaire, he is quoted as saying: 'There were three to four hundred men and they tried to cling to the over-crowded rafts. . . . On the morning after the battle the sea was covered with survivors trying to escape towards the Azores.'

The area of the Atlantic in which this happened was by no means deserted at the time. Indeed two U-boats reported that they spotted *Fidelity* in the daylight hours of that day. *Milne* and *Meteor* passed fifteen miles astern on their way to ONS 154. A massive search by six warships started at 1600 on 31 December and *Chediac* and *Battleford* passed close to *Fidelity*'s probable position on 2 January. Although the position of her sinking was not known, and she sent out no distress signal, her position at 1015 on 29 December was known and her course for the Azores, which would narrow down the search area very considerably.

Nothing more was ever heard from the people aboard HMS *Fidelity*. Not a single survivor, nor even a body, ever made land, nor was picked up from a raft. They all vanished from the face of the ocean. Strelow left his logbook ashore, but he himself did not survive to tell the story or to clarify the reasons why he did not give a direct answer to BdU's order or to explain what happened between the sinking of *Fidelity* and his visit to the scene of the sinking the next day. He and his crew went down with all hands when *U-436* was sunk by a Wellington on 9 September, 1943. So HMS *Fidelity* and her wreckage, her entire ship's company and the survivors from *Empire Shackleton* picked up on 29 December simply disappeared.

The truth about the disappearance of all on board HMS *Fidelity* will probably never be known. Either they all drowned or they were eliminated and all trace of them was efficiently obliterated. The majority did not go down with their ship according to Strelow. Between three and four hundred were struggling in the water when he surfaced to have a look. A massive search was carried out by six warships from dusk on 31 December until 11 January, covering thousands of square miles of ocean where the sinkings had taken place and not far from the point where *Fidelity* is known to have been sunk. Admiralty would know the probable area of search from *Fidelity*'s last signal and her intention to make for the Azores. This search picked up *Fidelity*'s MTB which had drifted ninety miles after it ran out of fuel. It is extremely unlikely that the sea swallowed up without trace over 350 bodies, most of which would have been wearing lifebelts, nor would the numerous life-rafts which floated off *Fidelity* have disappeared quite so suddenly. There are many examples, too many to mention, of survivors being discovered many days or even weeks later in lifeboats, on life-rafts or just perched on floating wreckage, dead or alive, still afloat or washed up ashore. Yet not one of the people on board *Fidelity* left any trace behind.

One is left with the strong suspicion that they were all 'eliminated', and here are some pointers that must be taken into consideration.

A lot has been written about the U-boat officers and crews, their training, morale, discipline, courage, loyalty and efficiency, and some of this is justified. But there were some notable exceptions. On the first day of the Second World War, Lemp, in *U-30*, sank the *Athenia* in flagrant disobedience of orders and with total disregard for the 1103 passengers, neutral as well as British, who were on board and who had sailed before hostilities were declared. He left them to drown – and 112 did drown – but when he returned to port, his official log was altered to show that he had sunk not the *Athenia* but other ships, and all reference to the *Athenia* was removed. The crew, on Admiral Raeder's orders, was sworn to silence. So much for discipline and example.

When they were successful, the U-boat crews were treated as an élite body of volunteers. They were certainly pampered ashore. Dönitz would greet them personally as they arrived in Lorient and hand out Iron Crosses. (Each member of the crew of *U-47* (Prien) which sank the *Royal Oak* got one from Hitler.) But when things went against the U-boats and the 'happy time' was over, the crews were sometimes taken on board at gunpoint[10] and those who attempted to get out of the U-boat service were branded as lacking in moral fibre and treated as pariahs. So much for volunteers and morale.

When the Commandos raided St Nazaire, Dönitz moved his U-boat headquarters from the neighbouring port of Lorient back to Paris. So much for courage.

As for training, Dönitz made such a bad miscalculation in the balance between training and front-line operations that during the whole battle there was only one short period, between October, 1942, and July, 1943, when there were more U-boats operational than under trials or training. Just before the U-boats surrendered, at their peak strength of 429 there were 263 under training and under trials and only 166 operational.

Some were less efficient and loyal than others. On 8 May,

1941, Lemp abandoned *U-110* to HMS *Bulldog*, leaving on board all his marked charts, his code books, his cypher documents and his Enigma coding machine. The scuttling charges failed to work and among the documents recovered by *Bulldog's* boarding party were the daily settings for the coding machine for the next eight weeks, thereby compromising the German Navy's vital code, 'Hydra', used by all U-boats, enabling Bletchley Park to crack this cypher, with a few breaks, until the end of the war.[11]

All Nazis were bound by a personal oath of allegiance to the Führer, an oath that they took very seriously. At a Conference in the Reich Chancellory on Monday 28 September, 1942, which ran from 1630 to 1830, the following were present:

The Führer
Grand Admiral Raeder
Field Marshal Keitel
Admiral Dönitz
Admiral Fuchs
Vice-Admiral Kranke
Vice-Admiral Maertens
Rear-Admiral Lange
Captain von Puttkamer
Baurat Waas.

The minutes record that:

[The Führer] considers it impossible that the increase in production of the enemy shipyards comes anywhere near what propaganda would have us believe. Even if the enemy should succeed in launching ships relatively fast, he would still not have the necessary engines, auxiliary engines, other equipment and most of all, crews for those ships. *In regard to the manpower problem, he calls attention to the fact that it is very much to our disadvantage if a large percentage of the crews of sunken merchantships is able to go to sea again in new ships.*
(Führer Conferences on Naval Affairs, page 294).

This is very close to an invitation to the naval officers present to take every possible step to ensure that crews of sunken ships did not survive their sinking.

There were some very brave and competent officers in the U-boat arm. There were also some butchers of the worst sort. Dönitz was himself accused, but never convicted, of issuing directions to fire on 'shipwrecked sailors', otherwise known as survivors of U-boat attacks. Instead, only a month after Hitler had raised the matter, he gave strong hints to his U-boat commanders by ambiguous orders, such as

> announcing in his U-boat training course in October, 1942, that the manning problem was the Achilles heel of the Allied merchant service and that the time had come to wage 'total war' on ships and crews.

Korvettenkapitän Karl Möhle, chief of the U-boats at Kiel, testified that he had briefed commanders that 'U-boat Command cannot give you such an order officially. Everybody had to handle this according to his own conscience.'[12]

An appalling example of one U-boat's Commander's interpretation of this briefing is given in Peter Padfield's book *Dönitz*, (Pages 354/6). It is based on the evidence of the accused at his trial.

> [Hitler] knew that behind Dönitz' ostensible orders to take Captains, Chief Engineers, Chief Officers and Navigators prisoner, lay secret instructions, given orally to Commanders, to annihilate survivors – so long as this did not endanger the boat.
>
> On 13 March, 1944, *Kapitänleutnant* Heinz Eck sighted *Peleus* and put in two torpedoes, sinking her but leaving many people in the water. He surfaced and picked up the third Officer and a seaman, interrogated them and put them back on their raft. He ran about half a mile, ordering machine guns, Mauser pistols and hand grenades to be passed up to the bridge, then turned back. Approaching the rafts again he or his watch officer hailed one on which the chief officer was trying to gather survivors and ordered it closer; as it neared he gave the order to his bridge group to open fire, and the survivors found themselves under a hail of machine-gun bullets. Then a signal lamp was trained on them and grenades were hurled, both at the raft and amongst men who had leaped into the water.
>
> Eck repeated this treatment with the Third Officer's raft, then

175

spent the rest of the night cruising amongst the wreckage, mainly timber beams and hatchboards on which the survivors were clustering, directing machine-gun fire at them. The guns were manned during this time by his watch officer, Hoffman – who also threw grenades – his engineer, Lenz, a petty officer, a seaman and, most extraordinarily, by the U-boat's doctor, Walter Weisspfenig – all according to the evidence, firing quite calmly, without excitement over a period of at least five hours.

Eck, his watch officer and his doctor were sentenced to death by shooting, the other accused to terms of imprisonment. He went to his death denying that Dönitz, and by implication any other officers at U-boat command, had any part in his decision to massacre the survivors of *Peleus*.

The opportunities to wage such total war unobserved were quite rare, because most ships were in convoy or in busy waters. *Fidelity* was on her own. The Germans involved in the *Peleus* massacre were brought to book because two men survived and got ashore. Perhaps not a single person survived from *Fidelity* because a similar massacre was more efficiently carried out and no one survived. Certainly some destruction of the survivors was implicit in the German signal quoted above, which asked Strelow to 'report if survivors in boats or whether their destruction in the weather prevailing can be counted upon'.

We shall never know the truth for sure because Strelow's U-boat went down with all hands on 9 July and no one has come forward with any other explanation. The whole truth would not in any case have appeared in Strelow's log because he was acting under the general order to U-boat commanders not to enter sinkings and acts in breach of International Conventions in their logs.

Chapter Twelve

KNIFE EDGE

In all the long history of sea warfare there has been no parallel to this battle. . . . It would be decided by which side could endure the longer. . . . It depended on whether the men of the Merchant Navy, themselves almost powerless to defend their precious cargoes of fuel, munitions and food, could stand the strain of waiting day after day and night after night throughout the long slow passages for the rending detonation of the torpedoes which could send their ships to the bottom in a matter of seconds, or explode their cargoes in a searing sheet of flame from which there could be no escape.[1]

Dönitz took over as Commander-in-Chief of the German Navy at the end of January, 1943. The U-boats' run of successes in November and December, 1942, had slowed down and he knew that the Admiralty's change of the convoy code had temporarily stumped B-Dienst. There were suspicions that leakage of information about the U-boats' locations had been the result of treason or that his U-boats' W/T traffic was being regularly decyphered, hence their inability to find the convoys. After an extensive investigation, he was inclined not to believe either theory and to blame the slow-down in sinkings to weather in the North Atlantic.

Meanwhile the suspension of the Arctic convoys had enabled him to transfer more U-boats to the North Atlantic, and he was pressing Hitler strongly for more support from Göering in the provision of aircraft support. He had never departed from the view that Germany's only hope of victory lay in the hands of the U-boats and estimated that it was essential to sink 600,000 tons every month to outpace American and Allied construction, but he was nowhere near this target.

Dönitz never received the air support he wanted, while a similar struggle was going on at top level among the Allies, first among the British Chiefs of Staff and later between the British and the US Army Air Force. The struggle in Britain was between Air Chief Marshal Joubert, who wanted to give first priority to offensive bombing of German targets on the mainland of Europe, and the Admiralty, whose priority was to protect the convoys by finally closing the Atlantic Gap. This could be done by converting B.24 Flying Fortresses from their high-level function to bombing at sea level and reconnaissance extending right across the ocean. Although over 19,000 of these aircraft were produced during the war, at the end of 1942 only fifty-two were made available for anti-U-boat operations and they were operated by the US Navy which had its own priorities. In February, 1943, Air Marshal Slessor became C-in-C Coastal Command which at that time had eighteen in all, nine in Iceland and nine in Northern Ireland, but none at all stationed west of Iceland.

Encouraged by his recent successes, but frustrated by the safe passage of the Torch convoys carrying the tens of thousands of Allied troops and their supplies to North Africa, Dönitz was spurred on to new endeavours. The more pressure he brought to bear on the UK-bound convoys, the greater the potential benefits for the German forces in Africa, which were going through a difficult phase. His exhortations to his U-boat crews at sea had always been grandiose and verbose, (in marked contrast to the British Admirals' and the Admiralty's almost embarrassed one-liners), but they now began to resemble Wagnerian calls to heroic death in service to the fatherland.

Meanwhile a great volume of urgent cargo and loaded shipping was accumulating in America waiting for convoys to Britain.

At this time the Admiralty was benefiting from the work that had been done in the collection and analysis of valuable statistics by Professor P.M.S. Blackett, who, after forming the Operational Research Unit for Coastal Command, had moved over

178

to the Admiralty in January, 1942. In the opening years of the conflict commodores reckoned that thirty, or at the most forty, ships was the maximum that could be controlled effectively; the HX and SC convoys had been limited to thirty up to the end of 1942. Professor Blackett had concluded that it would be more effective to run very much larger convoys, a conclusion that had not been accepted by the Admiralty, who were not yet ready to risk any big jump in size. The overall problem lay not only in handling and escorting this number of ships of varying characteristics at sea, but also in the complex administrative and physical task of assembling, loading and holding such huge gatherings until all were ready to go. An even greater problem could be expected when the convoy arrived in the Western Approaches, because of the need to find suitable berths to offload and because of the sheer volume of cargo that had to be dealt with simultaneously at the ports and an inland distribution system that was already overloaded and constantly disrupted by bombing attacks on the docks and the roads and railways that served them.

Many of the ships were manned by Chinese and Indians, who had little or no hope of seeing their homes while the war continued. Once alongside the wharfs, in spite of redoubled security, they had few problems in getting ashore from their ships, disappearing and picking up jobs where they could earn, in comfort and relative safety, a great deal more than they could ever hope to get afloat. As we have seen, desertion had become a major problem and was getting worse, which served to increase the congestion, since American law would not allow ships to sail if they were short-handed.

By the end of February the transport of the American forces and their supplies to Britain, the need for continuous replenishment of the Allied armies in Africa, preparation for the resumption of the Arctic convoys, and the build-up for a second front in Northern Europe presented the War Cabinet with a frightening situation. The graphs of sinkings, and of supply and demand, displayed in the War Cabinet Headquarters underground in Whitehall, were showing that there was a monthly deficit of 750,000 tons landed in Britain.

The main assembly centres for the UK-bound convoys had

been Halifax and Sydney, New Brunswick, until America entered the war. When the Americans took over the control of the western section of convoy control at the end of 1942, the convoys were planned by the United States Navy's Convoy and Routing Section, situated in Washington and headed by Rear Admiral Martin K. Metcalf USN [COMINCH] reporting to Admiral King.

The main departure point of the convoys was altered to New York, resulting in serious congestion and an increase in desertions. For deserters the prospects were much more attractive in New York than in Halifax.

By the beginning of 1943 the Admiralty had taken note of Professor Blackett's operational research and had pushed the numbers of merchant ships sailing in convoy up to sixty-four. The Americans wanted them to go higher. HX 228 had sailed with eighty-one, although, before setting off on the final leg, twelve of these had been detached and diverted to Halifax because the numbers were restricted by the availability of escorts.

In New York the anchorages and berths were crammed. In March there were 160 ships loaded and ready to go. In search of a solution, a plan was worked out to split them into three convoys sailing 36 hours apart: SC 122, a slow convoy, would sail first, followed by HX 229 and then by HX 229A. In three days three large convoys would pass 100–150 miles off Halifax. That was the plan. With hindsight it seems obvious that a fast convoy must catch up with a slow convoy not very far ahead. Their course would then take them on the northern route 40 to 200 miles south of Iceland, giving them the minimum period without air cover and hopefully drawing the U-boat concentrations away from the southern routes, particularly the UK–Gibraltar Torch supply routes.

In SC 122 fifty-one ships passed the Western Ocean Meeting Point (WOMP) under Commodore White, escorted by B5 group, thirty-eight with HX 229 under Commodore Mayall and B4 group, and thirty-seven under Commodore Casey with EG 40, a total of 126 ships in three convoys, close together. Twenty loaded ships and those turned back previously by the weather would have to wait for the next bus.

B-Dienst was fully aware of the details of these plans and routes. This was, after all, number 229 in the HX series: the convoys had been following the same routes and the same routine for a long time. B-Dienst even complained that one of the convoys had sailed a day later than scheduled, which was not acceptable to the German sense of good order.

The radio traffic necessary to set up and control the convoys inevitably fell into a pattern, and even when the Admiralty changed the code books the Germans did not take long to decypher the vital messages. Indeed, they knew more about the position, course and speed of two of the three convoys than the SOEs and the commodores, derived from the sighting reports and estimated courses and speeds of the shadowing U-boats as they transmitted them back to Dönitz' headquarters.

Unfortunately for the convoys, the Germans had also recently changed their codes and for a critical ten days, 10 March to 20 March, the information from Bletchley Park dried up. Only HF/DF fixes were available to the Admiralty to locate the U-boats, and these showed where the U-boats were when they transmitted, but gave no indication of their intentions.

Meanwhile Dönitz and his U-boats knew with great accuracy where the convoys were to be found, and their routes. Sure enough when they reached the meeting point off Newfoundland (WOMP), the two halves of HX 229 were only one and a half days apart and catching up on the slow SC-122 ahead. The plans for the timing of the convoys and the very similar route that all three followed before they set off across the ocean seemed almost designed to give the U-boats the very best chance of spotting them. Sod's Law was in operation to make things worse. HX 229, the faster convoy, was aided for a while by a following gale that pushed the ships along at ten and a half knots: inexorably this convoy closed up on SC 122 until they were only half a day apart. If the U-boats missed the leading convoy they had the chance of intercepting the second following close behind, and if they missed that one they had a chance of bumping into the third.

The method of selection of a commodore for one of these convoys was quite simple. Longest in was first out. So Commodore White was to take out *Glenapp* for SC 122, leading column eight, with his Vice-Commodore, the Master of *Boston City*, leading column eleven. Commodore Mayall led HX 229 in the Norwegian ship *Abraham Lincoln* and Commodore Casey led HX 229A in *Esperance Bay*. These three ships were comfortable, refrigerated ships, commanded by experienced masters. However, not all the crew were exactly fighting fit. *Glenapp* had been lying alongside the wharf in New York for some time: she had loaded palm oil, cocoa and copper in West Africa, but instead of joining the Sierra Leone convoys straight back to the UK had made first for New York where she was found to be in an unseaworthy condition due to engine problems. Although this had meant absence from home at Christmas, there had been compensations for the crew, since they were able to enjoy the bright lights of Manhattan. The Chief Engineer, R.W. Douglas, saw Frank Sinatra in his New York debut on 30 December, 1942, and there were night clubs along the wharfs. During their long enforced stay until March, when they were ready to go, the crew took part-time jobs ashore and made the best of the chance to enjoy the remains of a peacetime life ashore that had all but disappeared from the cities of Europe.

All the ships in the convoy were loaded to capacity. In addition to their normal cargo below decks they were required to take as much deck cargo as they could, within the limits laid down by their load lines; they also carried as many passengers as could be packed in. Among these were a number of Distressed British Seamen (DBS). This crude terminology, resented by many, embraced survivors who had been rescued when their ships sank, some twice or more, as well as men who had got into trouble with the police ashore and deserters who had been caught and arrested.

On 4 March Commodore White attended the convoy conference which was run by a senior officer from the US Navy, during which he went through the daily routine with the Masters, most of whom had done ocean convoys before and some who had done more than they would like to remember. The routine was standard. Each ship was allocated its place and the route to take if detached from the main body in an envelope not to be opened until they were at sea. No information on the main route was given to anyone. The Masters were advised about the known disposition of U-boats, warned for the umpteenth time of the need to keep closed up, a subject that was always a sore point with Masters of old, badly maintained ships sailing on routes for which they had not been designed, and about the use of illuminants, either accidentally or deliberately.

To Commodore White fell the task of sailing first. The ships in his convoy came from Canada, Britain, the Dutch West Indies, the Falkland Islands, Greece, Holland, Iceland, Newfoundland, Norway, Panama, Sweden, the USA and Yugoslavia. There were eight tankers, fifty-one freighters, four fast refrigerated ships and two small (1650 tons) Royal Naval Landing Ships, each loaded with cargo and with twenty Sherman tanks on deck. Among the crews was a rough bunch sent over from Britain to man *Fort Cedar Lake* and *Fort Anne*, built by the Canadians for the British. On the way to the convoy assembly point their crews had been so hung over that they had to call on outside assistance to raise steam.

Glenapp sailed at 0718 Local Time on 5 March, 1943, and there was confusion even at this stage. In spite of the briefing the day before, some ships were using Greenwich Mean Time and some convoy time, which would alter as the convoy moved east across the Atlantic.

There was a lot of ice coming down the river, making it hazardous for officers and crews anchored in the stream to get to and from the shore. In the crowded anchorage ships, while working their anchors, fouled other ships' cables or dragged their anchors and went aground; six were damaged in this way before they got to sea. Since final orders and last minute courses and emergency meeting points were passed by hand from launches to the Masters of the ships after they were back on board, this was a most unwelcome addition to the other problems that faced each ship before she sailed.

Commodore White had with him his Yeoman of Signals Fred Morris, who had been with him since 15 May, 1941. They made a good team, having already served together on several convoys, and were to stay together for fourteen successive convoys. White was in his mid-fifties, comparatively young by comparison with some of the other commodores, but he was very experienced. In

183

addition to his time in the merchant service in the Booth Steam Navigation Company, he had been commissioned as an acting Lieutenant in the Royal Naval Reserve on 1 March, 1909. His service during the First World War included a spell on the flagship HMS *Hannibal* and he moved up the ranks to Captain RNR on 31 December, 1932. He was recalled to serve as an Ocean Commodore in 1941. The *Glenapp* was a 'reefer', a refrigerated ship with good accommodation, under the command of Captain L.W. Kersley.

This was apparently a routine convoy, number 122 in the slow SC series, only differing from its predecessors in its size and the fact that it would have two faster convoys astern, setting off at much reduced intervals. It turned out to be one of a trio which marked a turning point in the Battle of the Atlantic and the course of the Second World War.

The full story of these three convoys has been carefully analysed and written about by many naval historians, and it is not intended to go over this ground again, but rather to present a picture of the action as seen by Commodore Sam White and his signals staff from the bridge of *Glenapp*.

At first light on 5 March it was obvious to the German agents ashore that there was something afoot as *Glenapp* moved slowly down the congested North Hudson River, picking her way through the ice floes. Other ships cast off and fell in astern. The SOE, Lieutenant-Commander E.G. Old RCNR, in the Canadian corvette *Le Pas*, and HM Canadian Ships *Blairmore*, *Rimouski* and *New Westminster* scurried round checking names and numbers as this long snake of ships in a column several miles long made for the open sea.

Convoys, at this early stage of American involvement in the war, left New York with lots of panache. Airships, aircraft, tugs, tenders, minesweepers and trawlers flocked round them until they left the safe swept channels. As they approached the open sea the escorting flotilla of little boats thinned out and disappeared.

Beyond the Ambrose Light Vessel the Commodore and his team started the business of getting the ships into their deep-sea stations for the journey ahead. At five knots he first brought up the column leaders in line abreast, seven on his port and six on his starboard beam; the others then fell in astern. In their final formation the ships occupied a thin quadrilateral of thirteen columns, each column consisting of three or four ships. Two more columns would join off Halifax. The least popular station was in the wing columns. Although the risk of collision was less, there was a feeling of vulnerability and exposure to attacks from the flanks. The ships were allocated stations that would enable them to disengage to various destinations with the minimum disruption as they came close to home. This was a simple manoeuvre on paper but not so easy in practice with the onset of darkness. It started to blow; the merchant ships were heavily laden; some of them were carrying cargoes piled high on deck which caught the wind and blew them off course as they ambled about seeking their proper places.

The first test of the ships' and the masters' ability and willingness to cooperate came as the speed was increased by stages to seven knots which was to be the nominal speed of the convoy for the next eighteen and a half days.

After the first night the Commodore sent one forty-year-old ship back into Halifax. Then the weather deteriorated to a full gale. The slow ships rolled and yawed about; the neat compact quadrilateral started to break down as the comparative abilities and weaknesses of each of the ships were revealed. The steering gear of one of the newly commissioned Royal Naval Tank Landing Ships broke down for the first time but not the last. The Commodore sent her to the rear of the column in disgrace where the danger of collision was reduced.

The storm continued through the night and eleven ships were missing when daylight came. Two had put back to New York and six to Halifax; two rejoined later. *Clarissa Radcliffe*, carrying a cargo of iron ore, straggled during the night and disappeared.[2] This was a bad start because there was no possibility of their tiny escorts rounding them up. One of the ships, a little Dutch freighter, *Kedoe*, took two days of determined steaming to get back in station, watched with admiration by the Commodore, who signalled, 'Well done. Look up Luke 15, 6.' This reads, 'And when he cometh home, he calleth together his friends and neighbours, saying unto them, Rejoice with me, for I have found my sheep which was lost.'

Ahead another Commodore was in trouble. SC 121, sixty ships under Commodore Birnie, carefully tracked by B-Dienst and running accurately to schedule south of Iceland, had run into a line of seventeen U-boats, the Westmark Group. The U-boats sank thirteen ships on 10 March. After commanding nineteen ocean convoys, Commodore R.C. Birnie lost his life when his ship, the Norwegian *Bonneville*, went down with all hands. He was the twentieth commodore to lose his life at sea. Commodore A. Cocks, on his first round trip as an ocean commodore took over from him.

Also running ahead, convoy HX 229 of sixty ships escorted by EG B3, had been caught by Group Newland. The SOE, Commander A.A. Tait RN, in HMS *Harvester*, had rammed and damaged a U-boat, but *Harvester* herself was also damaged. The French corvette *Aconit* rammed the U-boat again, depth-charged it and sank it. *Harvester* crawled away on one engine, picking up survivors from a sunken merchant ship as she went, but the shaft of her remaining propeller also broke and she came to a halt. She was then torpedoed twice and went down with most on board. *Aconit* came back and blew the U-boat to the surface: the little corvette at her maximum speed of 15 knots then rammed and sank it. A very remarkable record for any ship, but *Harvester* had a terrible price to pay. Commander Tait, her commanding officer, and another 144 of her officers and crew went down with her.

For the second stage, when SC 122 set off on its ocean voyage from the departure point off Halifax, EG B5 was allocated as close escort, under Commander Richard C. Boyle RN in the destroyer *Havelock*, consisting of the destroyers *Warwick*, a new frigate, *Swale*, and the five corvettes, *Buttercup* and *Godetia* manned by Belgians, *Pimpernel*, *Lavender* and *Saxifrage*. The destroyer *Volunteer*, delayed by 24 hours for repairs, was transferred to EG B.4. and replaced by the old US destroyer *Upshur* and the new *Campobello*, a small anti-submarine trawler built in Canada on passage to the UK.

The weather had already made a big reduction to the convoy's size: apart from the eleven ships that had put back to harbour, one ship had disappeared and the Liberty Ship *Stephen C. Foster*'s plates had split in the heavy seas: she put into St John's.

Fourteen ships joined from Halifax, including the specially fitted rescue ship *Zamalek*, always a very welcome and cheering sight. She was fully equipped with food and clothing reserves, an operating theatre, medical supplies, doctors and sick berth attendants. The rescue ships had most perilous roles: if a ship was torpedoed, the convoy lumbered on but the rescue ships made for and stayed in the danger area, locating and picking up survivors, simple targets for a U-boat to pick off as they lay stopped amid the wreckage. *Zamalek* had survived many convoys and was particularly well known among the merchant fleets and the escorts for her work after PQ 17. Her presence in the rear columns always lifted the morale of the merchant seaman. You never knew whose turn it would be next to go swimming and it was good to know that experienced and well-equipped rescuers were there to pick you out of the water.

Commodore White now had fifty-one ships deployed in eleven columns with his ship, *Glenapp*, in the centre. Ashore on both sides of the Atlantic there was a great deal of scheming and planning going on at BdU Headquarters in Kerneval as signals were decyphered by B-Dienst, and at the newly formed American Convoy and Routing section in Washington.

The fog and confusion of battle started on 12 March. SC 122 was turned 90 degrees to the north, on a mistaken appreciation of the position and length of the line of U-boats in Group Raubgraf. Had SC 122 carried on it would have missed the ambush, but instead the emergency turn increased the journey length and brought the ships closer to HX 229 and also closer to the position of the U-boat patrol.

At that point Group Raubgraf became involved in a skirmish with other westbound convoys, ON 170 and 172. The reports that this Group radioed back to Headquarters enabled the Allied HF/DF stations that circled the shores of the Atlantic to get a much better idea of the U-boats' locations. It was all bad news, showing as it did that the three convoys, HX 229, 229A and SC 122, were all heading for this area and that the gap between the slow convoy ahead and the faster convoys astern was narrowing.

By good fortune Commodore White and SC 122 had not yet been detected.

Another violent storm blew up on 15 March, during which for both the hunters and the hunted the priority shifted as both combatants fought for survival against the forces of the Atlantic Ocean and the dangers of collision in heavy seas and bad visibility. All the instincts of the Masters of the ships made them want to give every other ship a wide berth, but Commodore White had been warned by the HF/DF fixes and bearings from *Zamalek* and from the ring of shore bases that circled the North Atlantic of the numbers and locations of the U-boats, and needed somehow to keep his convoy in as close as possible formation consistent with the need to avoid collision. It was a delicate balance. If the ships straggled in an undisciplined herd into the Atlantic Gap ahead they would be easy meat if the weather moderated for the fifty-two U-boats which, at one time or another, would be involved in the battle.[3]

Meanwhile the ships were safe from the U-boats because it was quite impossible for them to stalk their prey in this kind of weather. Their duty officers and lookouts could stay on deck for limited periods provided they were lashed to the conning tower, but even then visibility was very much restricted by the huge waves and binoculars were covered in salt spray as the green waters swept over the decks and conning towers. Even in normal Atlantic conditions of wind force four or five, the belts with which the bridge crews were lashed to the conning tower sometimes parted and men were washed overboard. One commander's log gives a vivid account of the difficulties of operating a U-boat in big seas:

> In the attempt to run at high speed before the sea, the boat plunged twice. By means of extreme rudders, blowing tanks, and reduction of speed I succeeded in getting her to the surface. On the bridge, the C.O. and the watch, after half an hour of this, are nearly drowned. In a very short period 5 tons of water were shipped through the conning tower hatch, voice pipe and diesel air intake.

Due to the fine seamanship of the Masters the convoy kept in a compact formation, but in the middle of the night of 17 March, their luck ran out as the weather cleared and the visibility increased to twelve miles with a full moon silhouetting the ships. *U-338* was on its way to the estimated position of HX 229 but sighted SC 122 coming straight towards him, defended from a frontal attack by just two corvettes, stationed on either bow about four miles apart. He was not detected by either ship's 271M radar, and in clear visibility had no difficulty in slipping between them as he made his sighting signal. The bearing of this transmission was picked up by the HF/DF of *Zamalek*, stationed astern of the centre column, and also by *Havelock* on the starboard quarter, but it was too late. *U-338* was now among the ships of the convoy and fired two torpedoes at close range from his bow tubes and two from his stern tubes, hitting three merchant ships in quick succession. In the convoy there were many new ships which were manned by young and inexperienced officers and crew, and discipline was not good enough to prevent an immediate display of fireworks to which almost all the ships contributed further by loosing off snowflakes, which effectively illuminated and gave away the position of the whole convoy. *U-338* was still on the surface looking for further targets, but came under fire from the Commodore and two other ships, which forced him to dive. He then fired one of the new FAT torpedoes which circled inside the convoy until it hit *Fort Cedar Lake*.[4]

In a very short space of time a surfaced U-boat with a determined and bold captain had torpedoed three ships, come under fire from the Commodore and other ships, dived and torpedoed a fourth ship and disappeared below the surface. *Zamalek* and *Saxifrage* searched among the wreckage until 0900, picking up 131 survivors. It would be several hours before *Saxifrage* was back in station, and meanwhile the escorts had been reduced to five warships trying to protect forty-four merchant ships in eleven columns, as SC 122 steamed on into the nest of U-boats waiting ahead.

Commodore Mayall and HX 229, not far away, was in an even worse position. Eight ships, including his Vice Commodore's ship *Nariva* had been sunk; only two escorts, one each side of the convoy, were trying to protect his twenty-nine ships, a hopeless task once the U-boats found them. The rest of his group were astern heavily involved in picking up 325 survivors. Two did not get back to their stations until midnight.

Once again the SOE faced the insoluble dilemma, which no orders, however clearly stated, could cover. Should he leave men to drown or steam on to protect ships that might not ever be threatened? The orders for the SOEs of the escort groups were quite clear, but they were not always obeyed. The SOE was to ensure, 'the safe and timely arrival of the convoy'. But how long would the morale of the merchant seamen hold up if warships would or could not and merchant ships were forbidden to save their colleagues? And what further damage would be done to the relationship between the merchant service and the Royal Navy, following the PQ 17 disaster and abandonment of the merchant ships and their crews to their fates? Whatever the risk, merchant ships tended to pull up to rescue their shipmates if no rescue ship was nominated, and the Navy tended to drop everything to go to the rescue if one of their sister warships was severely damaged or sunk. When faced with totally inadequate resources, it was up to the man on the spot, the SOE, to make these agonizing decisions.

The acting SOE in *Volunteer* was in a desperate position: his force was reduced to two, under attack by day and night and unable to make any sorties away from the convoy to force the U-boats to submerge, with no air cover and fuel running low: he put out a call for help at 1310. It was a concise, understated, professional signal: 'HX 229 attacked, two ships torpedoed. Request early reinforcements for convoy.'

At 1437/17 he sent an amplifying signal to the destroyer *Highlander* which was coming up from astern She was carrying Commander Day, the Senior Officer of the Group, who had been delayed in St John's for vital repairs.

> Have *Beverley* and *Mansfield* in company. *Pennywort* and *Anemone* overtaking astern. Persistent attacks will not permit refuelling and situation is becoming critical. D/F sightings indicate many U-boats in contact.

Shortly afterwards two more U-boats were sighted right in the convoy's path, one eight miles away and another beyond. The

190

Commodore made an emergency turn to port while *Beverley* drove one U-boat to starboard, forcing it to submerge and keeping it down for two hours. This left just *Volunteer* as the convoy's single escort until dark when *Beverley* came back to resume station on the starboard beam.

Commodore White, with convoy SC 122 only 110 miles away, had picked up HF/DF bearings from five U-boats in his vicinity. But at long last help was at hand. A VLR had left Aldergrove at midnight and at 0850 arrived with the convoy, having sighted and attacked a surfaced U-boat waiting ahead of the convoy. Commodore White ordered an emergency turn to starboard, while the Liberator went off on another sweep, this time picking up another U-boat surfaced on the port bow of the convoy. Once again the aircraft's report enabled the Commodore to steer his charges round the U-boat's reported position. This was a crucial moment in the history of the Battle of the Atlantic. In the plotting room in Derby House it was apparent that a grim situation, long anticipated, had now to be faced. There were now so many U-boats at sea that it was no longer feasible to re-route all the convoys clear of the enemy's concentrations, even when their location was known. When altering the route of one outward-bound convoy there was the danger of pulling the U-boats closer to a convoy on the opposite course, or another convoy following close behind. Too many and too large alterations increased the ships' time at sea, delayed the cargoes, left the ships exposed even longer to enemy attack and caused fuel problems to the escorts.

The mangled and converging convoys HX 229 and SC 121 steamed on into the Atlantic Gap. As long as one of the forty-one U-boats was in touch with either convoy it could shadow and report the convoy's position, course and speed by watching the mastheads and the smoke, without itself being seen. With no aircraft cover, by working at this range on the surface and by taking a wide sweep around the perimeter, the U-boat could get ahead of the convoy and bring in its mates.

If the U-boats kept up the pressure there were not enough warships at hand to help the merchant ships. Those already involved were short of fuel and busily engaged in picking up the survivors of ships already torpedoed. These convoys,

191

however weakly defended, would have to be fought through: it would be the merchant ships and their crews that would go down.

The merchant seamen at this stage of the war were resigned to the dangers of the mid-Atlantic and their spirits sank as they came into the arena, knowing that the U-boats, in contrast, would be ploughing along on the surface at full speed with their tails up, unmolested, with five knots in hand over the corvettes and the knowledge that there were few destroyers with the speed to catch them and that most of the escorts would be busy picking up survivors from the previous night's slaughter. The option of surrender was not open to them; they could not turn back and their escorts were short of fuel, so short that the destroyer *Mansfield* had to leave her station and crawl off for Londonderry on one engine.

Only some heroic action could help these convoys.

The men to provide the solution were the pilots and crews of the VLRs which were at last released to fill their proper roles. Flight Lieutenant Burcher in his Liberator M 86 flew out and found the convoy in mid-Atlantic. It took him nearly nine hours and left him only four hours on station before he had to start the long journey back. In that four hours he completely upset the rehearsed routine of the wolf packs as they circled the ships just out of visual range, working into position for a night onslaught. This Liberator did five consecutive flights and, in a period of seventy hours, sighted ten U-boats and made nine attacks. Another VLR, flown by Flight Lieutenant Esher and his men, was in the air for 36 hours in just under three days, during which eight U-boats were sighted and five attacked. The pilots of the VLRs and their crews excelled themselves in their unflagging efforts to pull these convoys through the danger areas, and proved at last, even to the doubters, that their role was an essential element if the Battle of Britain was to be won.

The sight of a Liberator this far out cheered the seamen with the knowledge that they were no longer on their own and that they had a link with home. It was only just in time: morale had begun to show signs of breaking down. This was evidenced by ships not bothering to keep in station, dropping astern or making use of their superior speed to romp away independently. On board *Mathew Luckenbach* in HX 229 the Captain had called a meeting of all on board and with their agreement had sought permission to press on at her full speed of fifteen knots. Commodore Mayall, who knew the statistics and the number of U-boats around, refused this request, but nevertheless, in spite of a severe warning from the SOE, the Master went up to full speed and romped on ahead. They were forty miles clear and all happy when they were torpedoed by a U-boat chasing convoy SC 122 ahead. The ship took a long time to sink, allowing all the crew enough time to get away. Their luck held and they were picked up by the US Coastguard Cutter *Ingham*.

There were now hundreds of survivors on board *Zamalek* and the escorting warships. The survivors reacted in different ways after the first euphoria after rescue had worn off. Discipline tended to break down. In British merchant ships contracts ended, as well as pay, when the ship was sunk. Some of the British seamen refused to do any work at all, not even to clean their own quarters. A bunch of American survivors demanded overtime payments when asked to do some work on board the ship that picked them up. In contrast, Dutch and Norwegian seamen survivors set to willingly and polished their temporary quarters in *Pennywort* so that they shone like a new pin.

As the arrival of the aircraft helped to restore the morale of the ships in convoy, so the determination of the U-boat commanders seemed to waver. Urged on by signals from Dönitz calling for further results, they had expected another uninterrupted day on the surface during which they could get ahead and make ready for another devastating night attack. The U-boat crews had also been under great stress. They were not accustomed to the increased patrol lengths which were now becoming commonplace with the arrival of the milch cows to refuel and replenish their torpedoes at sea. In bad weather it was a tough job to get ahead of the convoys, even without interference from aircraft. To get into the best attacking position meant travelling all day at maximum speed on the surface with icy seas sweeping clean over their hulls and spray whipping the lookouts. Below decks conditions were as primitive as a pigsty, every inch of space stuffed with food, equipment or clothing. The crews were unwashed, the air was foul and the stench appalling. If forced to dive and attacked, the courage of each man and his endurance were tested to extremes as glass shattered, rivets leaked, the hulls groaned under the pressure of water at depths far deeper than designed limits and the massive hammer blows of exploding depth-charges reverberated through the tiny steel tubes in which they were sealed.

Nevertheless in the afternoon and the evening of 17 March continuous attempts were made by the six U-boats of Group Sturmer to get into attacking positions. Their attempts were frustrated by the air attacks and aggressive sorties by the escorts whenever a sighting or an HF/DF bearing was obtained. *Harvester*'s asdic was not working but this did not deter her from following HF/DF bearings, causing even the persistent *U-338* to lose contact.

At 2200 *U-305* crept through the three-mile gap between the escorts *Swale* and *Godetia* which were zigzagging on the starboard side. The determination of the U-boat's commander can be judged by the fact that while he was making his final approach he was not seen by the lookouts, nor the OOW, nor detected by radar nor asdics until, still on the surface and only 1000 yards from *Swale*, he was picked up by *Pimpernel*'s radar at a range of 4000 yards. He came under fire and not surprisingly missed his target, but his torpedoes ran on hitting *Port Auckland* and sinking *Zouave*. *Godetia* went back and picked up twenty-eight men from *Zouave* and thirty-two from *Port Auckland*. While *Godetia* was lying stopped, engaged in this rescue work, a second torpedo from *U-305* hit *Port Auckland*. Although her asdic was out of action, *Godetia* went straight to the scene, found the U-boat still on the surface, made to ram it, opened fire and forced it to dive. She then dropped one depth-charge – all she could afford – and resumed her tense and vital life-saving activity, taking on board another sixty-eight men from the lifeboats.

The convoy had been hammered by the U-boats, but now it was the turn of the Atlantic once more to hammer both convoy ships and U-boats alike. The weather deteriorated until the visibility had dropped to one and a half miles with snow squalls. As first light came, the convoy signalmen started to identify the remaining ships, but the formation which had so far doggedly held together was now being broken up by the power of the Atlantic seas as breakdowns and speed problems scattered the ships. The LST's steering had continued to give trouble and, with her blunt bow and high freeboard, she was quite uncontrollable.

The Commodore made a course alteration, not this time to dodge the U-boats but to ease the passage of his ships through the seas. This is an easy thing to write but for the convoy signalman it involved getting the signal across to all ships, making sure that they all understood, and monitoring their compliance. The risk of collision was very high. The ships' officers and crews had been under attack for five days with little sleep and had seen too many of their colleagues go down: the visibility was bad, coming down to nil in the snow squalls: a mistake by one column leader could result in mass collisions. But the ships came slowly and clumsily round to their new course and there were no collisions and no further attacks, another triumph for the consigs and for the seamanship in the convoy.

On that day a minimum number of VLRs had been operating at the outer limits of their endurance. However, their efforts had so impressed the Germans that the BdU attributed the disappointing results to 'very strong air escort and . . . constant air attacks'.

Commodore White endured the filthy weather on the morning of 18 March with some relief, as his depleted convoy ticked off the miles for home and looked for the reinforcements due. It was another busy morning for his signalmen as he redisposed his charges and put them back on course. Of the remaining ships afloat only *Empire Morn*, suffering from boiler trouble, had to drop back and make her own way. She got home safe.

Commodore White and the SOE both knew that they were not yet out of trouble. The SOE ordered the Liberator to fly round the perimeter of the convoy's visibility to keep them all submerged. The convoy was warned that there would be a 35 degree alteration of course to starboard at 2100 and then a resumption to the previous course at midnight, which would take the ships thirteen miles to starboard of their present track and so, it was hoped, dodge any U-boats waiting ahead. Once again all ships were warned not to reveal their whereabouts by putting on their habitual fireworks display.

The diversion didn't work. As the convoy turned to starboard the weather cleared and the ships were seen in the moonlight by *U-666*, which worked itself into an attacking position without being observed to fire a salvo of four torpedoes directed at two overlapping ships on the port beam of the convoy. Luckily one was a malfunction and the other three missed because the range was under-estimated and the firing coincided with the convoy's alteration of course. *U-666*, still unobserved either visually or by the escort's radar, did not give up. When the visibility again deteriorated, he reloaded his tubes and when he surfaced found himself on the other side of the convoy, going into the gap that had opened up between *Pimpernel* and *Swale* as they zigzagged. He fired two more torpedoes which hit the Greek ship *Carras*. Her crew abandoned ship as she started to settle, but *Zamalek* was there to pick up thirty-four of them to add to the 131 survivors that were already on board.

Considering the forces around him, Commodore White, with this single loss, had had an easy night, but HX 229, now only seventy miles away, had not been so fortunate. At 0800 on 18 March *U-60* sent off a shadowing report. The first attack came in the afternoon when the Liberty Ship *Walter Q. Gresham* and the *Canadian Star* were hit. The corvette *Anemone* saved sixteen from the Liberty Ship and fifty-one from *Canadian Star* to join the 163 already on board, but, without the specialized equipment and experience of the rescue ships, she had difficulty picking up survivors in the rising sea and wind. Many were lost in the cold and heavy seas. Survivors on board *Anemone* now outnumbered the ship's company by nearly three to one: shortages of clothing and food were added to her problems.

In the first ten days of March forty-one ships had been lost. When Commodores White (SC 122), Mayall (HX229) and Casey (HX 229A) brought their convoys home on 20 March the total losses in that month amounted to half a million tons of shipping. In these three convoys 144 ships had sailed. A quarter of these (thirty-seven) had either been sunk (twenty-one) or had turned back (sixteen), and a quarter (372) of the crew and passengers on board (1494) had lost their lives. The Germans had achieved this at the expense of a single U-boat. These were grievous wounds and could well have proved fatal.

The failure of these three convoys, coming so soon after the losses in SC 121, when, in spite of the most appalling weather with wind forces up to hurricane strength, the U-boats sank thirteen ships without any loss to themselves caused grave concern. Roskill records that the Naval Staff wrote a despairing note: 'It appeared possible that we should not be able to continue [to regard] convoy as an effective form of defence.'

The Naval Staff was tired. The First Sea Lord, who had borne the burden of his high office for over three years, was showing signs of the illness that would eventually lead to his death. It is clear that morale in the merchant service and its relationship with and regard for the Royal Navy had been shaken by the heavy losses during the year and the abandonment of the ships in PQ 17, a fact that Churchill acknowledged when he said:

> I cannot pass from this subject [the U-boat war] without paying tribute once more to the officers and men of the Merchant Navy whose losses have been greater in proportion than those even of the Royal Navy.

He could have added that up to that time twenty-one convoy commodores had lost their lives. They were all well known, well regarded and very experienced officers, including Admiral Sir H.J. Brownrigg KBE CB DSO, the most senior officer on either side to lose his life while serving at sea. In addition to Admiral Brownrigg, six Vice Admirals, five Rear Admirals, and nine Captains in the Royal Naval Reserve had lost their lives when the merchant ships in which they were sailing as Commodores had sunk.

The most serious sin of omission at top level was the failure to implement the recommendation made at the Casablanca Conference in January, 1943, immediately after the losses in convoy TM 1 and SL 125, to allocate eighty VLR aircraft to close the Atlantic Gap.

However, even at this dark time there was a lot to be pleased about. Above all, on average thirty-nine out of forty merchant ships were coming home safe. The need for new brooms had been anticipated. Admiral Sir Max Horton had succeeded Admiral Noble as C-in-C Western Approaches on 17 November, 1942. Sir Percy Noble's imperturbable charm and experience was brought to bear on the stubborn and expensive obstinacy of Admiral King USN. Air Marshal Sir John Slessor became C-in-C Coastal Command in February, 1943.

The British Naval Staff would have been less pessimistic if they had known that Dönitz, a man not easily beaten, had seen the writing on the wall in spite of these local victories. Allied radar, the extensive fitting of HF/DF, the deployment of the support groups with modern ships, the arrival of the first VLRs in the Atlantic Gap which with the escort carriers gave aircraft support from one side of the Atlantic to the other, and the involvement of USS *Bogue*, the escort carrier with the first American Support Group, were events that he had long anticipated and dreaded. They were the strongest warnings of the inevitable defeat of the present generation of U-boats and therefore the end of his dream of bringing down Britain by starvation of food, fuel and raw materials.

When the battle of these three SC/HX convoys moved into its final stage, Dönitz had already shifted his priorities to succouring the German troops in North Africa and had departed for Italy, leaving Admiral Godt in charge of the U-boats' daily activity. He was about to withdraw the present generation of U-boats from the North Atlantic, in order to conserve a nucleus of experienced U-boat crews to man the new generation of electric, high speed U-boats in which he pinned his hopes, but few of which were ever in action.

It is significant that his regular reports face-to-face with Hitler in March and April did not mention these critical convoys, but dwelt on his problems in the Mediterranean, his lack of long-range reconnaissance aircraft, the dismantling of Germany's big ships, the need to increase the output of submarines and E-boats and the shortage of steel.

In his anthology, *Other Men's Flowers* General Wavell quotes from Rudyard Kipling's poem 'Boxing'

> Man cannot tell, but Allah knows
> How much the other side was hurt!

and he comments: 'The last two lines illustrate my favourite military maxim, that when things are going badly in battle the best tonic is to take one's mind off one's own troubles by considering what a rotten time one's opponent must be having.'

Chapter Thirteen

COMMODORES IN THE ARCTIC

The raging ocean that covered everything was engulfed in total darkness and an awesome wind was moving over the water.

The above quotation, verse 2 of the first chapter of Genesis in the American Bible Society translation, accurately and concisely describes a mid-winter night in a full gale in the Arctic seas. The only element that needs to be added is the intense cold. As Admiral Bonham-Carter said in 1942, 'We in the Navy are paid to do this sort of job, but it is asking too much of the men of the Merchant Navy.'[1]

In contrast to their counterparts in the British merchant service the American Merchant Marine were paid large salaries and enormous bonuses. The American naval historian S.E. Morison tells us that, 'In addition to their daily pay of $100 per month for a forty-four-hour week, war bonus of the same amount, and overtime for work on Saturday and Sunday, a common seaman drew $5.00 per day for each day's detention in North Russia, 125$ for each air raid to which he was subjected after March, 1943, a seventeen per cent bonus for handling ammunition, and, on top of that, a $100 bonus from the Soviet Government. . . . For one round voyage that included several months' detention in North Russia, the least pay that anyone received on a certain American merchantman was $3200.'[2]

Nor were the Royal Navy's men paid any special money for service in these dreadful North Atlantic and Arctic waters. Look at the typical case of Peter Eustace, an HO signalman whose wartime service from 11 November, 1942, to 22 June, 1945,

200

included almost three years on Arctic convoys and Western Approach convoys in HMS *Starling*, which sank fifteen U-boats under the command of Captain F.J. Walker RN. He was paid no bonus other than his War Gratuity of forty-one months at ten shillings per month (£20-10s) and Post-War Credit of service as a rating for 1320 days at sixpence per day (£33). The author's pay as an ordinary seaman in the Royal Navy was two shillings and seven pence per day. It would have taken him seventeen years to earn as much as the lowest American seaman on this single round trip.

The Admiral was a great friend to the merchant service and much admired, but he was wrong when he said that it was asking too much of the men of the merchant service. The British and Allied merchant seamen continued to man the ships on the Arctic convoys and no American seamen went on a Russian convoy unknowingly, nor could they be ordered to go. Everybody assumes, quite rightly, that the question of pay related to danger rarely entered the minds of those serving in the Royal Navy. Did these seamen of so many nations go for the money, or for the adventure, or driven by some higher ideal?

The Arctic convoys were different from all other twentieth century ocean convoys, and indeed all the convoys in the long history of the Royal Navy. The nearest parallel was the operation of the Mediterranean convoys, but these were mainly military convoys, carrying troops and military materials in support of Allied Armies and bases. However, the Mediterranean convoys did not suffer from the same extreme weather conditions. The task of the Ocean Commodores reflected these differences. The Commodores continued to muster and to handle the ships in the convoys, but the escorting forces were much stronger and more numerous and there were many factors at work that went beyond the brief of a convoy commodore.

The protection of the merchant ships consisted of a number of concentric and interactive circles. The first layer was, as usual, composed of the warships of the close escort, but they were needed as much for anti-aircraft defence as for an anti-submarine screen. The next layer was the first line of defence against surface forces, such as the Z-class German destroyers; these were striking forces of destroyers, backed by cruisers. In

201

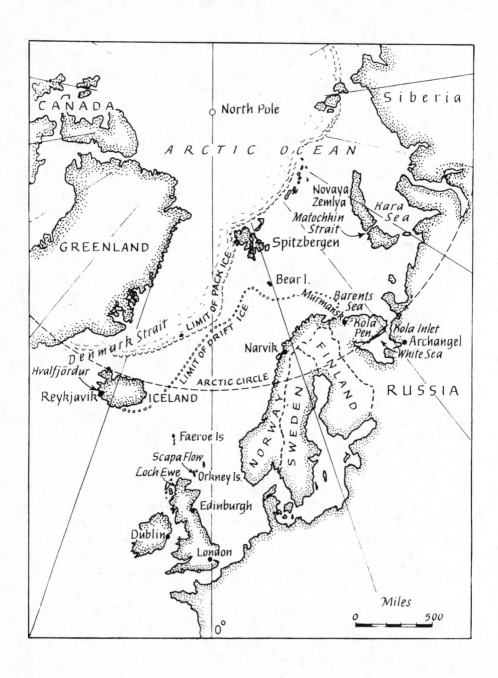

the background, and out of sight over the horizon, was the Home Fleet waiting to enter the ring if the German big ships could be tempted out of the Norwegian fjords. Sometimes the Home Fleet was a long way over the horizon, perhaps even lying at anchor in Scapa Flow at instant readiness, since its ships also had to prevent the German big ships from breaking out of the Norwegian Sea through the Denmark Strait and wreaking havoc on the Atlantic convoys. Hovering near the midpoint of the convoy route, out of range of the German aircraft, were the oilers with their own screen of destroyers, and, seldom mentioned, the Navy's submarines patrolling continuously off the coast of Norway.

Each convoy was in itself a major naval operation, in which the number of escorting warships often exceeded the number of merchant ships, and as such each section was under the command of an active service Admiral or Captain (D). The Arctic convoys were conducted on a much more formal basis than the Western Approach convoys, which were usually run and manned by teams in which Reserve and HO officers and men predominated. (The reservists were sometimes referred to, and still are, as 'part-time sailors', a description of which they are very proud.)

Seventy-six Arctic convoys were run, a small number in comparison to the thousands of other ocean and coastal convoys, but the whole operation ranks among the most magnificent achievements in the history of the Royal Navy and of the Allied merchant service.

The range and detail of each convoy has been covered admirably in the book *The Arctic Convoys* by Richard Woodman and this chapter's limited endeavour is to give an indication of the part played by the convoy commodores and their signalmen during the crucial year following the spring of 1942, during which the Royal Navy suffered one of its most humiliating experiences, and the merchant service one of its greatest single convoy losses, but during which those at sea conducted themselves in a manner which will be admired as long as men tell tales of endurance and fortitude at sea. A few veterans still survive to wear with pride the medal presented to all those who took part in the Russian convoys in commemoration of the fiftieth anniversary of these convoys. This medal was given by the Russians to all who sailed irrespective of rank or service, and it has been an individious task to choose who represents best the spirit that carried the men through. The choice has fallen on Commodore Dowding of the Royal Naval Reserve and his staff of convoy signalmen, sunk on the way out and on the way back.

All the seas in which the convoy battles were fought had their own characteristic discomforts and dangers. Only the convoys to and from the Arctic Russian ports of Archangel, Murmansk and the anchorages at Polyarnoe faced the same combination of extremes of cold, concentrations of U-boats operating not far from their bases, heavy German surface forces and, in summer or winter, days of continuous daylight or continuous darkness. The German battleship *Tirpitz*, probably the most powerful warship afloat in the European conflict, supported by the two 32,000 ton 11" gun battle cruisers *Scharnhorst* and *Gneisenau* and the large Z-class destroyers, imposed a threat which dominated all movement and worried people to death, from the greaser in the engine room of the tramp steamer to Churchill, Roosevelt and Stalin. The Royal Navy, which was responsible for all these convoys, had to be ready to overcome almost alone all these threats, whether encountered singly or simultaneously. Whether attacked or not, every convoy had to face close manoeuvring in fog, ice and dreadful seas. For the first six months, from September, 1941, until the end of February, 1942, there was the winter cold and the weather to endure, but little German interference. Thereafter, from March, 1942, until the last convoy in May, 1945, every convoy was under constant threat of attack and experienced a sense of immediacy that was absent from most of the Atlantic convoy routes.

Ninety-seven percent of the ships that sailed in Atlantic convoys came unscathed through the whole battle, but in 63% of the Arctic convoys ships were either lost or turned back due to weather: only 37% of the convoys got through intact to their destinations. The men from so many nations who manned the merchant ships travelled under a suspended sentence of death, knowing that they were sailing towards danger, and that the last part of their outward journey and their stay in Russia would be the worst part: concentrations of U-boats from their sheltered bases in Narvik would be waiting across the northern and eastern parts of their routes. Heavily laden on their outward journeys, the closer they got to their destination, the closer they would be to German air attacks. The German front line and the nearest enemy airfield were less than forty miles away from the badly battered quays in the Kola and the Polyarnoe Inlets: alongside or at their moorings, the merchant ships could expect to be bombed without warning at any time that they were offloading their cargoes, or waiting for the assembly of the homeward convoy.

They were long convoys. Even after reaching the departure points in Iceland, and after crossing half the Atlantic ocean, there were another 2,000 miles to be sailed. When the ice receded in the summer the convoys went further north to keep as far away as possible from the shore-based Luftwaffe, but this increased the distance to 2,300 miles. Even if all went well the eight-knot ships had ten to twelve days of terrible sea conditions and continuous threat from U-boats and bombers.

For the Royal Navy each convoy was a major naval operation, involving in the background, battleships, cruisers, destroyers, screens of anti-submarine and anti-aircraft ships, minesweepers, trawlers, submarines and, in the later convoys, aircraft carriers travelling either within or in support of the convoy. Apart from the trawlers and minesweepers, based in the Russian ports, the naval escorts ships tried to spend as little time as possible in the Russian ports, just long enough to refuel, turn round and start back with any ships from previous convoys that had discharged their cargoes and were ready for sea.

The crews of the warships had little to look forward to when they reached Russia. Facilities ashore were almost non-existent and made the desolate base of Scapa Flow seem like peacetime Piccadilly. The prospect for the crews of the merchant ships was even worse. There was no question of reaching a safe haven after arriving in port to deliver their cargoes. Recently, the vicar of a church close to my home announced a social event to take place before Christmas and ended with the words, 'Mince pies are available to those who bring them'. That was the way when the Arctic convoys arrived at their destinations in Russia. If ships needed repairs, fuel, food, medicine, medical attention or entertainment they had to bring them out. The crews could be reasonably certain that the unfriendliness of the Russians would not thaw, whether in winter or summer, and they could only hope that the much-needed tanks, planes and war materials wouldn't still be sitting where they had left them on the jetty when they came back a few weeks later, having fought another convoy through the U-boats, JU 88s and the threat of the *Tirpitz*.

The seas through which the ships would travel were dominated by ice – ice in the water, sometimes nine feet thick, ice soup all around full of lethal jagged ice croutons, known as growlers, icebergs a mile or more wide, ice shelves that had no end to the east or to the west, escape channels into the ice that had no exit, ice clinging to the rigging, ice on the gun barrels, ice on the binoculars and gun-sight lenses, ice on the anchor cables and in the hawse pipes, ice enshrouding the capstans, ice jamming the lifeboat blocks, ice on the duffel coats and freezing inside the cuffs and the neckbands, ice freezing solid on gloves, ice in the seaboots, ice up the nostrils, ice on the decks and the ladder rungs, ice on the depth charge rails, ice locking up the ammunition ready-use lockers, in the breaches of the guns, clamping up the firing mechanisms, ice on the flag clips and the signal halyards, ice freezing the signal flags into solid tight rolls, ice on the navigator's sextant on the open bridges.

The spray thrown up as the ships plunged their bows into the seas was immediately converted to ice as it whipped across the decks, adhering to the guard rails, the deck cargo and any part of the superstructure. In one of His Majesty's 300-foot sloops there were 200 men on board to cut away the ice with axes and steam hoses, but in the much larger merchant ships there were no spare hands to take on this additional work. The additional top weight affected the stability of the ships. As the ice formed aloft the roll of the ship would slow down and increase, until the ship seemed to be struggling against suffocation and crying out for release from the weight on her back. The Norwegian whaler HMS *Shera* went the whole way and was dragged right over by the weight of ice when looking for convoy PQ 12 in the ice.

Ice crept into the clothing of the crews. Down below in the dank and crowded messdecks ice formed on the deckheads of the messdecks and crept into the souls of the ships' companies. As the autumn rolled by, the moment approached when the sun would dip below the horizon and would not creep up again until the winter was over, three and a half months later. These seemed to be the most depressing times, when darkness reigned, but worse would follow when continuous daylight left the ships open to bombing round the clock.

On the Arctic convoys the use of evasive routeing was very much restricted because there was no sea room; the northern touchline was defined by the ice, the southern by the converging coast of north-eastern Norway and the proximity of German airfields. As the ships sailed closer to their destination the touchlines converged, until the ships were sailing almost due south down the Kola Inlet to Murmansk in the winter, or down the funnel to Archangel in the summer.

On the long journey, as in the approaches, the monstrous waves were as hideous and remorseless as the greybacks of the Atlantic Ocean; the feeble last effects of the Gulf Stream made little difference to the surface temperature of the water. In the winter, at the northern point of the route in the Arctic Circle, the temperature of the air plunged to twenty degrees centigrade below freezing point, causing a white freezing mist to rise from its surface, hiding the horizon and merging the sea into the air. Except by contact and observation on the spot, no one, not even the Russians in their home waters, had much precise knowledge of where they would find the ice. The icebergs sailed like monstrous juggernauts wherever the tides and winds took them, grinding their way remorselessly through pack ice which itself was not static, advancing in the winter as much as four kilometres daily.

The convoy signalmen worked at the topmost level of the ship, above the bridge, on ice-covered decks that were never still, hoisting the flags that controlled the merchant ships from platforms that had no protection. Signals could not be written down in these exposed perches and the signalmen could not keep their feet in the blizzard to man their signal lanterns.

Commodore Dowding in *Llanstephan Castle* took the first convoy from Hvalfjördur in Iceland to Archangel, sailing on 21 August, 1941, in Operation Dervish, the prelude to the convoys that were code-named PQ (outward) and QP (homeward), the first of which sailed on 28 September, 1941. (From December, 1942, their codes were changed to JW outward and RA homeward.) Seventy-seven convoys were run thereafter, the first seven pairs to PQ 7 and QP 7 sailing without commodores; thereafter, with a few exceptions, when the master of one of the merchant ships acted as commodore, the convoys were run by twenty-six ocean commodores. They were battle-hardened old salts, having already taken thousands of convoys to and fro across the Atlantic and round the coasts of the British Isles, but it is not surprising that, in most cases, each commodore's share of this white hell was limited to one trip out and one trip back. Only four Commodores did more. Rear Admiral Boucher RN did five; Captain Dowding RNR did four, including the two pathfinders; Captain Ullring, Royal Norwegian Navy, in his own waters, did four; Captain Meek RNR did three and Rear Admiral Leir RN did one.[3]

On the Arctic convoys six ships in which a commodore was flying his broad pennant were sunk. Commodore Anchor (*Botavon* PQ 15) and Commodore Casey (*Temple Arch* QP 10) were torpedoed, lost their ships, were picked out of the icy waters and went back to sea. Commodore Gale's ship *Ocean Voice* was so badly bombed she had to be towed into port. Commodore Dowding, on his third Arctic convoy lost his ship *River Afton* in the disaster of PQ 17 on 5 July, 1942. Three weeks later, on 27 July, he was back leading QP 14 when his ship, the repaired *Ocean Voice*, was again attacked and this time torpedoed and sunk. He handed over his duties to his Vice-Commodore, Captain Walker, in *Ocean Freedom*. On convoy JW 56A Commodore Whitehorn also escaped death twice when two ships in which he was sailing went down. The *Penelope Barker*, was damaged by exceptionally heavy weather and subsequently torpedoed; he transferred to *Fort Bellingham* which was sunk. Commodore Rees (*Empire Howard*) was posted missing and lost his life when his ship went down during the passage of PQ 14.[4]

In the initial seven months of the Arctic runs, up to 12 March, 1942, 109 escorted merchant ships had arrived safely in Archangel and Murmansk. Five ships had turned back due to ice or weather, but only two had been lost due to enemy action.[5] As the days lengthened the German invasion of Russia began to lose its impetus and the Germans became increasingly aware of the valuable war cargoes getting through to the Russians by sea to the railheads at Archangel and Murmansk.

Hitler was obsessed by Norway and that country's long exposed coast (and remained so, keeping some of his best regiments there until well after the Normandy landings). He believed that the Allies were planning an invasion of Norway which would cut off his supplies of bauxite, copper and iron ore and deprive him of the airfields which were a perpetual threat to the Arctic convoys. If the Allies could establish themselves in Norway this would make the convoy routes infinitely safer and even if Stalin claimed to be dissatisfied with the volume of supplies now coming in by sea, Hitler had no such illusions. Everything possible was done to encourage this phobia. A dummy Home Fleet was constructed at Scapa Flow and the intelligence services spread false rumours.

Hitler responded by moving heavy ships up to the North: *Tirpitz* actually put to sea with three destroyers from Trondheim on 6 March, 1941, to search for PQ 12. The force was sighted by the British submarine *Seawolf*, and C-in-C Home Fleet countered by fielding the battleship *Duke of York*, the battle cruiser *Renown* and the aircraft carrier *Victorious*, supported by cruisers and destroyers. The convoy ran into thick ice, which forced Commodore Hudson, ignoring Admiralty orders which would have taken him deeper into the ice, to alter course ninety degrees to the south-east, towards the enemy. For a while the two forces milled around in appalling Arctic weather unable to make contact. By the time that the skies had cleared B-Dienst had decyphered the information that the British had an aircraft carrier with them and *Tirpitz*, in accordance with Hitler's instructions, turned back.

The German Fleet was under crippling constraints. It did not possess a single aircraft carrier nor even the junior version, an escort aircraft carrier. Furthermore, Hitler had made it clear that his big ships were not to put to sea if there was any risk of meeting a superior force. Indeed they were not put to sea at all unless there was positive evidence that any Allied aircraft carrier had been put out of action. The ships' companies on board the German big ships lying idle in the Norwegian fjords were aware of the terrible casualty rate in their U-boat arm – and its many successes – but they and their wonderful ships were bottled up swinging round the buoys. The Commandos had destroyed the one dock, on the Atlantic Coast at St Nazaire, which was supposed to be capable of accommodating *Tirpitz* if that battleship needed repairs after a dash out to the Atlantic to raid the merchant fleets.[6]

Accidents occur and 'bad luck' strikes when morale is low. On 3 July, 1942, when eventually the pocket battleship *Lützow* (ex *Deutschland*) tried to put to sea from Altenfjord the ship went aground, followed in quick succession by three of the four screening destroyers. The German ships were not battleworthy, because they had had no opportunity to go to sea, and their crews, even though thought by their captains to be highly trained and efficient, would surely have suffered severe seasickness as a result; no one is immune unless conditioned by much exposure. They were badly and irresolutely led. Their morale was at rock bottom, and who could blame them?

The spirit of their service, undermined by a series of mutinies in the Baltic after the First World War, was once again systematically destroyed, from top rank downwards, by confused and clumsy communications. As a final blow to the hopes of the Grand Fleet and its train, the supplies of oil fuel for the Fleet were not getting through from their sole remaining source, the oil fields at Ploesti in Romania, because the initial impetus of the German attack had petered out hundreds of miles short of the Russian oilfields in the Caucasus. In one month fuel supplies to the ships fell to one tenth of the normal operational requirement. This shortage, helped by the impact of the Russian winter, so paralysed the German fleet that an order went out in February 1942 that: 'All operations are to be discontinued, including those by light forces. The sole exceptions to the ban on consumption of fuel are operations made necessary by offensive enemy action.'[7]

At the end of 1941 two events occurred that altered forever the thinking of both the German and the Allied fleets. On Sunday 7 December in a few minutes Japanese carrier-borne aircraft dealt a blow to the United States Fleet at Pearl Harbor from which no other country would have recovered. A few days later, off Singapore, the Royal Navy's battle cruiser *Repulse* and the battleship *Prince of Wales*, operating without air cover, were sunk by Japanese aircraft.

The emphasis shifted. The Germans brought up to the airfields in north Norway all their naval torpedo bombers, their Ju 88s, their Junkers dive-bombers and their long-range reconnaissance planes (KG 26 and KG 30). Against Dönitz' advice all U-boats putting to sea from the Biscay ports were ordered to return (northabout) to the Norwegian bases and concrete shelters at Narvik, to repel an invasion which was expected from Scotland by a phantom force of kilted Scotsmen on their way from Dumfermline. The thought was enough to strike a chill into any heart.

The Admiralty and the naval staffs had taken to heart the lessons of the losses of their two capital ships to aircraft in the Far East. The Admiralty and the Commander-in-Chief of the Home Fleet, although itching to get to grips with the German heavy ships, were now even more reluctant to allow their capital ships into waters that could be reached by aircraft from the German airfields along the coast of Norway. There were severe restrictions to prevent even cruisers going farther east than Bear Island, where their anti-aircraft fire was most needed, not only because of the threat from the air, but also because of the lack of docking and repair facilities in north Russia, should they be damaged.

So it was that the officers and seamen of the merchant ships, of His Majesty's destroyers, the old converted long-range escorts, the dreadful old four-stackers that the Americans had given us, of the stalwart corvettes, dogged minesweepers and of the little trawlers, sailed into the line of battle and inherited the privilege of facing up to the dive bombers, the torpedo bombers and the high-level bombing attacks which were to start in April, 1942.

On 8 April Commodore Rees (Captain E. Rees DSC RD RNR), who had completed eight Atlantic convoys, sailed in *Empire Howard* from Reykjavik leading twenty-five ships in convoy

PQ 14, escorted by one destroyer, two minesweepers and two trawlers. In the convoy there were eleven British ships, two Russian, one Dutch, one Panamanian and ten American. It is typical of convoys at this time that over half the seamen manning the ships were not British but from other Allied or neutral countries. The convoy had been due to meet its escort of six destroyers, four corvettes and two more trawlers under the command of Rear Admiral Bonham-Carter, flying his flag in the cruiser HMS *Edinburgh*, but two nights out the ships ran into dense fog and blocks of low-lying ice big enough to damage a ship's propeller, but very difficult and sometimes impossible to see. In the fog violent alterations of course took place to avoid these 'growlers' and in no time all semblance of order had disappeared. In the eerie whiteness of the freezing fog the air was full of the noise of ships' sirens and the thrashing of screws as ships went astern and made violent alterations of course to avoid each other and the ice. The confusion and damage that followed was so widespread that sixteen of the ships and the two minesweepers turned back.[8]

Only two American and six British ships succeeded in extricating themselves in sufficient order to reform and carry on in convoy. Two days later German reconnaissance planes located them and a Focke-Wulf Condor started its regular surveillance patrol, circling the ships, visible like an evil spirit in the haze and the mirage just above the horizon, but out of range of the guns of the escorting warships.

The memory of these aircraft, 'The Scourge of the Atlantic', dreaded forerunners of trials to come, is still indelibly printed on the minds of all who served on ocean convoys and particularly the Arctic convoys. Their presence meant that the convoy's course and speed were being reported and that either a U-boat or an aircraft attack, or both, would soon be under way. This was the rare occasion when seamen prayed for the protective blanket of a fog in which to hide.

In this case the Germans must have been aware of the weakness of the escort. Instead of the eighteen warships planned, led by a cruiser and including seven destroyers, the Commodore now leading the remains of the convoy towards the German airfields had initially to rely on an escort of one destroyer and two trawlers, and any firepower that could be mustered from the merchant ships. This precarious position had been brought about without any intervention from the Germans, just by the Arctic weather.

As the convoy turned south for its destination wave after wave of JU 88s put in a series of attacks that continued throughout the day. They didn't do very well. There were no casualties that day, but on 16 April the air attacks were intensified and combined with U-boat attacks. Two torpedoes caught the Commodore's ship, *Empire Howard*, one in the engine room and one in the boiler room, and a third exploded her cargo of ammunition, blowing her in half and sending her deck cargo of trucks cascading into the water. She went down in sixty seconds: those of her fifty-four crew who had survived the explosion had no time to launch any rafts or boats, leaping into the water to avoid being dragged down by the suction as their ship disappeared. The trawler *Lord Middleton* came charging in with a counter-attack to drive the U-boat down.

When a depth-charge explodes with a shallow setting, it flings thousands of tons of water into the air in a column which is several times the mast-head height of the attacking vessel. The impact of a monster Pacific roller on a surf boarder is as light as a feather compared with the weight of solid water that then descends like a vast and deadly sandbag on anybody or anything beneath, bending steel stanchions, breaking bones and smashing ribs like splitting firewood. Below the surface the power of the explosion is enough to crush like an eggshell the circular steel hull of a submarine built to withstand the pressure of water at a depth of 1,000 feet. When the charge explodes there is a split second during which the surface of the water remains undisturbed and no sound is heard, except through the hydrophones; then the surface shudders as if a great electric shock has been administered and concentric circles spread out in seconds from the point of the explosion. A shock wave in the air is not seen; a shock wave in the sea when a depth-charge explodes is clearly seen. Its impact on a man in the water, with his body below the surface and his head and shoulders supported out of the water by his lifebelt, is devastating and usually fatal.

The bodies of eighteen of the crew of fifty-four from the *Empire Howard* were picked up, but only nine survived. Twenty-nine of her crew were lost. Commodore Rees was last seen smoking a cheroot and hanging on to wreckage, but neither he nor any of his staff of convoy signalmen survived.

PQ 14 reached Murmansk on 19 April with no further losses. The arrival of this convoy brought to an end a sequence of outstandingly successful convoys. 154 ships had sailed in convoy and only seven had been lost to German attacks. The main enemies had been fog and ice which had turned back seventeen ships, sixteen of which were in the convoy that we have just reviewed.

However, the days of perpetual daylight, when the sun never drops below the horizon, were not far ahead, and this greatly increased the danger from German air attacks, a threat which the Royal Navy, operating beyond the reach of air bases and short of aircraft carriers, was not well placed to meet. It also stretched to the limit the endurance of all the seamen in the Allied merchant ships who had now to stay almost twenty-four hours a day close to their action stations. The time between the warning of an air attack and the arrival of the bombers did not permit the luxury of cruising stations, with only one third on deck around the guns, or even of defence stations, with half the armament manned. The crews of the merchant ships on the Arctic runs, particularly the new Liberty Ships now working from America, were often reinforced by additional gun crews, but the strain on the masters and watchkeeping officers increased, because of the longer hours when aircraft attacks could be expected and because many of the officers and crews in the newly built merchant ships were young and inexperienced, with little sea time behind them and no experience of sailing in convoy or of Arctic sea conditions.

In spite of the increasing risk to the convoys and the many other urgent demands on British and Allied maritime resources, Roosevelt still pressed for more convoys to Russia. Stalin, in his boorish, direct and insulting manner, continued to moan and chivvy to the point where Churchill's diplomatic veneer cracked and he instructed that 'Mr Maisky should be told that I am getting to the end of my tether with these repeated Russian naggings and . . . it is not the slightest use trying to knock me about any more.'

The next convoy sailed under Commodore Anchor in *Botavon*. He was an experienced merchant service officer with a fine reputation. He had completed his war apprenticeship in uncomfortable and unglamorous little ships on the east coast convoys, and had survived the mining of *Ahamo* near the East Dudgeon Bank in the North Sea in April, 1941, when thirteen men were killed and seven wounded. He had been promoted to Captain in the Royal Naval Reserve and to Ocean Commodore on 29 March, 1942. He was accustomed to the problems of commanding convoys from unsuitable ships. In convoy ON 227 he had been allocated a ship in which nothing much worked as it should have done. The compass was so unreliable that he, the Commodore who was supposed to be guide of the fleet, was forced to steer by using the ship astern as his guide.

PQ 15 was Commodore Anchor's first Arctic convoy, sailing on 26 April, 1942, when the battle of the Arctic convoys had suddenly ignited and was about to work up to its climax. Twenty-five ships sailed, including five that had turned back from convoy PQ14. Among them was *Empire Bard*, a ship fitted with gear for heavy lifts to expedite the poor cargo-handling facilities available in the Russian ports.[9]

The escorts were numerous and powerful, consisting of four minesweepers, a submarine, four trawlers, six destroyers, an oiler and her escorting destroyers and HMS *Ulster Queen* converted to an anti-aircraft ship by the fitting of six 4-inch high-angle guns and fourteen close-range oerlikons and 12 pounders, the same armament as a Modified Black Swan-type sloop. Two cruisers joined on 30 April and over the horizon, as an insurance against a sortie by German surface forces, were two battleships, an aircraft carrier, more cruisers and ten destroyers. There were more warships than merchant ships.

The journey had a bad start. On 1 May the battleship *King George V* ran over and sank the Tribal Class fleet destroyer *Punjabi*. The USS *Washington*, next astern, had difficulty in avoiding the stricken destroyer, but she remained afloat for long enough, and her discipline and drill was good enough, to allow 206 of her crew to be rescued. This collision risk was an additional hazard on the Russian (and Mediterranean) runs which was not usually experienced by Atlantic convoys, where the merchant ships were not so often in close company with large warships in close formation.[10]

As soon as the convoy came within the range of the German bombers it was located by a reconnaissance plane. On that evening, in low visibility and rain, HM Ships *Seagull* and *St Albans* picked up an asdic contact and immediately put in a model attack, blowing the submarine to the surface before it sank. Too late it was realized that it was the Polish submarine *Jastrzab*, on her first patrol and some 100 miles off station.[11] So this convoy started off with the score two-nil against, without attacks from the enemy but with losses of two warships and hundreds of their crew, due to human error and Arctic weather.

PQ 15 passed the partially loaded homeward bound QP 11 on opposite course, whereupon the Germans shifted their attention to the Russian-bound heavily laden PQ 15. On 3 May, as the ships passed Bear Island and made their way south for Archangel, Heinkel He 111s made a determined low-level attack. The convoy and its close escort put up a formidable barrage which brought down three of their number but one determined attack got through which spelt the end of *Botavon*, *Mutland* and *Cape Corso*. There was a heavy loss of life, *Cape Corso* losing her master and forty-nine of her crew of fifty-six, *Botavon* lost twenty-one of her crew but among her survivors was Commodore Anchor and his staff and her master, Captain J.H. Smith. This was the second time that he had been called upon to swim for his life, but the waters were very much colder than the North Sea and this time he was much further from land. There was no relaxation from the bombers as the ships came closer to their bases, but snow squalls hid them as they entered the Kola Inlet and there were no further casualties.

Homeward bound (QP) convoys were made up from any ships and crews that were ready to return and were usually lightly laden and not such attractive targets to the Germans. (Strange to relate, one ship had a consignment of goose feathers in her cargo.) Nevertheless, when the Germans lost track of PQ 15 in the snow squalls they transferred their attentions to the homeward bound QP 11. The death of Commodore Rees meant that

216

there was no Ocean Commodore available to command this convoy on its journey home, so the duty fell to Captain W.H. Lawrence in *Briarwood*. Both the Acting Commodore and his ship were veterans of many convoys, including PQ 3 and PQ 5. No better man could have been chosen, but he now had the double burden of handling his own ship and handling the convoy.

When he set out the convoy was escorted by four minesweepers, four corvettes, one anti-submarine trawler and eight destroyers to look after his eight merchant ships and, best of all the cruiser HMS *Edinburgh*, Admiral Bonham-Carter's flagship, as close cover, a sight that gave heart to the merchant ships. Bonham-Carter was a popular admiral, liked and respected not only among his own ships' companies, but also among the masters and men of the merchant ships, to whom he always had an understanding word to say.

From observation, from German agents ashore and from B-Dienst's decryptions, the Germans always knew when the convoys were due to sail from Russia and this time they had deployed seven U-boats outside the Kola Inlet. On 30 April the worst occurred. The cruiser HMS *Edinburgh*, ranging ahead of the convoy, was disabled by two torpedoes, whereupon three of the large German Z-class destroyers put to sea. Two of them, the *Z-24* and *Z-25*, mounted 5.9 inch guns (roughly the same calibre as HM cruisers *Edinburgh* and *Trinidad*) and eight torpedo tubes. *Hermann Schoemann* had five 5-inch guns. The convoy escort, with two destroyers detached to succour *Edinburgh*, mustered only six 4.7 inch guns. The German surface forces had at last found a chance to deal a blow at a weaker force.

But first they had to get past Commander Richmond in the aptly named HMS *Bulldog* and his flotilla. Before sailing, the SOE had conferred with Acting Commodore Lawrence and they had devised a plan to deal with just such an emergency. Now it clicked into action. The Commodore and his well-briefed charges made for the ice at their best speed and the escorts turned away to meet the enemy, staying between the merchant ships and the Germans. A deadly cat and mouse game was then played out in the snow squalls and the heavy seas along the edge of the ice shelf. For four hours Richmond and his destroyers laid smoke out of which they made sorties at full speed, while the merchant ships dodged along the northern touchline, weaving in and out of the leads into the ice. Richmond handled his destroyers brilliantly against the better armed and faster enemy force. Six times the Germans tried to get through to the convoy and six times Richmond and his flotilla foiled them. The only casualty was the Russian ship *Tsiolkovsky*, which had become detached. Shortly after 1800, running low on ammunition, the German ships, now actually pursued by the pugnacious and inexhaustible *Bulldog*, used their superior speed to disengage and seek out the disabled *Edinburgh*.

Bulldog lost touch and rejoined her charges just as the last one emerged from its hiding place in the ice. The convoy, now scattered over several miles, reformed and arrived safely on 7 May in Loch Ewe. Acting Commodore Lawrence and Commander Richmond had shown how an aggressive escort could ensure the safe passage of a well-handled convoy against a more powerful predator.

Edinburgh had suffered considerable damage. Four escorts[12] had been diverted from the convoy to endeavour to save her: a Russian patrol vessel, *Rubin*, a tug and minesweepers were sent out from Kola. The minesweepers *Harrier*, *Hussar* and *Gossamer* lent a hand, but, in spite of every effort, little progress could be made.

The German destroyers established contact with the crippled cruiser and her attendants at 0630 the next morning. *Edinburgh* immediately cast off her tow and worked up to full speed, although she was listing heavily and could not be steered. *Z-24* and *Z-25* failed to find their target, but when *Hermann Schoemann* came out of a snow squall she was met by the full fire of the stricken *Edinburgh*'s armament. The second salvo caught her and put her out of action. Meanwhile the two British destroyers had taken on the two remaining German destroyers. Outgunned, both *Foresight* and *Forester* were disabled. Meanwhile *Edinburgh* had been hit again and was about to break in half. The Germans concentrated on scuttling *Hermann Schoemann* and taking off the crew. They were so busy doing this that they failed to finish off the two British destroyers or to return to the task of annihilating the convoy. To the amazement of the British, the German ships, who then had a perfect opportunity to polish off two more destroyers broke off the action to return to base.

Two convoys which sailed simultaneously at the end of June suffered badly: QP 13, which ran into a 'friendly' minefield and suffered severe losses, and PQ 17, which suffered very severe losses, to which we will return.

On 27 June, when Commodore Dowding was leading PQ 17 out of Reykjavik, bound for Russia, Commodore Gale was leaving Russia in *Empire Selwyn* with QP 13 bound for Iceland, bringing back from Murmansk and Archangel a large convoy of thirty-five ships which had discharged their cargoes and were returning to Iceland, many of them in ballast, others with deck cargoes of timber and pitprops. In these two convoys, PQ 17 and QP 13, seventy merchant ships would pass on opposite courses within a few miles of each other when they skirted the southern edge of the ice-shelf as far north as they dared, and as far away from the German bombers as they could get. The largest national contingent came from America, thirty-five ships, many of them quite recently built, some now well armed but with many inexperienced crews and masters. PQ 17 had no less than twenty-seven warships as her close escort. QP 13 also had a large close escort of fifteen warships and one submarine. The two convoys passed on 2 July. Both had come through days of fog and neither knew exactly where they were. Having seen no sun or stars for several days, they were perforce navigating on dead reckoning, but in spite of these problems, the rendezvous was carried out at the halfway point, when the oiler transferred from the eastbound to the westbound convoy.

First we will follow QP 13. Apart from the weather and fog, this homeward-bound convoy enjoyed an uneventful passage up to 4 July, when the convoy split into two sections. Commodore Gale continued with nineteen ships and turned south for a safe arrival at Loch Ewe. From the safety of the shore it might have appeared that the same simple voyage lay ahead of the other sixteen ships escorted by two of His Majesty's minesweepers, a corvette and two trawlers, under the command of the SOE in

219

HMS *Niger*, bound for Hvalfjördur under acting Commodore J. Hiss, an American who was master of the merchant ship *American Robin*.

It was always an anxious time as convoys approached the land from a passage where murky weather had for several days prevented the navigators from taking star or sun sights to give them an accurate position. Dead reckoning navigation was made more difficult by the very large alterations in magnetic variation which characterize these high northern latitudes. This was Hiss's problem as he closed the coast of Iceland. It was an unusually difficult approach, because there was a British minefield to the north of Iceland, laid to impede the German surface raiders' exit into the Atlantic through the Denmark Strait. Captain Hiss was not a regular Ocean Commodore and this minefield was not marked on his charts.

Niger scouted on ahead to make a positive landfall. She picked up the coastline a mile ahead and signalled the convoy to alter to the west on the last stretch for port. In the murk it looked like land. But it was not land, it was a monstrous iceberg with vast tentacles below the surface. To avoid it the convoy, led by *Niger*, now wheeled away to starboard on a course that led them straight into the minefield. *Niger* blew up. In quick succession another five ships hit mines and were sunk and a seventh was damaged. In the fog, with unexplained explosions all around, confusion reigned. Some of the merchant ships thought that a U-boat attack had polished off the escorts, others that the convoy had run into an ambush of German surface ships. A few realized that they were in the middle of a minefield that was not on their charts. Only HMS *Hussar* knew exactly where she was and where the minefield was; she led the remaining eleven ships out of danger. At enormous risk to herself, *Rosselyn*, the French corvette, spent a hair-raising six and a half hours smelling her way around and into the minefield to pick up 179 survivors, who otherwise would certainly have perished – a heroic action.

We now return to Commodore Dowding and convoy PQ 17. The events leading up to this tragic convoy have been mulled over and discussed by many professional and amateur historians, armchair master mariners and naval captains. Books have been written, a well-publicized libel case has been fought in court and the discussion will doubtless go on and on. The facts are that a convoy of thirty-six merchant ships sailed from Reykjavik bound for Archangel on 27 June, 1942, carrying very important supplies to Russia, acccompanied by a fleet oiler. Two merchant ships turned back before reaching Bear Island. It was very necessary at this time to provide a solid mass of close escorts capable of fighting the ships through the U-boats that were certain to be waiting, and to provide protection from the German high-level bombing, dive-bombing and torpedo-bombing that would be met once east and south of Bear Island. There was an imminent threat from the German heavy ships lurking in the fjords. *Tirpitz* had left her moorings in Trondheim and her whereabouts was not known. *Scheer* and *Lützow* had left Narvik.[13] If – and this was the big if – the heavy German ships put to sea to attack PQ 17, then there was no doubt that support from Home Fleet battleships, an aircraft carrier and escorting submarines and destroyers would be vital if the convoy was to have a reasonable chance of getting through. No such support could reach the convoy in time. The First Sea Lord decided that the German Fleet was making for the convoy and ordered it to disperse and then to scatter.

This chapter is limited to a description of the impact of this decision on the Commodore, Captain J.C.K. Dowding CBE DSO RD RNR, and Convoy Signalman Leslie Thompson. This was the first attempt at a joint Anglo-American force supporting a convoy. The Royal Navy deployed twenty-seven warships around the thirty-six merchant ships. They included three rescue ships fitted with HF/DF, two submarines and a good mix of anti-submarine and anti-aircraft ships, but nothing with any heavy guns. These were provided by Admiral Hamilton's four cruisers (two US Navy) and three destroyers (one US Navy). This force cruised forty miles away to the north, (the opposite side to the probable approach of the enemy), endeavouring to keep in touch using a very ancient Walrus, a joke even in 1942.[14] The First Lord, from the Admiralty bunker in London, could never expect to be in very close touch; even the SOE of the convoy and the Flag Officer commanding the cruiser force disagreed about the actual position of the convoy, estimates varying from ninety-five to twenty miles which are long distances for an eight-knot convoy to cover, and seem even longer when dense fog descends. They also disagreed about the best course for the convoy to follow.

The convoy's departure had been reported by a German agent in Iceland, which was normal, and its progress had been monitored by B-Dienst's decryption of subsequent unwary radio signals. The merchant ships were led by Commodore Dowding, an experienced Commodore who had started his Commodore's career in coastal convoys. He had been promoted to Captain in the Royal Naval Reserve in December, 1940, and had started his duties as an Ocean Commodore in April, 1941. He led the first pair of Arctic convoys, code-named 'Dervish', which reconnoitred the return route to Archangel in August and September, 1941. His ship in convoy PQ 17 was *River Afton*; she had already completed two pairs of convoys, PQ 1 and PQ 13, with Commodore Casey on board. She was a familiar sight unloading in the Russian ports.

On 1 July, after four days at sea and getting near the halfway mark, the convoy was in good heart, having fought off the first U-boat attacks. In the afternoon the first shadowing aircraft appeared. This also was something which every convoy dreaded but expected. On 2 July PQ 17, outward bound, passed QP 13 on its way home. There were attacks from U-boats and from Heinkels on 2 and 3 July, all of which were repelled without loss.

Captain Broome's report on 4 July said, 'My impression on seeing the resolution displayed by the convoy and its escort, provided the ammunition lasted, PQ 17 could get anywhere.'

Although SOE, he could have no knowledge of the uncertainty and painful indecision that now overwhelmed Sir Dudley Pound, the First Sea Lord, and his staff at the Admiralty. The only positive information was that *Tirpitz* had definitely left her moorings at Altenfjord. In the fogs and snow squalls, the German battleship might be anywhere. The Commander-in-Chief had to cover the possibilities that a German raiding force was making for the Denmark Strait to break out into the North Atlantic or that it was setting course to intercept the seventy merchant ships now on their way to and from Russia, or that it was just shifting berth in the fjords. The Arctic Ocean is small in comparison to the Atlantic, but it still covers over five million square miles bordering on the immensely long coastline of Norway, with its scores of fjords in which ships can hide from aircraft. This coastline is often shrouded in fog and snow squalls.

Somebody had to make the decision. On the information in front of him, the First Sea Lord decided that *Tirpitz* and supporting forces were probably at sea on a course to intercept PQ 17, and that the Home Fleet would not be able to get there in time to protect the convoy. If *Tirpitz* found these ships, the supporting cruisers and destroyers would never get within range of her 15-inch guns and would have no chance of protecting their charges. He decided to intervene and to take the action that he thought would best minimize the slaughter of the merchant ships and their escorts if *Tirpitz* got among them. On 3 July, the SOE, Captain Jackie Broome RN, received a signal: SECRET AND IMMEDIATE, OWING TO THREAT FROM SURFACE SHIPS CONVOY IS TO DISPERSE AND PROCEED TO RUSSIAN PORTS; and thirteen minutes later a further signal; SECRET, MOST IMMEDIATE, ADMIRALTY TO ESCORTS OF PQ 17, CONVOY IS TO SCATTER.

The SOE had received not one but two explicit orders to break up his convoy. He had two alternatives: not to obey two clear orders from Admiralty, or, however reluctantly, to conform and to pass on these instructions to the Commodore for action.

Aboard *River Afton*, Leslie Thompson was the nineteen-year-old convoy signalman on watch. He remembers:

> The signal passed to me via the SOE in *Keppel* by Aldis lamp was headed: Most Immediate and Urgent: 'To all ships. Scatter fanwise and proceed independently to your ports of destination.'
>
> As I was on watch I bent on the flags – first flag and pendant eight and called the Commodore and Chief Yeoman to the bridge. They immediately told me to haul it down until they got further confirmation, which caused more confusion than ever.
>
> Eventually I won the argument, but had to pass it to a lot of ships by Aldis Lamp to convince them. That was the last signal made to the convoy apart from wishing all ships good luck.

HMS *Keppel*, the SOE's ship, then closed the Commodore's ship, flying the signal. Neither the Commodore nor his Chief Yeoman could believe their eyes.

Three years of hard-won war experience had taught Dowding and his fellow Commodores that the ships in a convoy must stick together, whatever happened. His unusually strong close escort formed a protective shield round the merchant ships, which the U-boats had not succeeded in penetrating. The anti-aircraft ships and the merchant ships had already proved that they could put up a formidable barrage against air attack. Behind the convoy there were three specialized rescue ships, with doctors and equipment to pick up survivors. Why break up any convoy, let alone this one which had done so well up till then?

The Commodore instructed the Chief Yeoman to confirm the signal, which was now flying at the dip, by Aldis lamp: he did this twice. Eventually Captain Broome brought *Keppel* up alongside *River Afton* and confirmed the instruction by megaphone to Dowding and her master, Captain Charlton, Broome's reported comment, 'It looks like being a bloody business', probably referred to the surface action which he thought would now take place between his destroyers and the mighty armament of eight 15-inch guns carried by the *Tirpitz*, which he thought was just over the horizon. He could imagine no other reason which could justify abandoning the merchant ships in the convoy and breaking up their formation.

The two flags were hoisted close up. When the Commodore ordered 'EXECUTE', convoy signalman Leslie Thompson brought them down with a run. This was the fatal executive signal. Until then the convoy had been a compact, well protected and quite powerful entity: from that moment each merchant ship was on its own. There was not a man in the eight-knot merchant ships who had not seen with his own eyes that the area was swarming with U-boats and who didn't know that they were now within easy range of the German bombers massed in the northern airfields. They too assumed that the German Fleet was at sea with its big guns and watched in horror as the destroyers formed up and disappeared over the horizon, abandoning them to their fate.

The merchant ships made off as fast as they could. They sailed north to the ice to get as far from the German airfields as possible before coming down along the west coast and desolate anchorages of Novaya Zemlya. The small escorting warships followed their orders and made for port. The destroyers and cruisers made off to the west, expecting at any moment to meet the heavy ships of the German Fleet in a bloody battle.

With the signal to scatter, the Commodore ceased to have any responsibility for or authority over the merchant ships. *River Afton* under the command of her Master, Captain Harold Charlton, aimed for the edge of the ice to the north. She didn't get far. Thompson takes up the story:

Within 30 hours of scattering, we heard one after another of ships being bombed and torpedoed and then came our turn. I dumped Confidential Books, (I was on watch once again). I thought immediately of my other signalmen in a cabin below the bridge.

I found the door jammed and the lads who had been sleeping beginning to move around. As the door wouldn't budge I kicked the panel through and they managed to scramble out of the bottom panel. I went with them to our boat station: the boat was already lowered and had DEMS gunners in it. I let the other signalmen go down first in front of me.

The boat was almost in the water – I had one foot on the boat – when a second torpedo hit the ship on the opposite side and our boat disintegrated, emptying its human cargo and carrying them astern. I was the only one to come back up the ladder: although I threw a lifebelt to them, the ship was still doing about 5 knots so they were all swept away.

On climbing back on board there was about ten of us gathered on the midships hatch. We got the Chief Engineer who was badly injured. We put him in a float-type stretcher and fastened all the buckles. Before we could lower him, a third torpedo hit the ship amidships and we were thrown about, as the ship broke in two. A seaman and myself ran towards the bow jumping from one army tank to another. (These were the deck cargo on each side of the forward holds.) On reaching the foremast we used an axe to release the life-rafts: my shipmate had a bottle of rum saved for this occasion which I had to throw to him on the raft. Unfortunately he missed it and it didn't float, as the ship slid below. I swam for the raft, even though I was dressed in duffel coat, seaboots and balaclava.

On boarding the raft with my seaman mate, we proceeded to paddle round to pick up other survivors, including the Chief

Engineer who later died. He already had a broken back. While we were doing this the U-boat surfaced and took two of the lads off one of the rafts and gave them a bottle of water and two black loaves, and asked for the Commodore and the Captain, who couldn't be identified because he was wearing a Louis Mountbatten survival suit, which looked just like a boiler suit in navy blue. The U-boat came around all of the rafts, his machine gunners on the rails each side, trying to identify officers. He spoke excellent English, we thought he was 'Oxford educated'. After his little speech through the tannoy system he said, 'Sorry I can't take any of you off, I have other urgent appointments.'

Then he played the hunting song, 'A'hunting we will go' as he sailed away at about 18 knots. After that we settled down in our heavily laden rafts for the night or even longer: we fastened four rafts together and put our awning up to help avoid the icy wind. The Commodore was on one of the rafts that joined up.

Only life-saving rafts remained afloat for the few men who had survived the torpedoes. They were rough wooden frames containing empty oildrums which provided buoyancy, and an awning, if it could be rigged, gave some inadequate shelter from the Arctic wind, which cut like a knife, but no protection from the icy water. The Commodore, his Chief Yeoman and his surviving convoy signalmen were on four rafts lashed together. The bodies of the survivors on the rafts were out of the water but their legs were in it. Men soon started to die as the seawater penetrated their sodden clothes and ice formed. A thick white fog rose like wisps of steam off the water. Any life that German torpedoes had failed to finish off would shortly be extinguished by the grip of the sub-zero waters.

But *Lotus* had turned back to the westward along the edge of the ice to search for survivors and she was now on her way back to join other warships which were making for the Matochkin Strait in Novaya Zemlya, about as far as they could get in the Barents Sea away from German aircraft and the threat of surface forces.

It was some hours later we sighted the corvette *Lotus*, which had received our distress signal and came back. I signalled with my semaphore flags to do an asdic sweep in case the U-boat was still

226

around, but she came right in and picked us up with scrambling nets. *Lotus* had already picked up a crew from another ship, so you could say 'she was rather crowded'.

The Commodore had seen the outline of a ship coming through the mist and let off a few smoke floats, but they made very little impression as the long Arctic twilight had started to close in and the low-lying sea fog enveloped the rafts. From *Lotus* the lookouts peering through the fog could pick out some little coloured objects apparently floating in the fog. It was enough. Suddenly they resolved into balaclavas being waved by the men in the rafts, and next moment they were amongst them and hauling them on board.

Lotus was now packed with survivors. She had no doctor on board, just an inexperienced sick berth attendant. Conditions were appalling, with every inch of deck space taken up by injured and shattered survivors, many in a very bad way, and too terrified to go below, even in the Arctic cold. The ship's company were hard put to work the ship and get to their action stations. *Lotus* bore the news that *Tirpitz* was at sea. It was a bit of false information which cast further gloom over an apparently hopeless position but at least temporarily seemed a logical reason why the convoy had been ordered to scatter, as it seemed that the Royal Navy's small ships had disappeared in order to take her on.

Lotus, with Commodore Dowding and his surviving signalmen on board, made for the Matochkin Strait, out of range of German aircraft, arriving there at midnight on 6 July to be joined by HM Ships *Lord Austin*, *Lord Middleton* and *Northern Gem*. On that day *Tirpitz* and her destroyers poked their heads out, but were ordered to put back as soon as the Home Fleet was reported, to the disappointment, even fury, of *Tirpitz*'s officers and men.

Tirpitz or no *Tirpitz*, the fate of the merchant ships was sealed. Their tight anti-aircraft and anti-U-boat screen of warships had been broken up, not by a superior force, but by the possibility of a superior force. As isolated units the merchant ships were almost defenceless. One by one they would be picked off either by U-boats or by aircraft.

227

Signalman Thompson continues:

After a 24-hour rest at anchor the Commodore organized a conference aboard *Palomares* and unanimously decided we should sail next day to Archangel. After numerous attacks and ice and fog, we lost two merchant ships from air attacks. Some of these were several hours long, so we were very pleased to have the two A/A ships with us. We were almost in sight of the Russian coast and we in *Lotus* and *Poppy* were dashing around in these attacks, dropping depth-charges as we got sub contacts during the air attacks. We had the greatest admiration for *Lotus'* Captain, his manoeuvring saved the little ship time and time again.

One of the trawlers was on her way back to Iceland with many survivors when the Admiralty ordered her to turn about and make for Archangel: she ended up having to burn furniture and anything else they could find: God knows what they lived on, but they arrived a week or more after everyone else.

Once ashore in Russia, Dowding was in a difficult position and under even more physical and mental pressure than the other survivors. He was a career merchant service officer and naturally sympathetic to the disillusionment of the masters of the merchant ships which had sailed and seen the Royal Navy's warships disappear and abandon them to their fate. One of their colleagues had lost his life. Twenty-two others had lost their ships and were now stranded ashore in Russia with nothing to do. They were in bad shape. The sinking of a ship is a sad and moving moment. To a seaman and particularly the master of a ship, it is the loss of a home and a mistress. Only eleven had brought their ships safe into port. Like many of the crews of the sunken merchant ships, Dowding had finished up in the water. As Commodore, he had had the ghastly duty of passing on the Admiralty's orders for the convoy to scatter, an order that ran contrary to the instinct and inclination of everyone in that armada of ships. However, he held the rank of Captain in the Royal Naval Reserve and even now was one of the most senior officers ashore in Russia.

Although he had not got a convoy any more, he did not stop working after he was picked off his raft and brought into harbour. The load on his shoulders increased as he put to sea again, scurrying from remnant to remnant, restoring order and a semblance of discipline to the scattered ships hiding in the fog and ice in the anchorages of Novaya Zemlya.

His efforts to save ships had not been very successful and he had little to look back on with satisfaction when he climbed on board *Ocean Voice* as Commodore of convoy QP 14 for the return journey with his faithful Yeoman of Signals and team of convoy signalmen, including Leslie Thompson. He heaved a sigh of relief: on the return trip only four ships had been lost to U-boats and aircraft in the thirteen convoys that had sailed home from Russia since the start of the series. Another two or three weeks and he might get home for a few days' leave.

Convoy QP 14 sailed from Archangel on 13 September with fifteen merchant ships, heavily escorted by an equal number of warships in the close screen and a cruiser, an aircraft carrier with thirteen Hurricanes and three Swordfish, an anti-aircraft cruiser, a submarine and seventeen destroyers in support — thirty-six ships to protect fifteen merchant ships, a far cry from the early days when Atlantic convoys had sailed with one sloop to protect twenty or thirty ships.

Cocooned in this impressive protective package, the only immediate apparent threat to the merchant ships lay in the presence of numerous icebergs, and, when visibility permitted, the usual shadowing aircraft. With the ice at its extreme summer limit, the convoy was routed as far north as possible towards Spitzbergen, where the destroyers would refuel. Convoy discipline was not good. *Winston Salem*, a survivor of PQ 17, straggled and lost touch on the first day. Her Master had been sent home suffering from a nervous breakdown after his shattering experiences on convoy PQ 17 and had been replaced. In spite of the impressive escort *Troubador* also lost touch.

A patrolling Catalina reported surfaced U-boats ahead of the convoy, but prejudiced the reception of its report by giving the wrong recognition signal. A Swordfish reported another some distance astern and attacked it.

The comparatively peaceful passage was disturbed by homing signals from another U-boat ahead on 19 September, and it soon became apparent that these were not isolated signals from solitary U-boats on passage but chatter between a large group lying in wait across the convoy's track. The pattern began to emerge: after the German victory in July, it was to be a test case between the German forces trying to inflict maximum damage on the convoy. If the bombers and U-boats could maul this homeward bound convoy as well, even Churchill would have to think again about the feasibility of continuing the Arctic convoys. On the other side the Royal Navy was determined to redeem its reputation.

After seven days of patrolling in the bitter cold, the aircrews of *Avenger*'s aircraft were exhausted. The Sea Hurricanes were not suitable for this work and the open cockpits of the ancient stringbags gave their crews no protection from the weather. (Talk about wind chill!) Admiral Burnett sent *Avenger* home, escorted by *Scylla* and had himself hauled across in a bosun's chair to the destroyer *Milne*.

The first casualty on 20 September was the minesweeper *Leda* at the rear of the convoy, torpedoed by *U-435*. Then the U-boats struck again, hitting the Tribal Class destroyer *Somali*. She did not sink, but the whole compact package around the convoy started to break up as the destroyer *Ashanti* was despatched to take her in tow and others to screen the operation. On 22 September, nine days out and in waters where an undisturbed run to port would be normal, *U-435*, which had been trailing the convoy since sinking *Leda*, got through the screen again and sank three ships: *Bellingham*, ex-PQ 17, the oiler *Gray Ranger* and, cruel stroke, the Commodore's ship *Ocean Voice*, with Dowding aboard, his socks hardly dry from his immersion when leading PQ 17.

There was one casualty, a baby born on this ship, to a Russian delegation woman some days before and now taking passage to UK. All boats got away safely, some picked up by escorts, including Commodore Dowding. The two convoy signalmen went aboard *Zamalek* to continue their journey.

Zamalek had hundreds of survivors on board, a lot of stretcher cases and no food. *Ocean Freedom*, being Vice Commodore, now took charge. Commodore Dowding had made this arrangement before sailing, perhaps because he had a premonition.

The convoy signalmen had a rotten home-coming when they reached port. They fell between two stools: they didn't get the treatment given to the Royal Naval ratings and didn't get the royal reception laid on for once for the DBS. Leslie Thompson continues:

When our small convoy arrived at Loch Ewe we went aboard *Leinster Castle* where we were given good baths and civilian clothes measured up by West End tailors, hair cuts etc, but everything we queued up for we didn't get because we were Royal Navy so we were left to travel in our woollen survivors' gear. On arrival at Glasgow all the merchant navy men were invited to a town hall welcome party and as they went off by luxury coaches. We reported to NCSO. All we got was railway warrants to our base in Liverpool.

After our survivors' leave, we reported back to our office headquarters at Liver Buildings. We saw lists of people who had been awarded medals: our names were not on them. Fourteen medals were to *River Afton* crew and to Commodore Dowding and the Chief Yeoman.

My next convoy after my leave was to Philippeville in North Africa, when I was again torpedoed 3 times in 6 months. It could have been a record. The following year I did another Russian convoy. Rather quiet by then, with Commodore Boucher who was a real gentleman. On returning home he called me into the office to tell me he was recommending me for a mention in despatches for my conduct throughout, but I still had no confirmation of this.

There was a lighter side to our convoy work, when I sailed to Canada, America, and West Africa, living very well compared with our folks at home.

Commodore Dowding had been torpedoed and lost his ship on two successive convoys. He is described as:

a very able officer but a bit remote from his staff preferring to give all his orders through his Chief Yeoman who was RNR. Commodore Dowding I admired for his determination to stay with the convoy even when he was offered a flight home to UK, as convoys had been cancelled indefinitely: he refused the chance and said, 'As long as ships are there I will stay to form a convoy.'

231

Leslie Thompson, who served with him as a convoy signalman and in the course of his duty hoisted one of the best known signals in the history of the Royal Navy, had been torpedoed five times, and had gone back to sea, all before his twenty-first birthday. But when he applied to the Admiralty for the Russian Convoy Medal, to which he surely was entitled, he was told that he couldn't have one because there were not enough medals to go round. Disgusted at this mean treatment, a friend acquired one for him from a medal merchant over fifty years later.

The pressures on Allied shipping continued to get worse. The entry of the Americans into the war had increased the load enormously. The preparations for the landings in North Africa, in itself another huge maritime commitment, made it impossible to continue simultaneously with a regular succession of Russian convoys. Whether or not to sail PQ 18 after the losses in eight out of the last ten convoys was a crunch decision. Forty-nine merchant ships and ten warships, including two cruisers had gone down. It was plain that surface ships without strong air cover could not be sailed into the reach of the Luftwaffe airfields without the high probability of further heavy losses which could seriously injure the Allied Navies' strength, not only in the Arctic but also in other vital spheres.

Another slaughter like PQ 17 could not be borne and might damage relationships with both Russia and the United States further, perhaps beyond repair, putting the credibility of the Royal Navy into question. The Home Fleet's priority in August shifted to getting a convoy through to Malta (with serious losses), and no convoys were run to Russia in that month.

However, there was a fleet of laden merchant ships waiting to sail in American ports and Iceland. There were ships and men, including hundreds of survivors, languishing ashore in Russia. Their enforced stay in a hostile and barren environment was becoming dangerous, and they were badly needed for the new ships.

The Prime Minister pressed the Admiralty to 'fight another large convoy through', using all available aircraft carriers to provide air cover while running the gauntlet of the full length of the north coast of Norway, all the German airfields, the lurking

German Fleet and the U-boat concentrations. The Naval Staff had a hard time with him and it is greatly to their credit that they diverted him from this rash attempt. Even Churchill couldn't persuade or bludgeon the admirals into risking the Navy's full aircraft carrier resources in a foolhardy gamble to satisfy the Russians. Instead they set about another formidable task as an alternative – to build up a balanced force of Catalinas, Hampden torpedo bombers and reconnaissance Spitfires in North Russia. They succeeded against all difficulties, but at some cost in lives and in aircraft. On their 2000-mile journey eight of the thirty-two Hampden torpedo bombers were lost and the Russians made a further demonstration of their friendly cooperation by sending back the medical unit in the next convoy home, while they grabbed and held fast for their own use its medicines and stores.

Tirpitz, *Scheer* and *Hipper* were now based in Narvik, *Scheer* and *Hipper* had made sorties through the Barents Sea and beyond Novaya Zemlya, laying mines as far into Russian waters as 100 degrees East and seventy-eight degrees North. The US battleship *Washington* and her four destroyers had been with-drawn from the Home Fleet, but had been replaced by *King George V*.

In the end it was a political decision to sail convoy PQ 18, and an Admiralty priority, influenced by the need to restore the Royal Navy's credibility in the eyes of the Americans and the men of the merchant service, not to mention the self-respect of the Royal Navy itself. Whatever happened, the merchant ships and their cargoes must get through.

Bodham-Whetham in *Temple Arch* was chosen for the job of Commodore. Rear-Admiral E.K. Bodham-Whetham, to give him his full title, had retired on 1 August, 1939, but came back almost immediately as one of the first Ocean Commodores. He had plenty of hard experience in the job, going back to the first days of the war in November, 1939, when he sailed in *Glenport* with a convoy of twenty-eight ships, most of them in ballast. It had taken him the whole of the first night and until noon the next day to form up the convoy in its eight columns. Three days later, in a full gale, the ships started to get hopelessly out of station. On that occasion, the ship which the Naval Control

Service had allocated to him, and which was supposed to be the guide of the convoy, became unmanageable and impossible to steer. She would not answer her helm; the bows would not come up into the wind, and he was forced to wear ship, (turn before the wind through an almost complete circle), which took him thirty minutes and left the convoy leaderless. In a spell of bad weather that convoy took twenty-four hours to cover forty miles.

The C-in-C adopted a completely new approach to the protection of PQ 18. His problem was to get thirty-nine merchant ships, a rescue ship and three oilers, with three minesweepers, over a route of 2,300 miles with minimum loss. He deployed a close escort of nineteen small warships, a mixture of destroyers, corvettes, minesweepers and trawlers around the convoy to provide an anti-submarine fence. Inside this fence, for the first time ever on these convoys, an escort carrier, HMS *Avenger* and her two destroyers sailed in the rear ranks astern of the merchant ships. The main power was provided by the Fighting Destroyer Force, the cruiser *Scylla*, sixteen destroyers and three more cruisers. At the ready, but still an awfully long way away in Iceland, lay the battleships *Anson*, *Duke of York*, and the cruiser *Jamaica*, their screen pared down to only five destroyers. Six submarines patrolled off the coast of Norway. Two fleet oilers and their escorting four destroyers waited in Spitzbergen. That a total of sixty-one warships were deployed to protect a convoy of thirty-nine merchantmen is a clear indication of the Admiralty's determination to get this convoy through. It is also an outstanding example of the awesome power of the Royal Navy at that time when called upon in an emergency.

The Commander-in-Chief, Admiral Tovey, relied on the fighting power of the Destroyer Fighting Force, and the aircraft carrier. This force was commanded by Admiral Burnett, a typical ex-destroyer officer, as was the Commodore, in the powerful new cruiser *Scylla*, whose station was at the head of the column of ships adjacent to the Commodore. As a last resort, using the loud hailer was the most direct and simple way of minimizing communication difficulties that were the rule in the Arctic murk.

The convoy sailed on 2 September, routed as far north as the

234

ice would allow, in spite of the extra distance. Through B-Dienst these plans were known to the Germans. They had brought up forty-two HE 111s from Norwegian bases and thirty-five JU 88 torpedo-bombers all the way from France, planning to attack at high level and low level simultaneously, a technique designed to confuse the anti-aircraft defences and to make it very difficult for any aircraft support to deal with both attacks at the same time.

On 13 September, 150 miles north-west of Bear Island and 450 miles north of the German airfields, the shadowers arrived and the air attacks started. They were at first ineffective, but the intensity and determination of the Luftwaffe pilots built up to a climax when a wave of forty JU 88 torpedo bombers came in on the starboard bow. The Commodore ordered an emergency turn together forty-five degrees to port. Eight of the ten columns turned and emerged unscathed.

The fog of war defeated the two starboard wing columns, who never executed the turn and were annihilated in seven minutes. Eight ships went down: only one, *Mary Luckenbach*, survived, but she had not long to live.

The whereabouts of *Tirpitz* was not known; she had been lost to our reconnaissance planes from 14 to 18 September. Later it was learnt that Hitler's personal instructions to Admiral Raeder to take no risks and two feint sorties by the Home Fleet had kept her in port once again. She was exercising inside the fjord while the battle went on at sea.

The convoy was subjected to sporadic attacks from the air and from U-boats right up to the time when they were entering the White Sea. Thirteen ships were lost, ten to aircraft and three to U-boats, but twenty-seven of the ships that sailed arrived in Archangel on 17 September. The Luftwaffe had thrown their full strength against the ships but had lost forty aircraft; and three U-boats had been sunk. This was a severe blow to the Allies and to the Russians, but it had done the Germans a lot of damage too, and the convoy had held together. The crack German torpedo bombers had done their worst in one of the rare occasions when they cooperated fully with Dönitz' U-boats.

But it was a final flash in the pan for the Germans. Shortly afterwards the priorities changed and the crack squadrons were transferred to the Mediterranean. On the Arctic convoys the Luftwaffe and U-boat arms never again got their act together with such effect.

The enemy's assaults on the convoy at sea ceased, but, as the convoy came into soundings, once again the Arctic maritime hazards were waiting to trap the unwary seaman approaching his moorings. The leading lights that should have been lit to guide the arriving merchant ships over the bar of the River Dvina were not operating.

Did the ghost of Nelson whisper in Admiral Bodham-Whetham's ear 'Anchor Hardy! Anchor!'?

A gale blew up. The ships anchored in the mouth of the river, but five ships dragged their anchors and drove up onto a lee shore, where they were attacked again by JU 88s. Those that survived this final hazard ran straight into a full-scale air raid on the town.

When the ships were finally off-loaded a month later for once a big banquet was thrown by the Russians. But Commodore Bodham-Whetham was too exhausted to attend. He returned to active service, but never recovered his full health after that convoy and died in hospital in Gibraltar on 27 March, 1944, having completed thirty-five ocean convoys in his thirty-six months in harness. In most records, for some reason, he is not listed among the select band of commodores who lost their lives during the Second World War, perhaps because he didn't die at sea.

After QP 14 and PQ 18 no more convoys sailed to or from Russia until the long nights of winter in November and December. The codes for these convoys altered to RA homeward and JW outward. In December the great victory by Admiral Fraser when he sunk *Scharnhorst* in the Battle of the Barents Sea finally swung the balance in favour of the Allies. The Heinkels and JU 88s had been relocated to the Mediterranean to support Hitler's armies in North Africa; the warship escorts were now supported by aircraft carriers sailing in the convoys and, after March, 1943, the U-boats had lost much of their drive, following their trouncing in the Battle of the Atlantic. The hazards reverted to an on-going struggle against the cold, the blizzards and the

236

navigational problems of the Norwegian Sea. The commodores came to do their stint of a pair of convoys, one out and one back.

So ended one of the hardest fought series of battles in the long history of the Royal Navy. As in the Mediterranean, no convoy could be slipped through by cunning evasive routeing. Each convoy had to fight against an enemy on the sea, under the sea and in the air. In addition each convoy to Russia had also to fight against ice and fog, both of which took their toll.

The handling of the ships and their escorts were feats of seamanship and considerable naval operations in their own right. Twenty-six Commodores, each assisted by a Yeoman of Signals and a tiny staff of very young convoy signalmen, had led the convoys. There were many inexperienced American officers and crews in newly launched Liberty ships which presented additional problems. There was a dreadful period in the long Arctic summer days of 1942, between March and September, when the battle hung in the balance, but at the end 97.2% of the ships completed their journeys: The merchant ships were manned by seamen and officers of many countries. At the start, most of the merchant ships were British. In the later months, most of them were American, but it was not uncommon to find the ships in the convoys manned by crews from a dozen different countries, – Americans, British, Belgians, Canadians, Chinese, Dutch, Estonians, Frenchmen, Indians, Irishmen, Lascars, Norwegians, Panamanians, Poles, and Russians. Their courage and endurance was put to the test on countless occasions and in the end the spirit of the seamen won through. The protection of the convoys on their journeys was almost exclusively provided by the Royal Navy, and in numbers of lives lost, if this is a measure, theirs was the greatest sacrifice.

POSTSCRIPT

Few ships were engaged from the start of the Arctic convoys through the rough days from September, 1941, into the quieter convoys of 1944, when casualties were no longer so horrific. Among the exceptions were His Majesty's minesweepers *Britomart*, *Hussar* and *Salamander*, which had swept the channels and escorted ships in the Russian convoys since day one with 'Dervish' and PQ1, and then formed part of the First Minesweeping Flotilla based at Kola. They were familiar sights to all the ships in the northern convoys, and it was because of their unrelenting accuracy that not one ship was lost to mines in Russian waters, in spite of the Germans' efforts by mine-laying aircraft, U-boats and the minelayer *Ulm*. They were fine, versatile seaboats and manned by very tough battle-hardened reserve ratings and officers. All three not only survived PQ 17, but were busy for many days afterwards at sea rounding up the surviving merchant ships that had sheltered around Novaya Zemlya and taken refuge in the Matochkin Strait. *Britomart* then joined the Russian White Sea Squadron in the Kara Sea, providing minesweeping and anti-submarine protection for the ships that the Russians' icebreakers forced through the Siberian waters during June and July of 1943.

They went on to escort the RA and JW convoys until the priority shifted to the English Channel and the Normandy invasion in the summer of 1944. The three ships then formed part of the minesweeping force that cleared the way for the landings.

In August, 1944, they were sweeping off Arromanches, enjoying the unusual luxury and contrast of the warm sun.

Hands on deck waved at an RAF plane as it flew over. Soon afterwards, without warning, a formation of Typhoon fighter-bombers came out of the sun and in a series of attacks blew *Hussar* and *Britomart* out of the water and damaged *Salamander* beyond repair. Some of the few survivors left in the sea drifted towards the land and were then killed by shell fire from German shore batteries.

NOTES

Chapter One (pp 1–7)

1. The position has not altered. In the closing decade of the twentieth century over 90% of Britain's trade by volume is still carried by sea. But most of it is under 'Flags of Convenience' as the Red Ensign disappears from the oceans of the world.
2. PRO CAB 3/8 CID 316A
3. To pass the time, and 'for exercise', guns' crews would carry out target practice at mines drifting around afloat and unattached. In some areas this might happen daily, or even several times daily. The mines were also there at night and in confused seas were unlikely to be seen. The Navy's escort ships had enough men to provide a continuous watch of lookouts, whereas the merchant ships carried minimum crews and any increase in manpower was unacceptable to the owners.
4. See Chapters 8 and 13 on Liberty Ships and Arctic convoys.
5. B. Perrett, *A City At War*.
6. PRO ADM 1 15675.

Chapter Two (pp 8–22)

1. What is a Commodore? The rank is first encountered in the Royal Navy after the accession of William III. It is derived from the Dutch 'Kommadeur', modified to 'Commadore' and was later established as 'Commodore'. It became a rank granted to an officer in command of a small squadron who had a second captain in his ship, with entitlement to fly a white broad pennant with a blue cross. The distinction between a Commodore 1st Class and a Commodore 2nd Class was never very clear. Anson sailed from England in 1740 as a Commodore 2nd Class in charge of six small warships, two supply ships and 1500 men, 500 of whom were Chelsea pensioners. 1300 of his force perished

from disease. On his return journey he promoted himself to the 1st Class by promoting his First Lieutenant to be Captain. Two classes of commodore were officially recognized in the regulations of 1824. An Admiralty order of 26 September, 1958, refers to Queen's Regulations and Admiralty Instructions Article 0123: it abolishes the distinction between 1st and 2nd Class and states:

> 'In future officers will be appointed as Commodore and this will be equated for all purposes to the present Commodore 2nd Class.'

The rank has always been a temporary, non-substantive rank, going with the job. In the Second World War a Commodore was senior to a captain and junior to a Rear Admiral. In any case, more through good-will and common sense than through a good structure and clear chain of command, the question of rank didn't cause problems, although the Senior Officer of the Escort Group was in command of the convoy, he was nearly always junior to the convoy commodore.
Abstracts from Instructions in ADM 199 5.

> The convoy is under the command of the senior officer of the escorting warships [SOE], while they are present.

> ### Commodore of the convoy
> The direct charge of the conduct manoeuvring and general proceedings of the convoy will be vested in the Commodore of the Convoy who will sail in one of the merchant ships of the convoy and be responsible to the Senior Officer of the escort for everything appertaining to ships in convoy. In the absence of an escort he will take the entire command. (But see below).
> The Vice-Commodore will take over the duties of the Commodore, should the latter be incapacitated or be absent from the convoy for any reason.
> Should both the Commodore and the Vice-Commodore be absent from the convoy, the Rear Commodore (who may be the master of a merchant ship), or the ship detailed will take full command.
> Masters are always responsible for the safe navigation and handling of their own ships.

Noon Position. Each master will keep his own reckonings. All ships will hoist their noon position (convoy time) at 1300, unless otherwise ordered by the Commodore.

All ships must take in the Commodore's Noon position, which is the reference position of the day.

To confuse matters further, since a convoy was defined as one or more merchant ships escorted by one or more warships, if no warship was present the convoy ceased to exist.

2. In 1877, the year before this Commodore was born, there had been a strong move in Parliament to abolish flogging with the cat-o'-nine tails. The Naval Discipline Act declared that a sailor could be flogged for 'any act, disorder or neglect, to the prejudice of good order and Naval discipline'. The move was defeated in the House of Commons with the help of some ancient Admirals who reckoned that flogging was necessary to prevent mutiny. Mutiny was defined as 'insolence, desertion, rudeness, disobeying the commander, or striking a petty officer'. Although flogging had fallen into disuse, the Admiralty refused to give up the right to use it in wartime until 29 March, 1939.

3. This attitude persisted for a long time. The writer remembers a speech day at Pangbourne College in the 1960s. To the dumbfounded amazement of the cadets, their teachers and their parents, the guest speaker, an enormously distinguished and successful Field Marshal, in full regalia, told the officers of the future who had already had four years of preparation for their life at sea, that they now had four main responsibilities: to own up, pay up, put up and shut up. He elaborated by explaining that they must own up when they made a mistake, pay up for all the advantages of education that had been thrust upon them, put up with whatever treatment they might receive, and keep their mouths shut. If they have followed his instructions on points 3 and 4, they have perhaps contributed to the disappearance of the British merchant service referred to above.

4. Jago's Mansion was the name for Devonport naval barracks.

5. The model for this part of the Fighting Commodore's life is the early career of Vice Admiral Sir Gilbert Stephenson KBE CB CMG, who served as a Convoy Commodore from September, 1939, in six ocean convoys. He set up the Western Approaches establishment at Tobermory, training 1132 ship's companies. Over 200,000 men passed through his hands there before going to sea in the Battle of the Atlantic.

243

His brilliant contribution to the victory of the escorts in the Second World War is fully described in Richard Baker's book *The Terror of Tobermory*, W.H. Allen, 1972.

6. He was instructed in the system of gunnery control which was modified only slightly after Jutland and taught, nearly 40 years later in the Second World War, to gunnery control officers in convoy escorting warships, although it was useless in the many surface actions at night or, in reduced visibility, against U-boats. In practice every gun in every ship, including merchant ships, loosed off as many rounds as possible without much idea where they were going, and everybody was happy so long as the requisite number of dull red glows on the enemy's hulls indicated that hits on the enemy were being registered.

7. See page 296, *The Sea Heritage*, Admiral Sir Frederic Dreyer's autobiography.

Chapter Three (pp 23–32)

1. The convoy Commodore flew a fish-tailed pennant, (a broad pennant) with a blue cross on a white background.

2. This was an early example of the conflicts that arose between masters of the merchant ships and the Commodores who sailed in them. With all his seniority and experience, the commodore had, in theory, no authority over the handling and navigation of the ship in which he was carried, which could and did give rise to difficult situations, because the Commodore's ship was Guide of the Fleet, the ship on which all others had to keep station. It was a very serious matter of which the Commodore made light, at any rate in his report.

3. It is said that when the depot ship HMS *Tyne* attempted to move from her moorings in Scapa Flow, where she had lain so long as an invaluable depot ship, she was found to be aground on gin bottles, a rumour no doubt spread by the lower deck men who only drank rum.

4. For this information I am indebted to Mrs Peggy Matthews, who allowed me to study the extensive records compiled by her husband, the late Len Matthews, a convoy Yeoman of Signals with a remarkable record, and to Tom Bainbridge, another consig, who continued this work after the war and has compiled comprehensive files giving details of consigs who passed through these courses, including names, dates and service numbers.

Len was more fortunate, or more cautious, than Tom Bainbridge, who also jotted down a rough record of the convoys in which he served.

When ashore waiting for another trip, one of the shore-based staff happened to notice his scribbles and reported this. He was 'in the rattle' at once and sent to 'chokey' for his sins, a very humiliating, uncomfortable and cold experience, with a hard bed, basic food and water and one blanket in mid-winter. The operation of the security regulations was very unfair: it is obvious to the reader of this book that many people, from admirals downwards, kept diaries without retribution. Indeed personal diaries kept by three convoy commodores can be studied by anyone in the Imperial War Museum in London.

Chapter Four (pp 33–46)

1. All this 'navigation made easy' depends on American satellite systems over which the British have no control. The Americans can alter the degree of accuracy, or deny access entirely, whenever they wish. The satellites are also destroyed by solar storms, the severity of which vary over an eleven-year cycle. The whole of the city of Quebec suffered a blackout in 1989 when its power network was paralysed by a solar storm attacking the earth's magnetic field.

2. Rescue Ships, properly fitted out to pick up survivors, with doctors on board to give them medical assistance, were attached to later convoys.

3. It has been argued that the Royal Navy was slow to learn this lesson and, before Admiral Stephenson set up the Western Approach training base at Tobermory, we were making the mistake of sending escorts to sea before they were ready to operate as teams. It can also be argued that, since the Battle of the Atlantic was always a race against time, with one side and then the other leading, Dönitz erred on the side of perfection.

4. In June, 1940, Admiral Gensoul, commanding the French fleet at Mers-el-Kebir, near Oran, was given the alternatives of sailing with the British, turning his ships over to the British, sinking them or sailing them to the West Indies for the duration of the war. He turned down all four options, so the British Force H, under Vice-Admiral Sir James Somerville, opened fire and destroyed or severely damaged all but one of the French ships.

5. Later Creighton commented that 'the priest told them his prayers had been answered from above and they would all survive the journey. To some that might appear pathetic. But I don't think his work was in

vain. He may have comforted people so that when the sea swept the life out of them they were at peace in their minds.'

Chapter Five (pp 47–74)

1. The Yantlet Gate is named after a sandbank in the Thames estuary near the anchorage where the ships mustered for convoys. The entrances to the Port of London were barred by booms and nets. A small 'gate' was opened and closed by boom defence vehicles to allow passage of ships.

2. PRO ADM 1/15675, letter from C-in-C Western Approaches to the Secretary of the Admiralty dated 7 September, 1944.

3. Acoustic mines were set off by the sound of a ship's propellers or machinery passing over them. Magnetic mines could be set to explode by the magnetic fields of ships passing over them. Because of their knowledge of the waters and seamen's skills in handling fishing nets and trawls, most of the crews manning the minesweepers were fishermen and trawlermen, with officers who came from the RNR or from the fishing fleets. Theirs was a particularly unpleasant task, but without them convoys could not have left port and the East Coast ports, including the Port of London, would have become unusable.

4. The LL (Double L) sweeper towed two electric cables astern, generating strong magnetic fields.

5. 'The Coal-Scuttle Brigade' was the nickname given to the colliers which continued to supply the power stations of the south, even when all other traffic had been stopped in the English Channel.

6. Commander Knapp, a highly experienced and efficient officer, was involved in a similar incident, the mining of SS *Dagenham* on 16 November, 1940. In his report he says, 'From the experience of the mining, both of this ship and the *Houston City*, there is no doubt that a little more action in attempting to stop water entering these vessels by their crews might well have saved both of them. There appears to be no organization for damage control and no equipment kept ready for stopping leaks. In the case of *Dagenham*, this ship continued to steam for some twenty minutes, and about five minutes after the explosion *Dagenham* reported no hull damage. Engine room subsequently flooded through leaks in the tunnel door and fractured condenser door. Condenser inlets were apparently not closed. My First Lieutenant and Engineer Officer were sent over but by the time they arrived, it was too late.'

Source notes (pp. 64–86)

Conditions aboard these hard-run old merchant ships were very different to those aboard the heavily manned and trained warships. In merchant ships the officers and crew were cut down to a minimum and had not joined, and were not trained, to fight a war. Commander Knapp's comments are an example of the great gap in understanding that could exist between the Royal Navy and the Merchant Service, particularly in the smallest and over-worked ships.

7. Confidential Book '*Manual Of Smoke Signals – 1940*'.

8. A modern lifeboat would halve this time.

9. A make and mend was a time for the ship's company to dance and skylark. At sea, at least one third of the hands were always on watch on deck at their cruising stations, in the engine room, round the guns and the depth charges, or on lookout, and there was room below to sling a hammock. But once in harbour, there wasn't enough room for all the hands to sling their hammocks. They slept where they fell – on and under the mess tables, on the locker tops or in the passageways. The knowledgeable stayed on deck, cocooned in their duffel coats, clustered round the warmth at the base of the funnels, not much better off than tramps.

Chapter Six (pp 75–91)

1. Lemp was in command of *U-110* and lost his life when it was captured by HMS *Bulldog* and the Enigma code machine was taken out before the U-boat sank.

2. To comply with the Prize Regulations merchant ships could only be 'defensively' armed, which meant that no guns could be fitted that could be fired forward of the beam. The same regulations laid down that a U-boat should surface and then halt and examine its prize and cargo. If satisfied that it was entitled to sink the ship, it must first ensure the safety of all on board. Although these regulations were soon generally ignored, the Trade Division of the Admiralty, when fitting guns on merchant ships, still stuck to this restriction on merchant ships' armament. The lack of means to fight back was a lasting source of dissatisfaction to merchant seamen and led to incidents when ships refused to sail without guns of some sort. Admiral Sir Frederic Dreyer, who was one of the first ocean convoy commodores and deeply conscious of the wonderful work of the Merchant Service, was appointed Inspector of Merchant Navy Gunnery in early 1940, but plans laid at his suggestion in peacetime took years to implement. It

was a mammoth task, both to find the guns, and then to fit them. Although a lot depended on the wonderful service given by Dutch and Norwegian ships sailing in the transatlantic convoys, as late as August 1940, for instance, Dutch seamen refused to sail from Canadian ports without a gun, and Norwegians without a promise of one.

3. The last ship of SC 7 to be sunk went down at 0504. *Leith* could not know that *U-99* was already on her way back to Lorient to stock up with more torpedoes and that others of the wolf pack had broken off to chase HX 79 where a further massacre was about to take place.

4. Some, but not all, shipowners recognized their crews sacrifices in a tangible form. The generous owners of *Trident* gave the crew a £5 bonus and three days' leave, and their officers £10.

Chapter Seven (pp 92–107)

1. Analysis with access to German records has shown that the bombing of industrial targets in Germany was unproductive or even counter-productive. German industrial productivity improved as bombing was intensified. The bombing of the U-boat pens was also counter-productive: it was left too late, until the concrete had set, and served only to impose great hardship on the French population and the towns in the vicinity of the shelters. The Allied bombing did not penetrate the layers of concrete once it was set and no U-boats were sunk or seriously damaged once home.

2. In HMS *Valorous* on the east coast convoys, as a further check on any serious straggler, the Doctor and Asdics Operator, armed with stop-watches, took the merchant ship's 'pulse' by listening to the noise of the propellers and signalling results to the Master, much to the annoyance of the Chief Engineer. If that didn't do the trick, the Commanding Officer, Lieutenant-Commander Wentworth Fitzroy RN, played the sound of the heart beat back to the ship over the loud-hailer.

3. This information is based on *The Sea Heritage*, Admiral Dreyer's autobiography.

4. This injustice, under which the contract, and so the pay, of those serving in the merchant service ended when their ship went down, was not remedied until 1 July, 1943.

5. There were strong indications that Hitler and Dönitz had passed on verbal orders, or at the least very strong hints, that U-boats should not pick up merchant ship survivors, except masters and chief engineers,

but this suggestion was never proved, even under intensive interrogation at the Nuremberg trials. One U-boat Commander only was found guilty of shooting survivors in the water after a sinking. He was tried and executed. U-boats, in any case, had little enough space for their own crews, and certainly would not have been able to carry numerous prisoners on extended patrols.

6. *Everleigh* survived until 6 February, 1945, when she was torpedoed off Cherbourg with the loss of six crew.

7. The International Mercantile Marine Officers' Association, International Transport Workers Federation and the Allied Shipowners (Personnel) Committee in Britain combined to put forward strong recommendations to prevent this, but failed.

8. Captain Richard H. Oland OBE RCN started the Naval Boarding Service and died on 7 September, 1941. His work was carried on and expanded by Commander F.B. Watt RCN who describes the history of the NBS in his book *In All Respects Ready*.

9. It is not clear whether the Chinese picked up this addiction from British Trades Unions or vice-versa.

Chapter Eight (pp 108–115)

1. The last seagoing Liberty Ship sailed across the Atlantic in June, 1994, under the command of Captain Jahal. She was moored in the River Thames by the Tower of London. Built for a life of five years, she had survived fifty. Visitors on board were most impressed by her immaculate turnout, attributable to the enthusiasm and hard work of her American volunteer crew.

2. This was a North Atlantic convoy. Many similarly ill-equipped Liberty Ships sailed on the Arctic convoys, another 1400 miles further north, where the sea conditions rank amongst the worst in the world.

Chapter Nine (pp 116–127)

1. The number of operational U-boats reached a peak of 240 in May, 1943.

2. Group Streitax: *U-103, 510, 509, 572, 134, 409, 203, 604, 659.*

3. The introduction of the fourth wheel increased the time to test by a factor of 26. The new code book was captured by HMS *Petard* when she sank *U-559* on 30 October, but it was not until 13 December that Bletchley had broken the code again, with a huge backlog of signals to

decypher, interpret and analyse. A small percentage contained vital information, but which were they? At this point Winn, the key man at Bletchley Park, collapsed from exhaustion.

4. This account was given to the author by Nobby Clarke in 1996 and is the verbatim transcript of an interview which he gave to the BBC.

5. Account by R. Borrer in April, 1989.

6. In fact twelve ships were sunk. *Anglo Maersk* was torpedoed but made it to Lisbon with forty-eight survivors on board.

Chapter Ten (pp 128–143)

1. Dönitz blamed the fall in sinkings in the second half of December on the weather, which was atrocious, even by normal Atlantic standards. The wind force reached or exceeded Force 7 on the Beaufort Scale 100 days out of 150. Dönitz recorded that the U-boats found they were hard put to remain at sea or to carry out any methodical system of search.

2. The statistics in this section are based on 'OIL', Payton-Smith, HMSO, 1971.

3. Files relevant to convoy TM 1 are contained in the PRO series ADM 199 223.

4. PRO ADM 199 series. January 1943 Monthly Anti-submarine Report.

5. *Albert L. Ellsworth* was sunk at 1743 on 9 January by *U-436*.

6. Both were finished off by *U-522* that evening.

7. It took two more torpedoes from *U-442* to sink her nearly twelve hours later.

8. Dönitz was surprisingly unenthusiastic about these results, perhaps because the U-boat commanders were making wildly optimistic claims. In this case they claimed to have torpedoed fourteen tankers of 141,000 tons. *German Naval History*, Volume 11, section 290, reports, 'The F.O.U-boats considered the results generally satisfactory as more than 100 hours had elapsed between the original sighting and the contact.' He also says that the convoy escort was 'unpracticed and lacking in perseverance, consisting of old gun-boats and corvettes.'

9. *Empire Lytton* (Captain John Andrews) was delayed at the start of the journey, and her master's duties as Acting Commodore were taken by Captain A. Laddle, *Oltenia II*, (second choice), torpedoed on 3 January. Captain J.D. Millar was the second acting commodore in *British Dominion* (third choice), sunk just after midnight on night of

10/11 January. There is no record of a third Acting Commodore (fourth choice) when only two ships remained. All these officers were experienced and reliable masters of tankers, but none of them held the rank of Ocean Commodore (Commodore 2nd Class Royal Naval Reserve). The losses in this convoy demonstrated painfully that the job of an Ocean Commodore required skills, knowledge and authority beyond those required for the day-to-day running of a tanker.

Chapter Eleven (pp 144–176)

1. *Bloody Winter* p. 24, and Roskill, Vol 1, p. 457 Note 2.
2. Between June, 1940, and September 1946. Commander Watt RCN's people had boarded over 50,000 ships.
3. Vice Admiral Egerton's diary is in the Imperial War Museum.
4. As the war went on, Dönitz got the balance between training and front-line operations wrong. Except for a period between October, 1942, and July, 1943, there were more boats in trials and training than operational. After August, 1943, the proportions got worse and worse. By December, 1943, there were two boats under training to each one operational. The U-boat fleet reached its peak strength of 459 in March, 1945, but by then only one in three (160) were operational: 299 were in trials, or on training duties. When the U-boats hauled down their flags, the Germans had a great fleet of very powerful boats devoting their time to trials and training when many of them might have been creating havoc cutting their communications from America to the Allied invasion armies in Europe.
5. *Soekaboemi* was sunk a few hours later by another torpedo from *U-441*.
6. Neither were credited as kills when the records were examined.
7. An HF/DF bearing from a ship at sea or from any one of the shore stations that circled the North Atlantic gave a single line of bearing. Two or more nearly simultaneous bearings were needed for 'fixes' which varied in accuracy. The specialist officers carried in some ships could also estimate distances by the strength of the signal and deduce the amount and nature of activity from the volume and characteristics. Routine daily reports had a standard format, giving, for example, position, course and speed, torpedo, food and fuel state, as did sighting and attack reports. Experienced interceptors could recognize

individual operators by telltale 'handwriting' in the morse transmissions. It is interesting to note that they could often recognize a German from an Italian operator. One was tense, demanding and abrupt, the other flowing, elegant and laid back. As mentioned, *Toward* had left her specialist officer behind, but her HF/DF reports were nevertheless very valuable.

8. New Edition, 1943. A U-boat commander was expected to be able to recite the contents from memory. Wartime translation by the US Navy.

9. International law permits this ruse provided that fire is not opened while flying false colours. For example HMS *Campbeltown* flew the German naval flag on the St Nazaire raid in an attempt to delay momentarily the land batteries from opening fire as she came up the estuary leading to the dock gates. When fired upon she immediately switched back to the white ensign, before returning the fire. With all the daily atrocities of the Battle of the Atlantic and disregard for international law, it is strange to see signals dealing with protocol given immediate priority.

10. PRO reports on interviews with German prisoners from *U-202* when sunk by HMS *Starling*. Fighting Captain.

11. This was one of the most important events in the Second World War and was of enormous value to all naval operations. For example, within a few weeks the three supply ships and six tankers strategically placed to replenish *Bismarck* and *Prinz Eugen*, and U-boats in a breakout into the Atlantic were eliminated.

12. Testimony at Nuremberg.

Chapter Twelve (pp 177–199)

1. Roskill, Vol 2, p. 355.

2. Her fate was a mystery for many years but German records show that she was probably sunk when sailing independently on 19 March by *U-663*, after the storm broke up SC 122.

3. The number of U-boats engaged at any time varied: they came and went, either from the need to replenish torpedoes or to refuel from the two milch cows which accompanied them, or by falling behind and losing touch.

4. FAT torpedoes ran at thirty knots for a set distance and then started to zigzag across the course of the convoy, on the chance of hitting any one of the merchant ships.

Chapter Thirteen (pp 200–237)

1. Rear Admiral Bonham-Carter in early 1942 after the loss of the cruisers *Edinburgh* and *Trinidad*. Five ships had been sunk under him.
2. *History of United States Naval Operations in World War II* by S.E. Morison, Volume I, page 374.
3. Commodore Leir spurned the comfort of the room provided for Ocean Commodores waiting for their convoys in the luxury of the Adelphi Hotel in Liverpool, using lodging rooms. On one occasion he turfed the duty signalman out of his bunk in the Liver Buildings head-quarters for a night's sleep before he put to sea.
4. But of these gallant old seadogs who led the Arctic convoys, two more were not to survive the war. Commodore Bodham-Whetham died ashore in Gibraltar in March, 1944, after an illness, and Commodore Gale had only four months to live before he lost his life in the North Atlantic in September, 1942.
5. These were the Russian *Ijora*, separated from QP 8 and sunk by German surface ships, and the *Waziristan* on the two-ship convoy PQ 7A sunk by a U-boat. HMS *Shera*, the Norwegian whaler, capsized while looking for convoy PQ 12 in the ice.
6. Admiral Darlan, the keen Vichy France collaborator and Anglophobe, warned Admiral Schultze in strong terms at a dinner on 3 December, 1941, not to take a 35,000-ton warship into the St Nazaire dock. If it could not be done between quarter of an hour before and after high water, presumably Springs, he described any such attempt as the certain loss for this ship for a year. A meeting was arranged for him to meet Grand Admiral Raeder on 28 January, 1942, when he repeated the warning not to take large warships into St Nazaire as chances of getting them out were doubtful. *Tirpitz'* declared tonnage was 35,000 tons but she displaced 41,700 tons which made it worse. (Minutes of Fuehrer Naval Conferences, pages 249–254).
7. The U-boats and pocket battleships were not affected by this shortage of oil fuel. They used diesel oil. The shortage of fuel oil affected all other activities. The Channel Dash by *Scharnhorst*, *Gneisenau* and *Prince Eugen* used 20,000 tons of the tiny stock of 150,000 tons available.
8. More by good luck than good judgment, the ships that turned back did better than the eight that plodded on so doggedly. Six of them tagged on to QP 10 westward-bound under Commodore Casey in

Temple Arch, and five of these eventually picked up the next east-bound convoy, PQ 15, which arrived in Murmansk on 1 April, a month after they first left Iceland.

9. *Empire Bard* was to have a long stay in Russian waters. She was scheduled to come back with RA 57 in March, 1944, but had to turn back and eventually returned with RA 59A which arrived in Loch Ewe in September, 1944, after a stay of over two years. If it had been an American crew, they would have been, deservedly, very well off.

10. The circumstances were similar to the tragedy on 2 October, 1942, when HMS *Curaçoa*, pursuing a suspected U-boat contact, cut across the bows of *Queen Mary*, carrying 15,000 American troops. *Queen Mary* struck the light cruiser and sank her with the loss of twenty-five officers and 313 ratings, continuing on her way without serious damage. Large ships at slow speed take a painfully long time to alter course or speed. *King George V* was also involved in another near collision when travelling in convoy HX 115, when the Commodore's ship had to put her engines full astern to avoid the battleship.

11. Instead of complaining about the destruction of their submarine, the Poles, with typical single-minded courage, clamoured for an immediate replacement.

12. The destroyers *Foresight* and *Forester*, and the Russians *Gremyashki* and *Sokrushitelni*. Whereas it was a major decision to divert one single escort to protect a damaged merchant ship, the same hesitation was not evident if one of H.M. Ships was badly damaged: it takes much longer to replace a warship than a cargo carrier, and the number of trained seamen on board is much higher. One of the major German errors was to go for the merchant ships rather than the escorting warships: if they had sunk escorting warships in preference to merchant ships right from the start of the war, the convoys would have been unprotected and they could have picked off the merchant ships at will.

13. *Lützow* had returned to the Baltic to repair the damage suffered when she grounded.

14. On its second patrol, the Walrus ran out of fuel and had to be towed behind a trawler. It had, however, an enormous capacity for survival, did some valuable work and eventually reached Archangel under tow by *Palomares*. Here it was claimed by the Russians as a valuable part of the shipment consigned to them and only reluctantly released to return to its parent ship.

INDEX

255

258